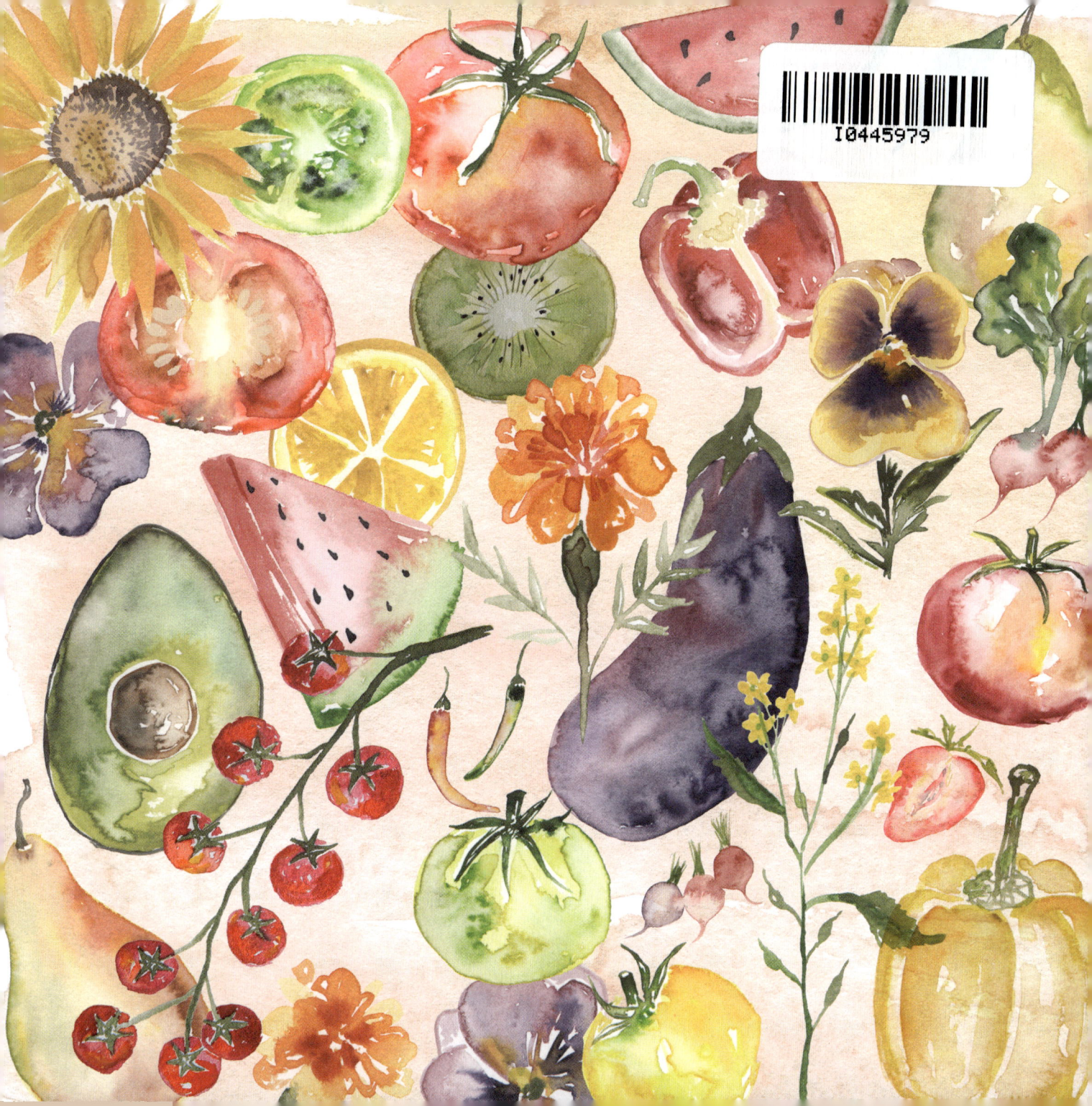

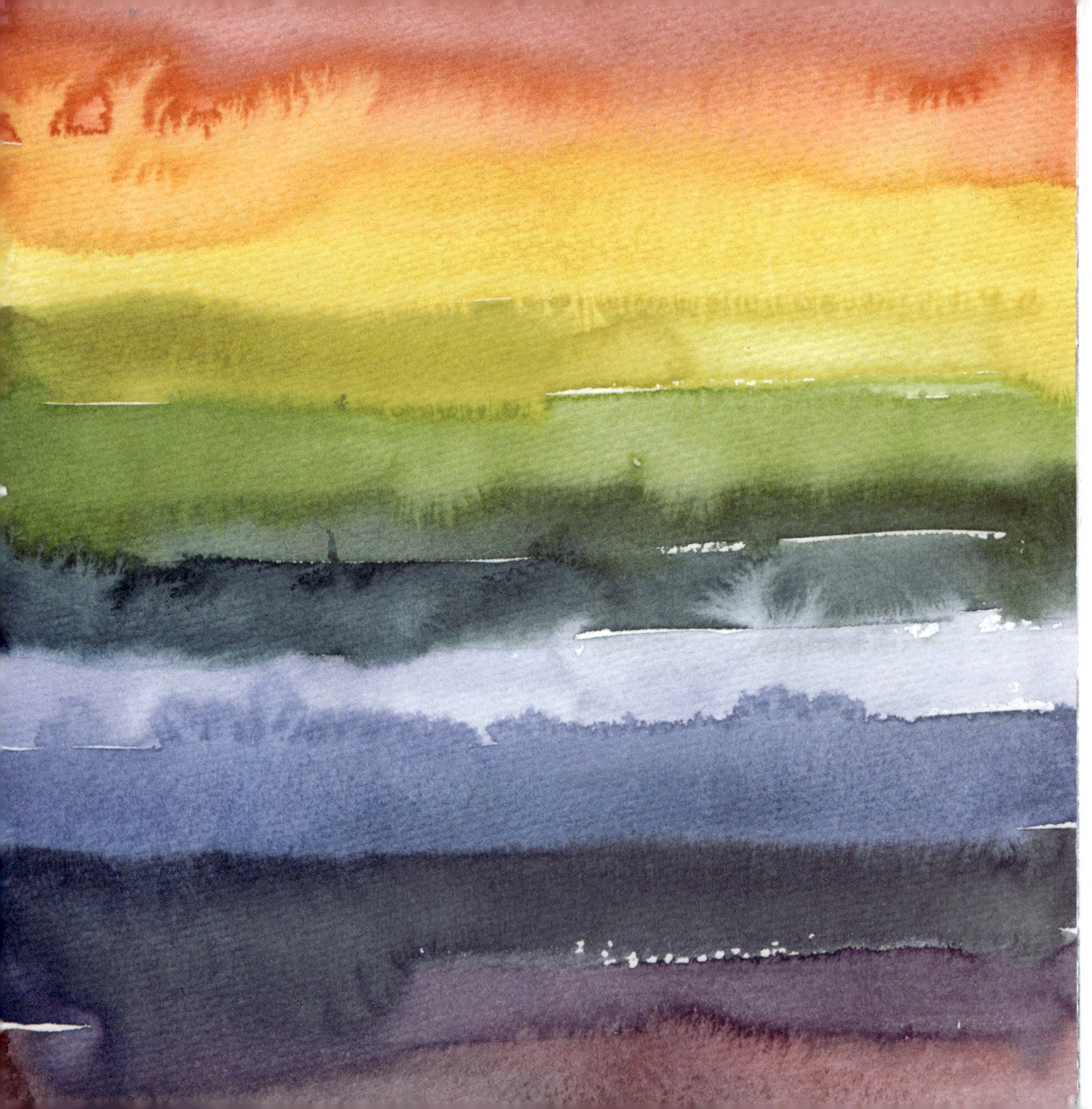

THE
watercolor
FEAST

Learn to Paint Simple Fruits,
Vegetables, and Edible Flowers

erin gleeson

ABRAMS, NEW YORK

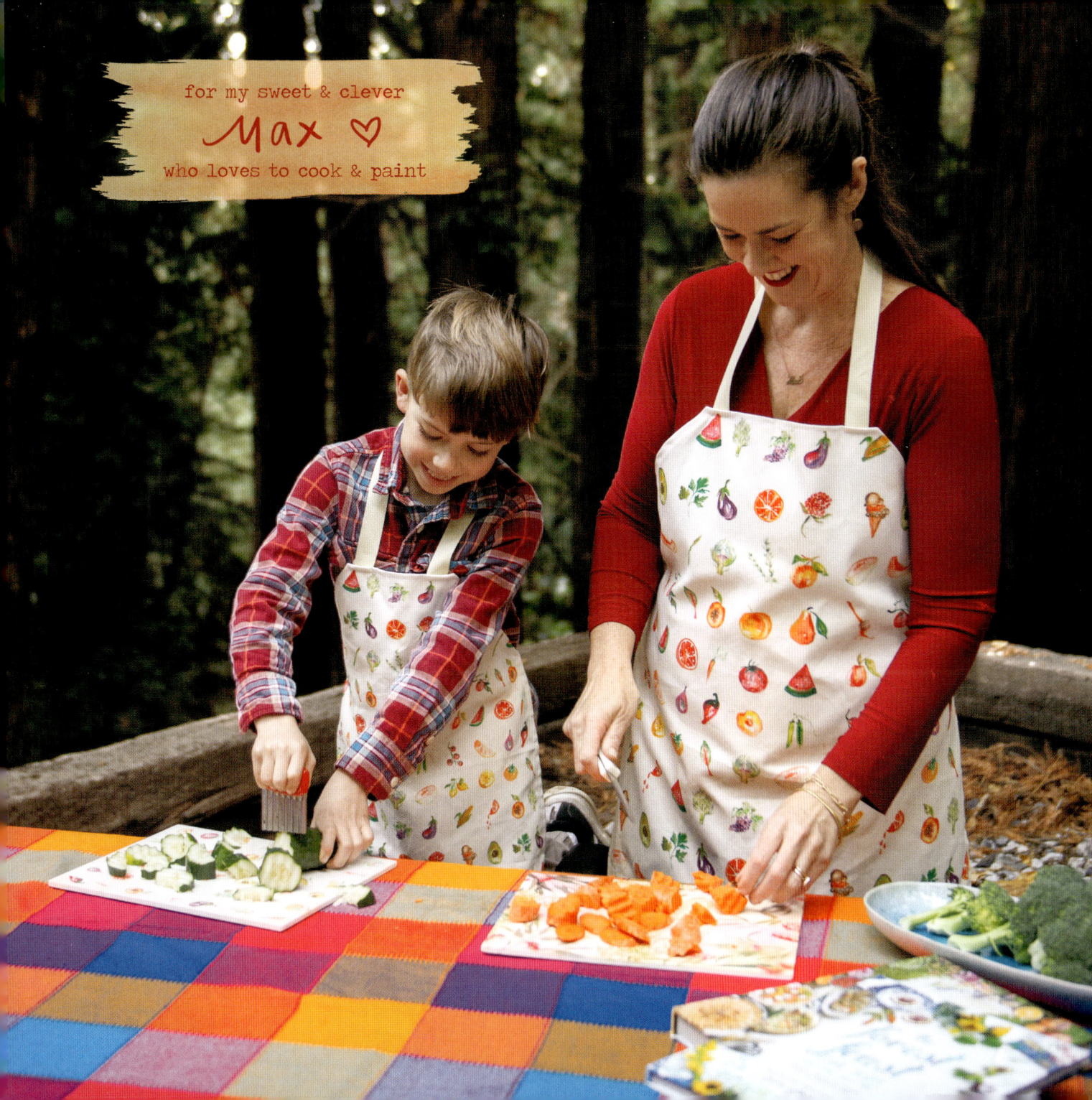

for my sweet & clever
Max ♡
who loves to cook & paint

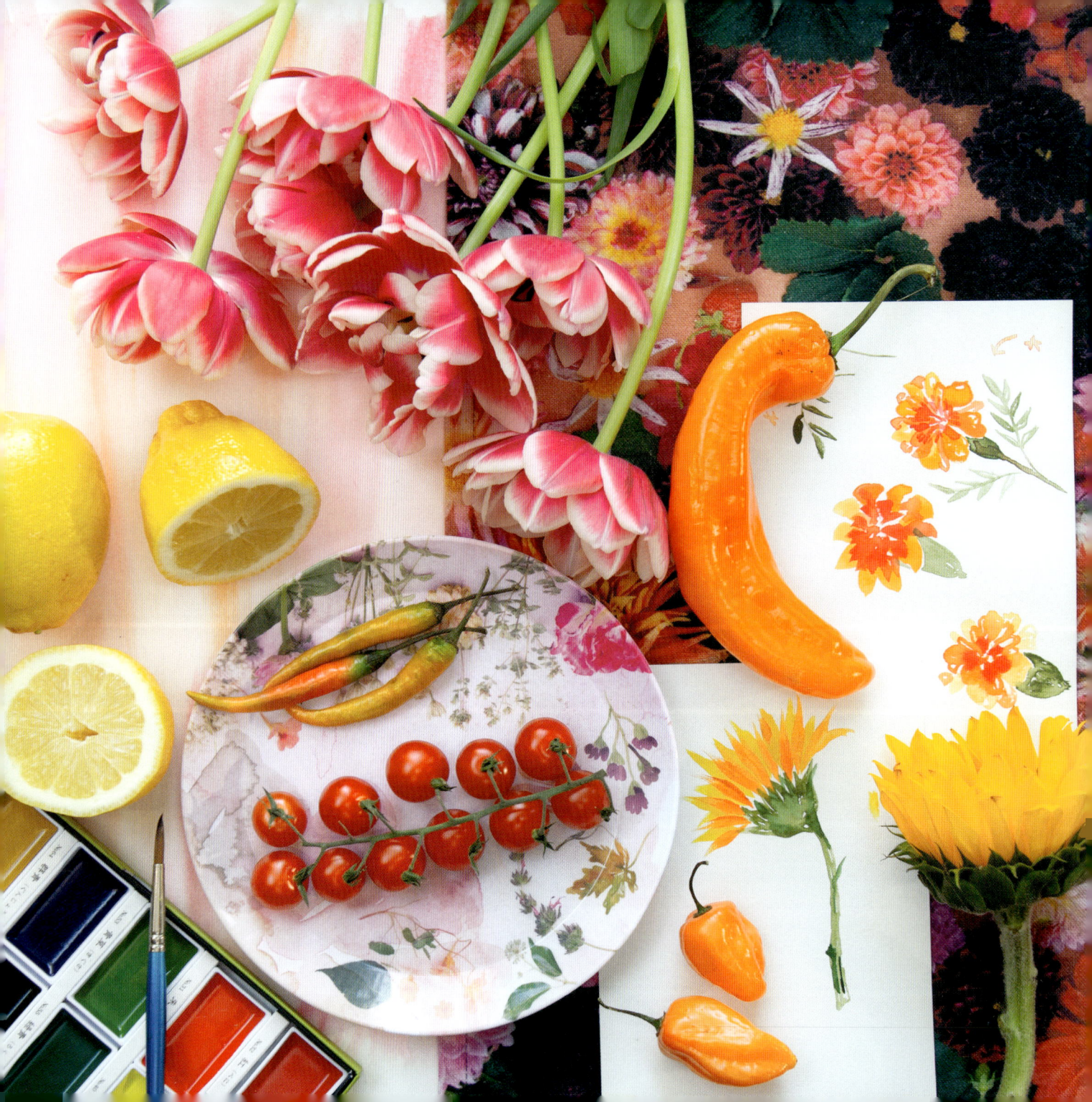

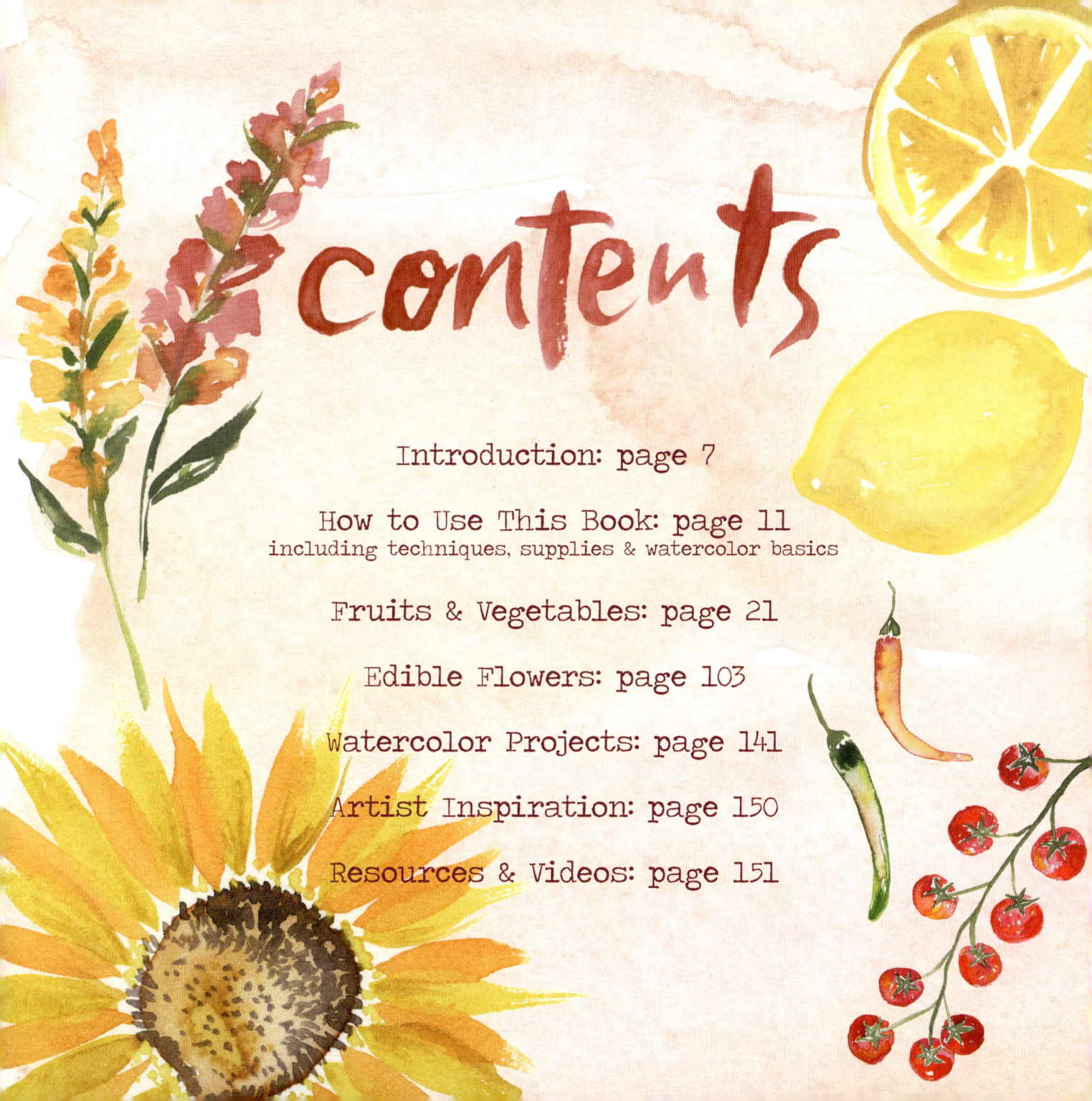

contents

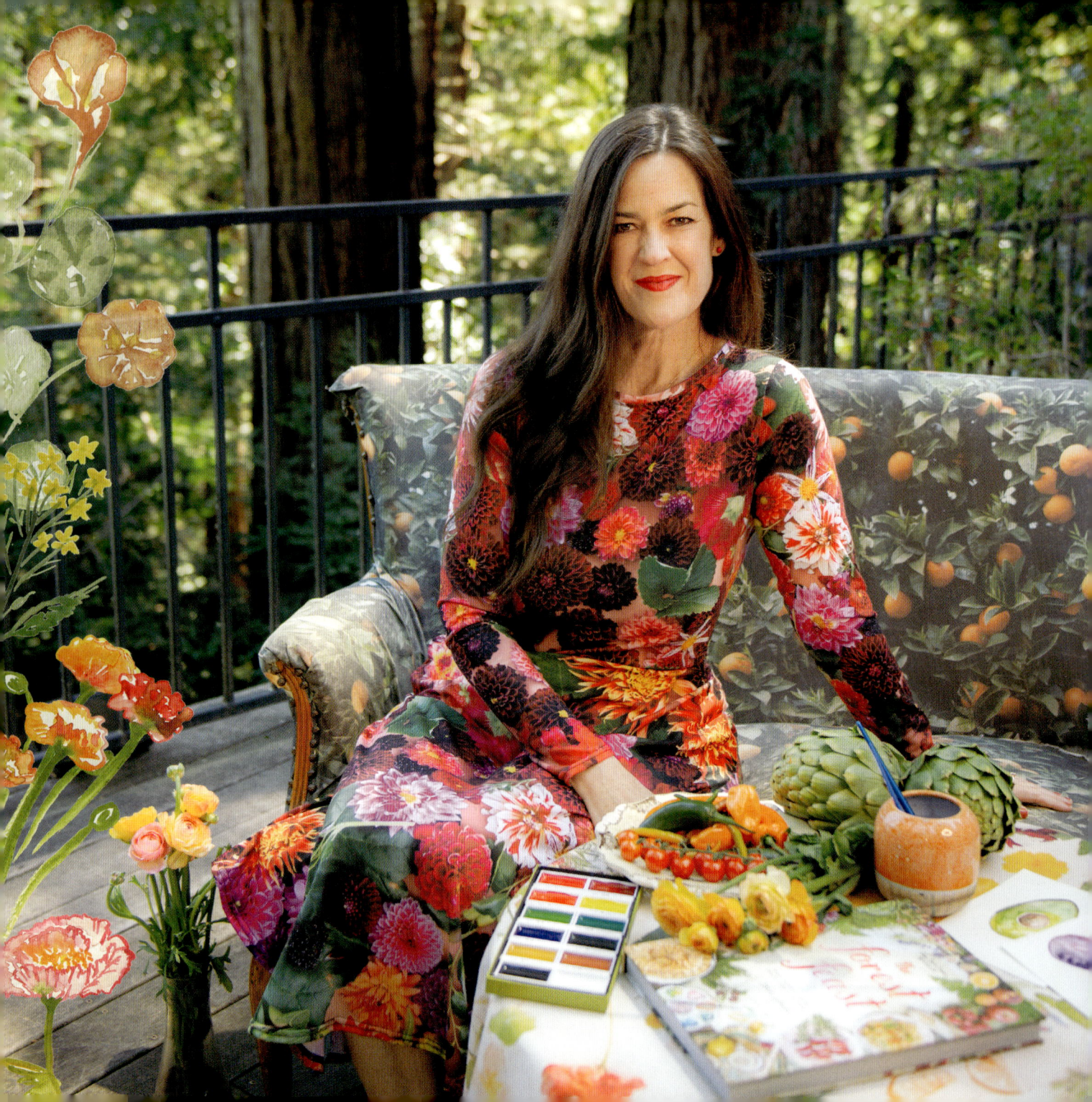

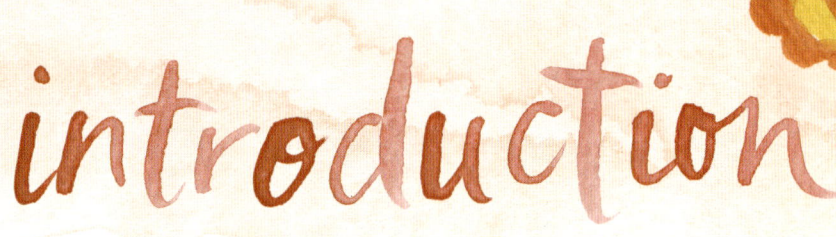

introduction

My three small children are prolific artists. They make art at school and come home wanting to make more. I watch as they fearlessly create and experiment using an abundance of colors and materials. When they are done, they feel proud and ask to tape their art on the wall.

Somewhere along the way, many of us lose this sense of creative wonder. As we get older, creative time is no longer offered or prioritized by teachers, parents, and later ourselves. An idea of whether or not we are "good" artists starts to form, and some of us begin to believe we are not artistic at all. Sure, some are born with remarkable artistic talent, but I truly believe we are all creative. Painting is a skill that can be practiced, like anything else.

I have always loved to paint. I began taking watercolor classes at age five and went on to major in art in college. I am lucky to come from a family that encouraged me to pursue a career in the arts, and I continued on to do an MFA in photography. While I taught photography at a college in New York City, I also worked as a food photographer, and watercolor painting was pushed aside as a hobby.

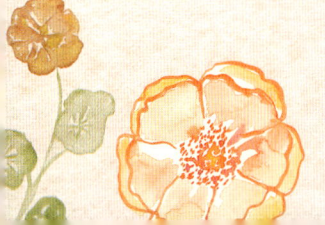
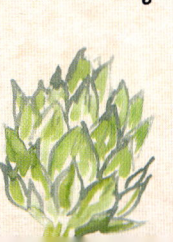
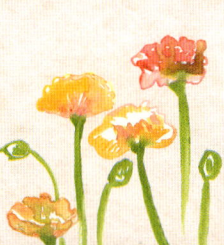
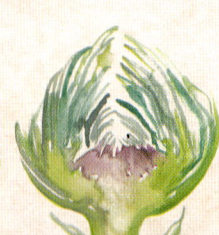
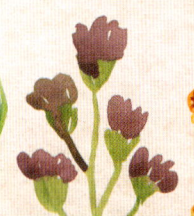
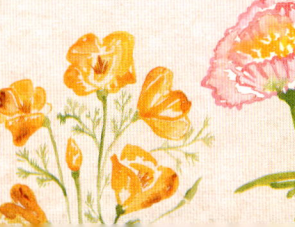

But one day in my thirties, in need of a creative reboot, I started to experiment by overlaying my photographs with watercolor illustration. My husband, Jonathan, and I had just moved to California, and because I love cooking, my creations were inspired by colorful local produce. These new collages I was making were centered around the little cabin in the woods we'd found, a huge contrast to our Brooklyn apartment. I began to share this artwork online, calling the project "The Forest Feast," and to my surprise it got noticed by editors. This launched me into a whole new career of writing, photographing, and illustrating cookbooks. With my bestselling cookbook series, The Forest Feast, I hope to encourage people to exercise their creativity through cooking and hosting. Now, with <u>The Watercolor Feast</u>, I hope to inspire you to make time for creativity by painting with watercolors. You never know what it may spark!

Whether or not you've painted before, this book has something for you. My simple tutorials for painting fruits, vegetables, and flowers are meant to be done on postcard-size paper in about 15 minutes. My intention is that you'll use my tutorials as a starting point to make your own unique paintings. No need to follow them exactly—there's no right way to paint a vegetable.

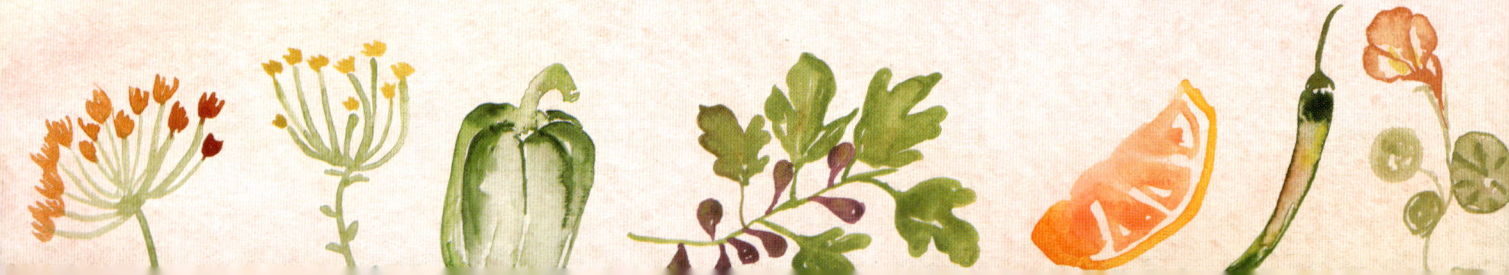

Have fun exploring! And once you've completed a painting, I have a recipe idea alongside each tutorial. If doodling is more your speed, I offer ideas for abstract color exercises. Perhaps you'll leave your paints out in a corner of your office and spend five minutes making art when you need a break. Or maybe when you invite friends over for a drink, you'll pull out the paints (see my Watercolor Cocktail Party on page 146). I turn my paintings into clothing and textiles to sell in my online shop, which you can preview in the Watercolor Projects chapter (page 141), and I hope you'll try this, too. I also suggest some of my favorite illustrators to follow on social media, in case you're just looking for inspiration (page 148).

Painting is rejuvenating. Vibrant color can bring so much joy, and engaging with color in the form of paint is quite powerful. I find that the simple act of running my brush over paper for a few minutes brings clarity, calm, and new ideas.

You are creative. You are an artist! Painting is one easy way to make time for creativity in our daily lives. My hope is that you'll feel inspired to start today.

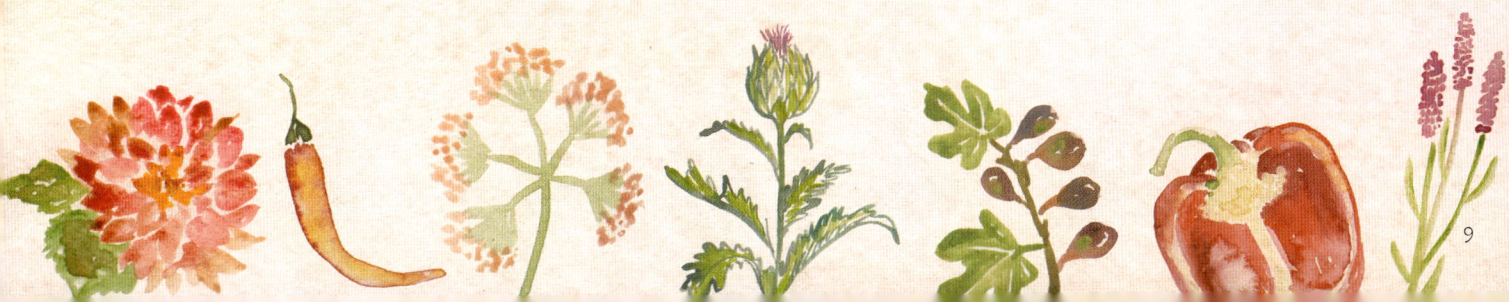

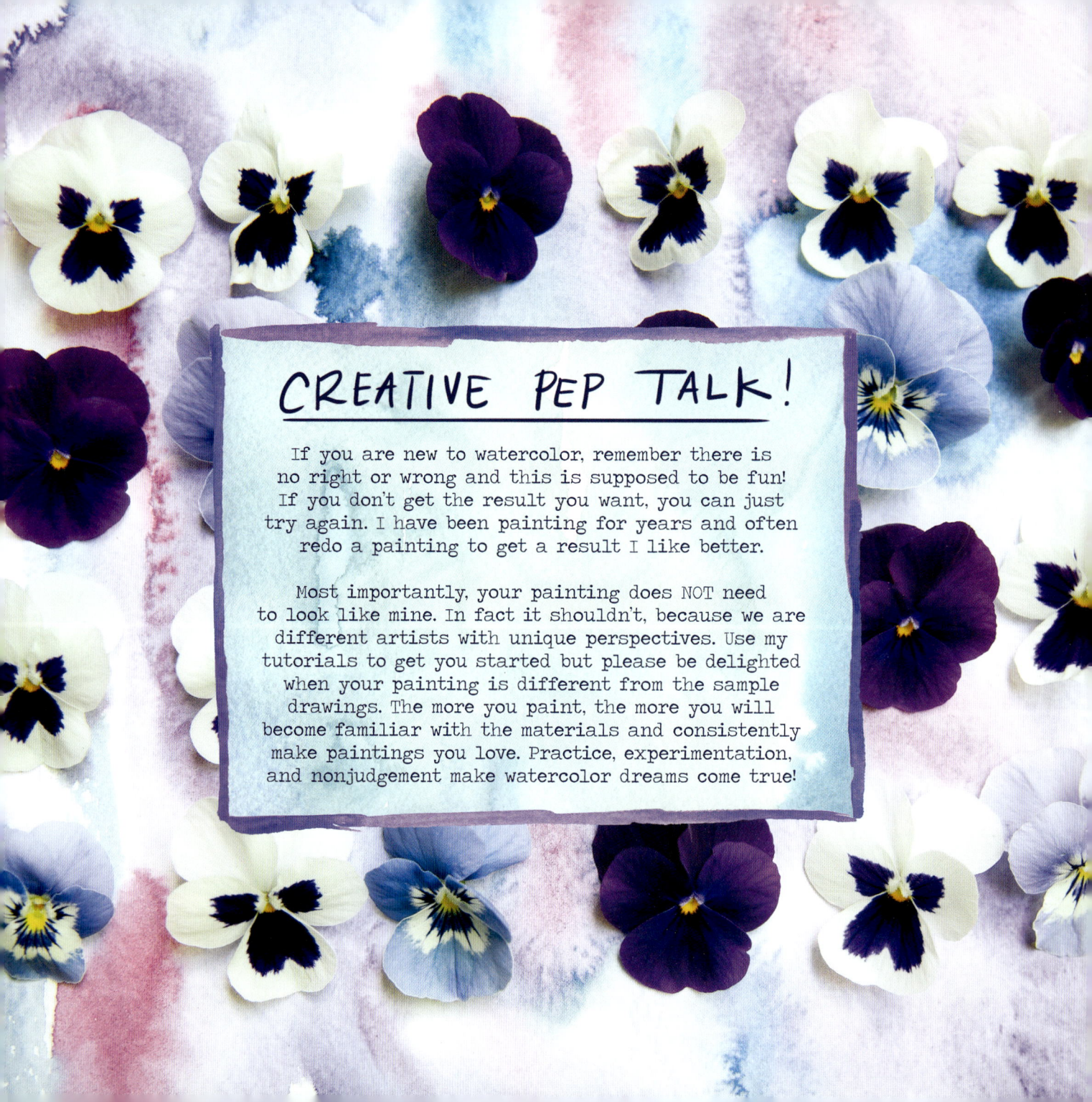

CREATIVE PEP TALK!

If you are new to watercolor, remember there is no right or wrong and this is supposed to be fun! If you don't get the result you want, you can just try again. I have been painting for years and often redo a painting to get a result I like better.

Most importantly, your painting does NOT need to look like mine. In fact it shouldn't, because we are different artists with unique perspectives. Use my tutorials to get you started but please be delighted when your painting is different from the sample drawings. The more you paint, the more you will become familiar with the materials and consistently make paintings you love. Practice, experimentation, and nonjudgement make watercolor dreams come true!

how to use THIS BOOK

{ The goal of this book is for you to make time for creativity through simple watercolor painting. }

OVERVIEW

* Easy 15-minute painting tutorials on postcard-size paper
* Visual step-by-step instructions
* Prompts for loose, abstract color exercises
* Recipe ideas for each vegetable, fruit, or edible flower you paint

This book is meant to be more exploratory than technical, with visual prompts to make simple paintings inspired by the farmer's market, the garden, and cooking. Although I've studied and practiced watercolor for years, I wanted to offer a more intuitive explanation of how I approach painting. My hope is that you won't copy my tutorial steps exactly, but instead use them as a guide to create your own unique paintings.

In the following section, I walk through some of the basics, like mixing your own colors and my favorite supplies. I invite you to play around with your materials and paint along with me as I show you a few fun methods I have used to illustrate my cookbooks. To me, painting on smaller paper feels more carefree because I know the painting will be relatively quick, it doesn't feel like I'm diving into a masterpiece, and I can mail it as a card afterward. Painting on smaller paper makes the creative session feel more approachable, which allows me to actually carve out the time to do it.

Remember that you never know exactly how a watercolor painting will look when it dries. It often surprises you, and that's the fun of it. Embrace that and you're free!

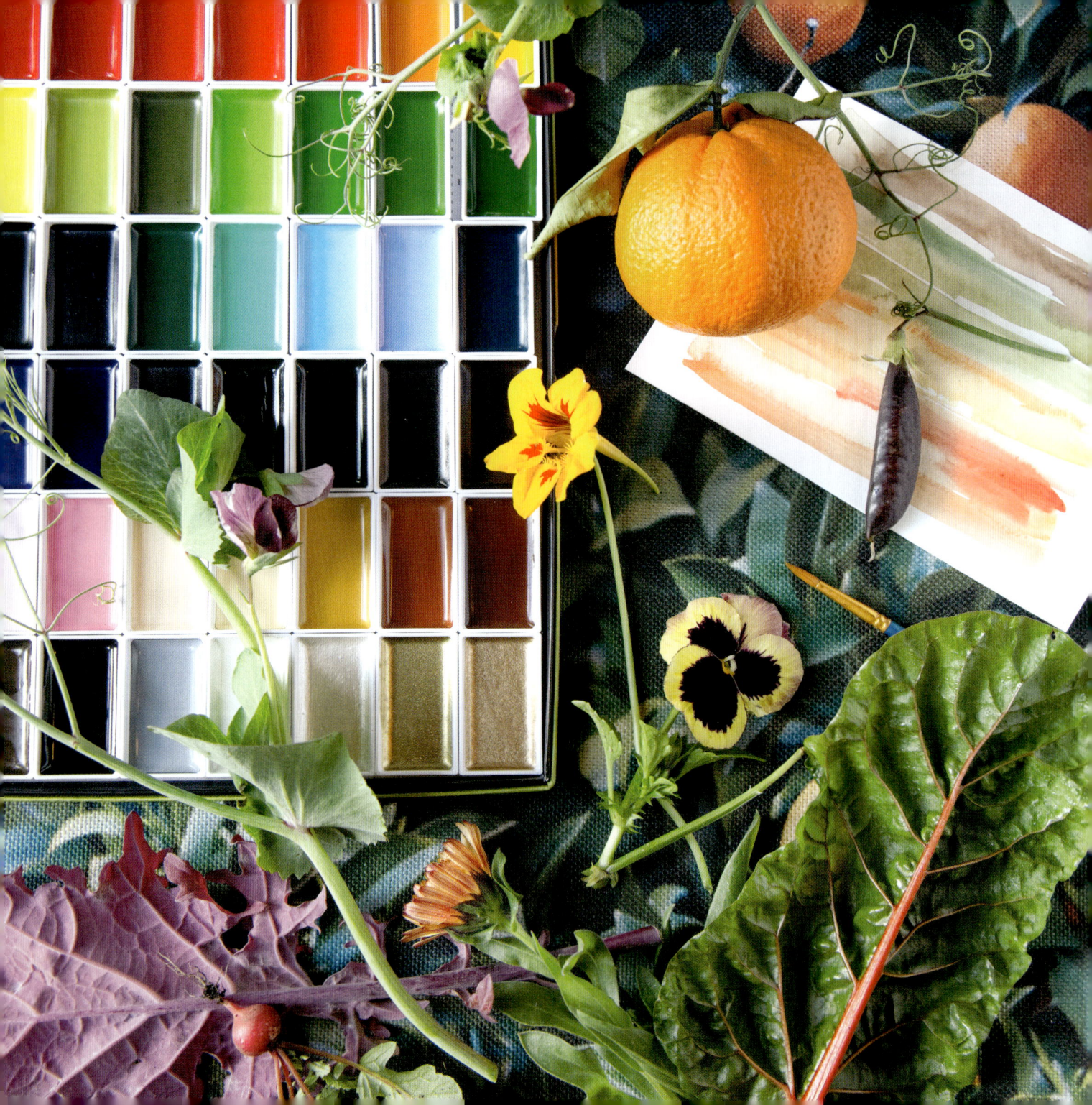

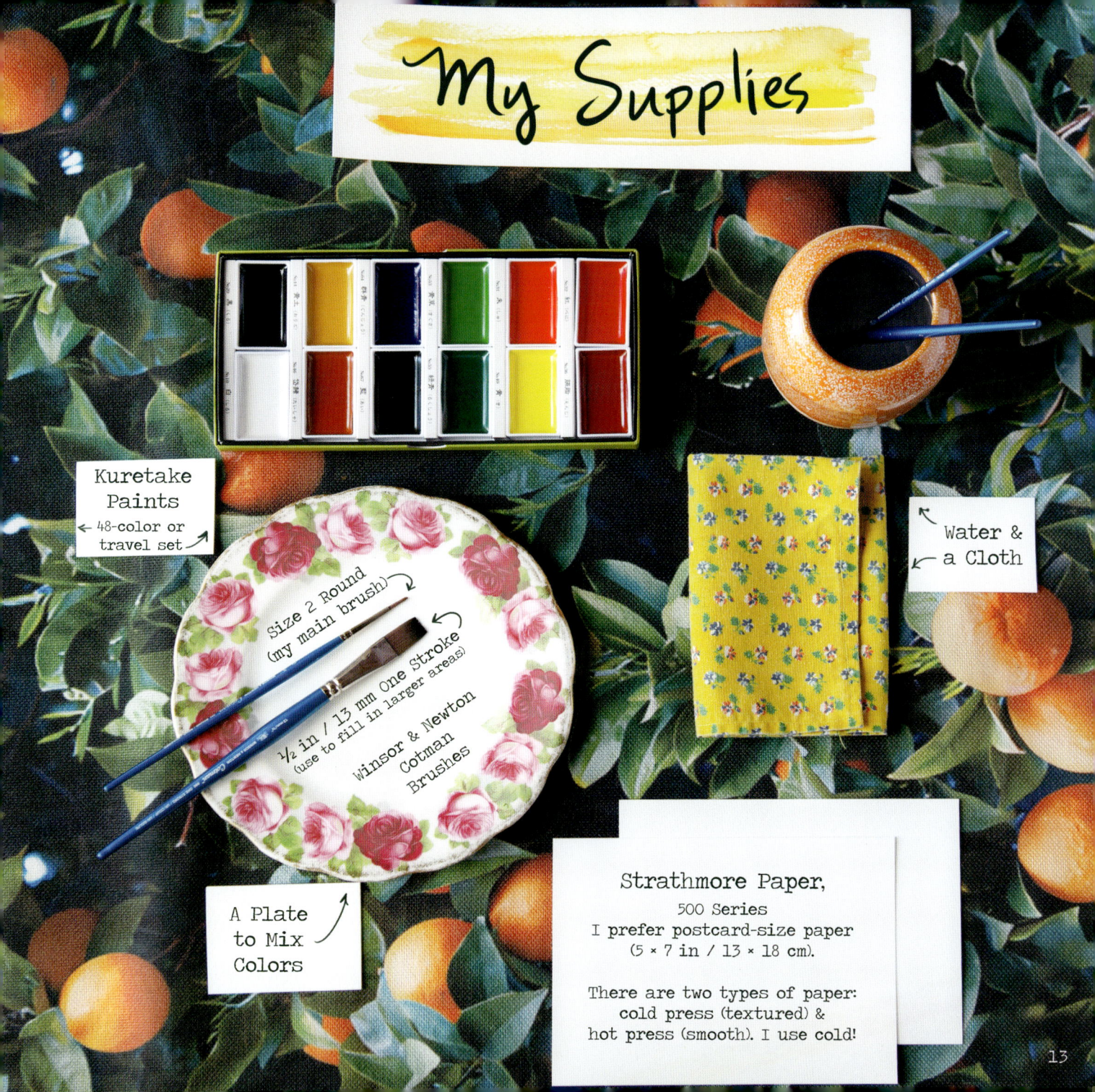

My Supplies

Kuretake Paints
← 48-color or travel set →

A Plate to Mix Colors

Size 2 Round (my main brush)

½ in / 13 mm One Stroke (use to fill in larger areas)

Winsor & Newton Cotman Brushes

Water & a Cloth

Strathmore Paper, 500 Series
I prefer postcard-size paper (5 × 7 in / 13 × 18 cm).

There are two types of paper: cold press (textured) & hot press (smooth). I use cold!

13

Color Mixing

I always think my paintings look better when I mix my own colors instead of just using what comes in my set (even though I use a 48-color set)! I generally combine 2 or 3 colors (in varying amounts) to create my custom colors. Some paint sets come with a palette to mix paints on the side, but my Kuretake paints do not, so I use a white ceramic plate that I wash at the end of every session. Think of each custom color as an addition math problem: $X + Y = XY$. If you don't like the first result, you can always add more of one color to change the shade, or add water to make it lighter. Or start over! Dark colors seem to really pack a punch, so I usually add them in small amounts.

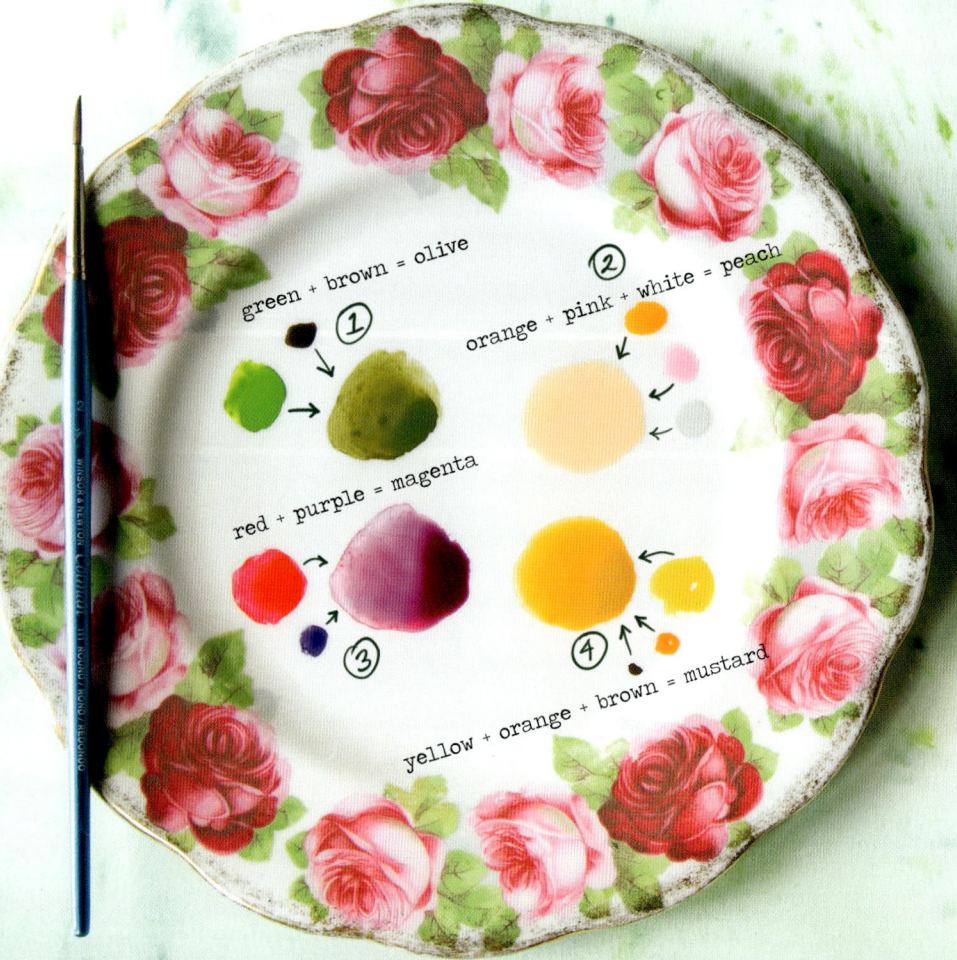

green + brown = olive

① ②

orange + pink + white = peach

red + purple = magenta

③ ④

yellow + orange + brown = mustard

1) Green plus a small amount of brown will make an olive shade of green. If you add too much brown & it gets darker than you intended, add more green to balance it out. I use this balancing act for every shade!

2) To create this peachy shade, I combined about the same amount of orange, pink & white.

3) Purple can be powerful, so I added just a tiny bit to red to mix this magenta shade.

4) To create a mustard yellow, I added orange & a tiny bit of brown to yellow, which made it feel richer.

Brushes & Water

The amount of water you have on your brush mixed with paint makes a big difference.

Use a size 2 brush for every tutorial in this book unless otherwise noted. Add water to your brush to move paint around more easily. If you have too much water on your brush, wipe it on the side of your water cup or on a cloth. Using the same small size 2 brush, I made these 3 different lines & this pea painting:

I press lightly with a solid amount of paint & water on my brush (wet but not dripping) to create thin, delicate lines.

With a lot of water & paint on my brush (almost dripping), I can make thicker lines & fill in larger areas when I press harder.

If I don't have enough water on my brush, the result will be dry-looking strokes.

Brushstrokes

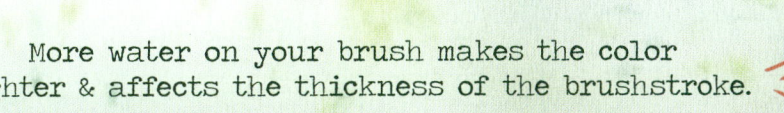

More water on your brush makes the color lighter & affects the thickness of the brushstroke.

Watercolor Basics

- <u>MORE WATER = LIGHTER COLOR</u>. Adding a lot of water to paint on your plate makes the color lighter.

- <u>DARK OVER LIGHT</u>. In watercolor, you generally always paint light colors first & paint darker colors over them. Light colors don't really show up on top of dark colors (like they do when painting with acrylics or oils).

- <u>WET COLORS BLEED</u>. Colors will bleed or mix together when they are wet, but not when one of them is dry.

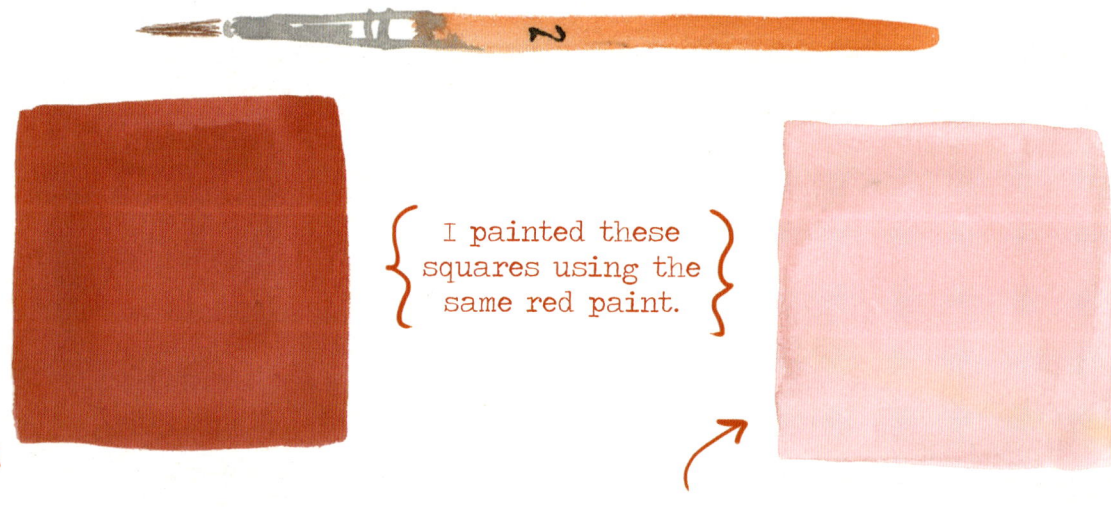

{ I painted these squares using the same red paint. }

For this one, I had a lot of red paint pigment on my brush & just enough water to easily spread it around.

For this one, I mixed a small amount of red paint with a lot of water on a side plate. When a color is really watered down, it becomes a lighter shade of itself (in this case, pink!). Try this yourself.

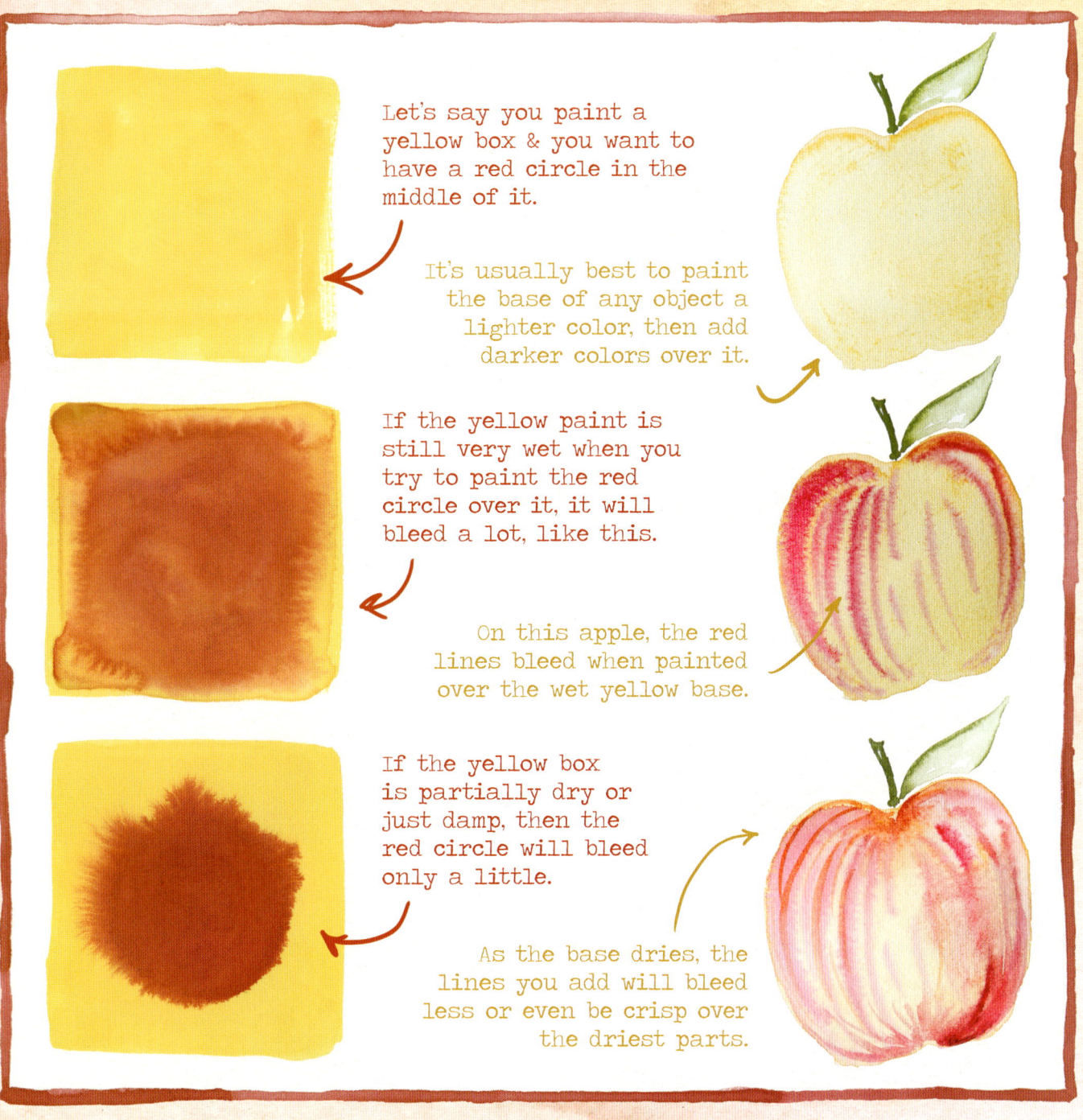

Let's say you paint a yellow box & you want to have a red circle in the middle of it.

It's usually best to paint the base of any object a lighter color, then add darker colors over it.

If the yellow paint is still very wet when you try to paint the red circle over it, it will bleed a lot, like this.

On this apple, the red lines bleed when painted over the wet yellow base.

If the yellow box is partially dry or just damp, then the red circle will bleed only a little.

As the base dries, the lines you add will bleed less or even be crisp over the driest parts.

Preventing Bleeding

If you want colors to stay separate &
not bleed into each other,
you have to wait
until one dries.

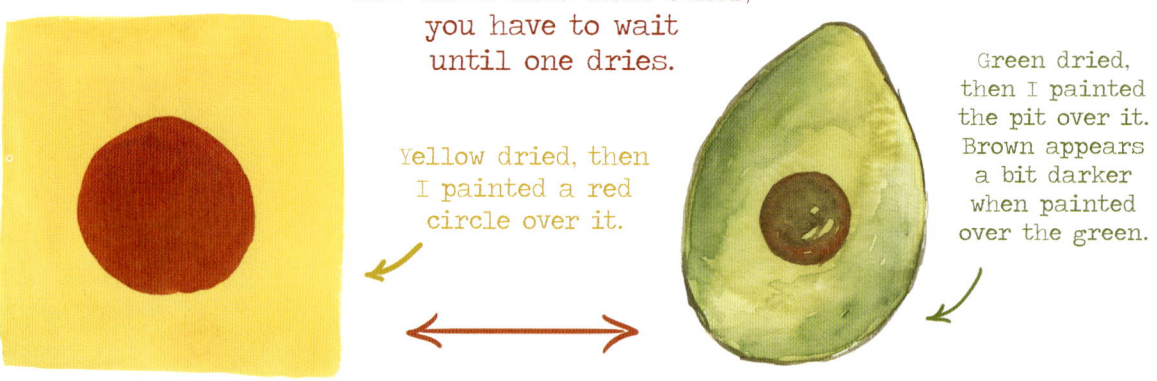

Yellow dried, then
I painted a red
circle over it.

Green dried,
then I painted
the pit over it.
Brown appears
a bit darker
when painted
over the green.

If you're impatient (like me!) & don't want to wait for the base color to dry, you can
leave a small amount of white space between the colors. If they don't touch, they
won't bleed. I used these 2 different methods for an avocado; which do you prefer?

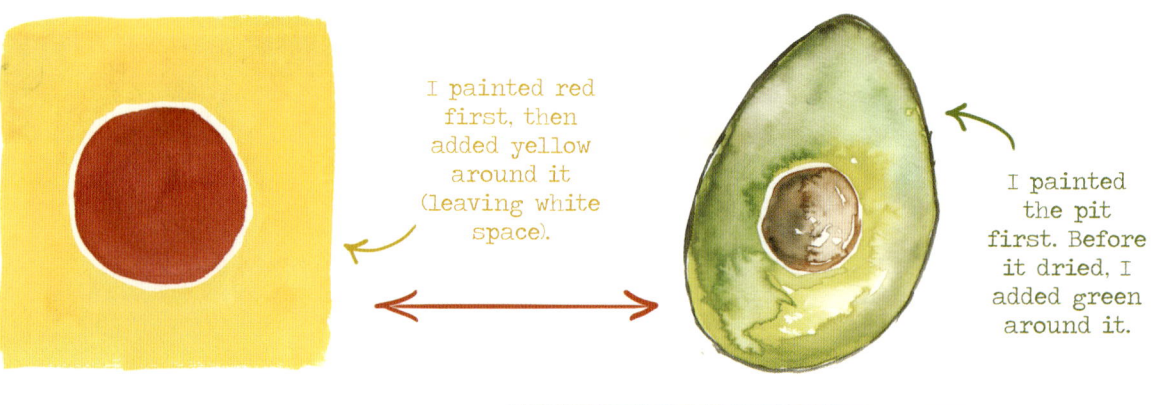

I painted red
first, then
added yellow
around it
(leaving white
space).

I painted
the pit
first. Before
it dried, I
added green
around it.

A NOTE ON PENCILS:

I occasionally use a pencil to draw an outline before painting. For this
avocado, I erased the line before painting so it was very faint & not
visible in the end. Tip: Once pencil is painted over, it's hard to erase.

Other Ways to Affect Color

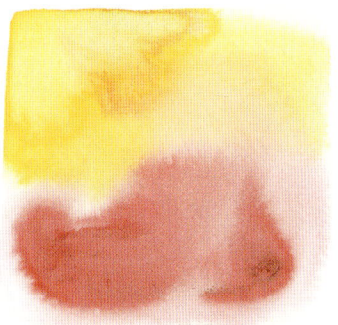

Using just water on your brush, paint a square. Then dab red & yellow paint on the watery square & watch the colors run together.

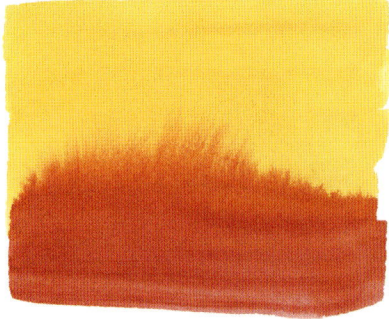

Here, I painted a yellow square. While it was still damp, I painted a stripe of red across the bottom.

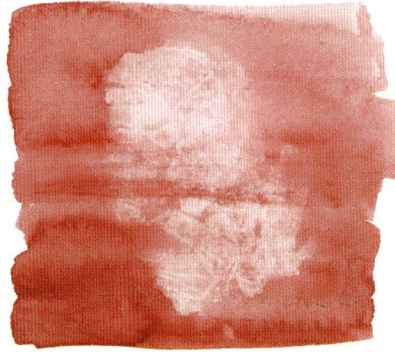

You can remove some color & water by blotting wet paint with a cloth, like I did above.

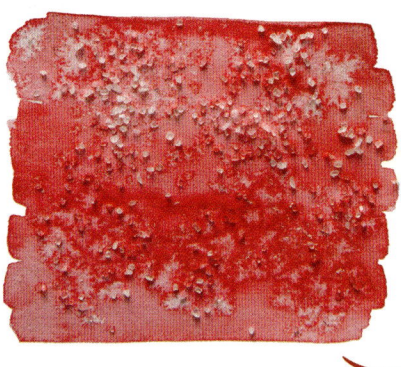

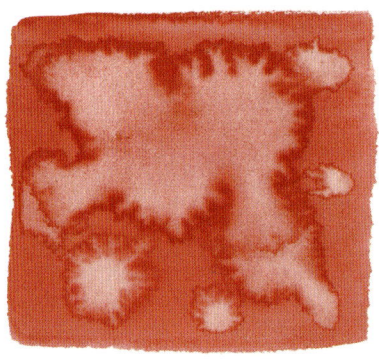

If you sprinkle coarse salt on wet paint, it absorbs some color. Let it dry, rub the salt off & you're left with a speckled pattern. I sometimes do this to show texture, like on the lemon peel on page 63.

If your painting is very wet, or if you drip water over dry paint, it will create "blooms" once dry.

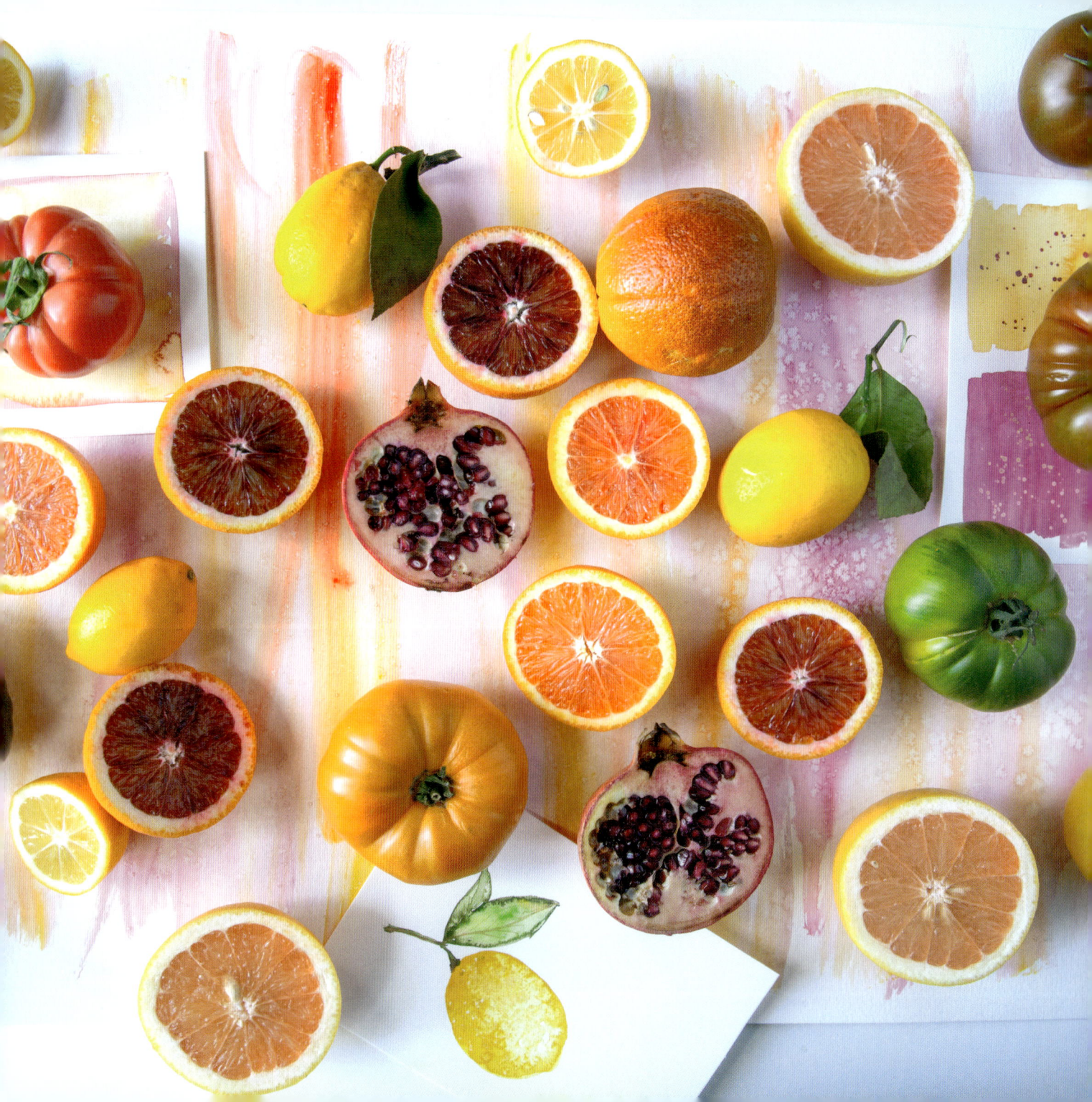

FRUITS & VEGETABLES

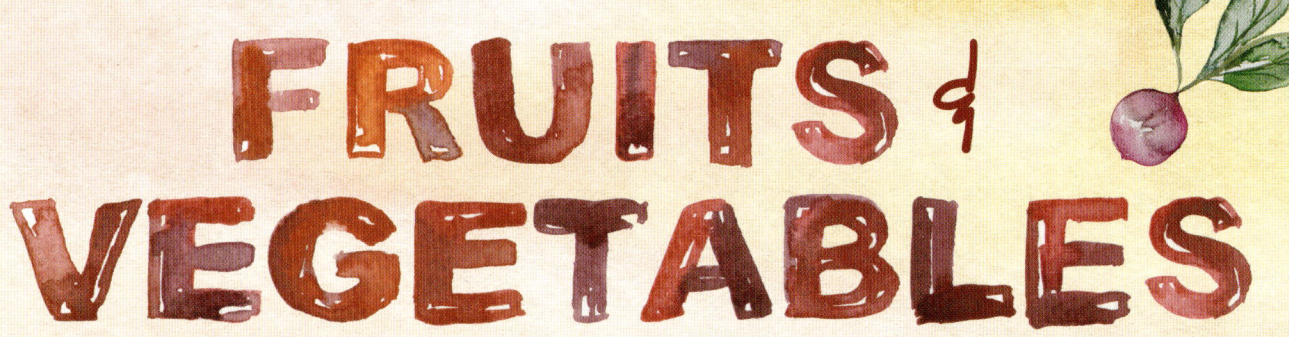

In this section, follow step-by-step instructions to make simple paintings of fruits and vegetables. Start each tutorial with a size 2 brush. Most of the time I use small brushes (size 0–2) and a larger brush (such as size 6) just to fill in larger areas. See my color mixing tips on page 14. To give your page a background color (see my peppers on page 37), paint the entire paper with a light, watered-down color. Let it dry, then paint your item over it. Get inspired by bringing home goodies from the farmer's market or just the grocery store! Because I use postcard-size paper, these paintings generally take about 15 minutes, but sometimes a little more if you need to let a layer dry between steps. I also offer recipe suggestions so you can enjoy the produce after you paint it.

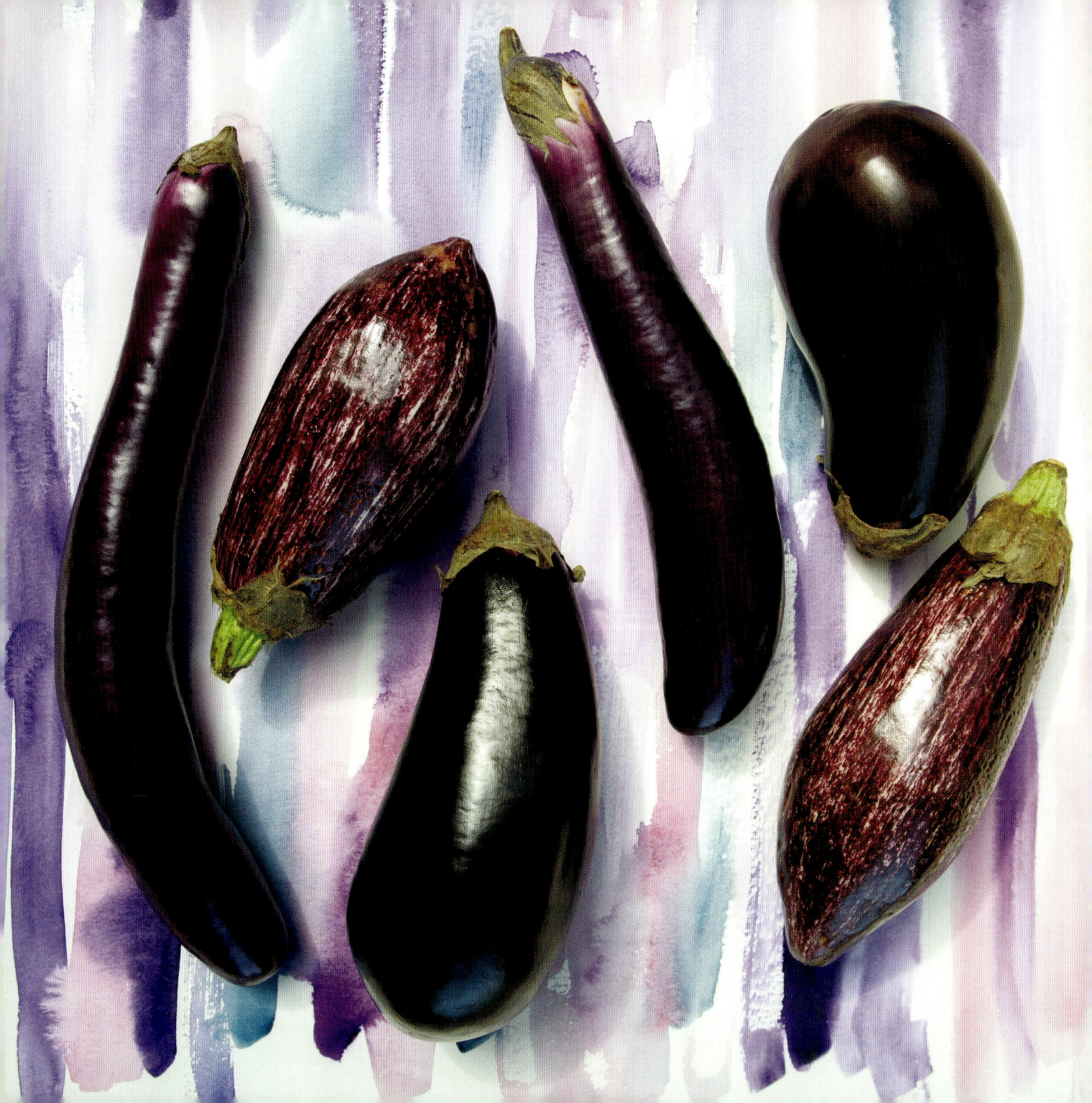

Eggplant

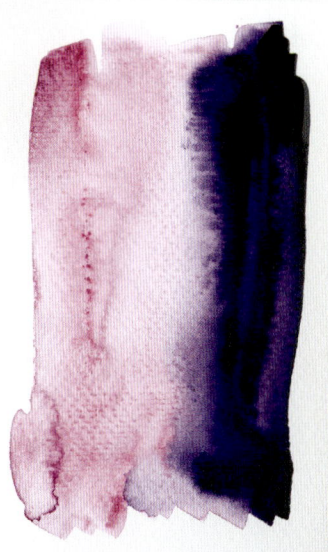

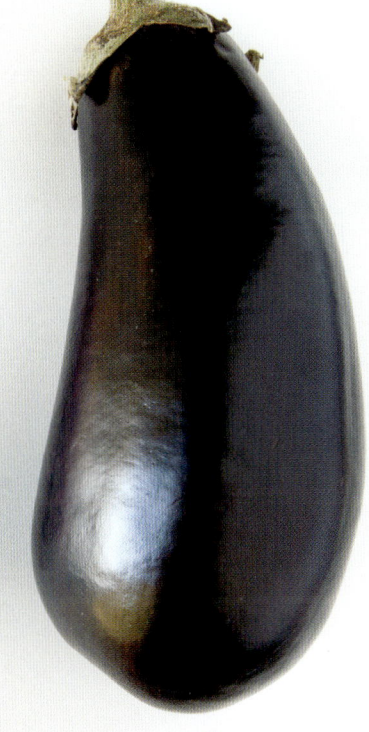

Color Exercise

On your plate, try mixing a few
different shades of purple.

{
purple + red
purple + red + brown
purple + black
}

Using lots of water & your new colors,
create a wash of purple on your paper.

Recipe Idea

Sauté cubed eggplant & red onion
with a good amount of olive oil &
a dash of sesame oil. Cook until
tender then stir in a splash of soy
sauce before removing from heat.
Top with cilantro & chili crunch.

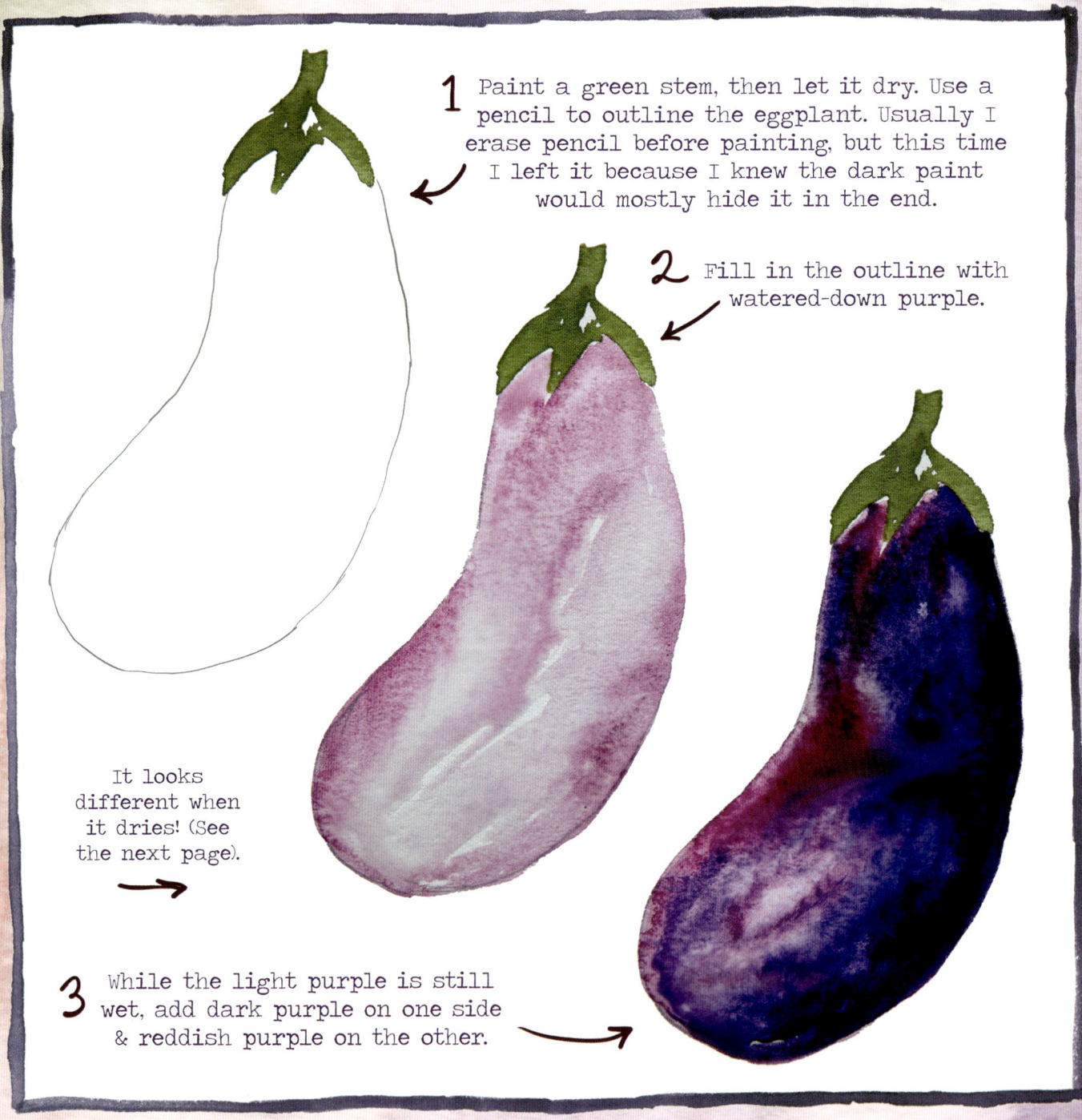

1 Paint a green stem, then let it dry. Use a pencil to outline the eggplant. Usually I erase pencil before painting, but this time I left it because I knew the dark paint would mostly hide it in the end.

2 Fill in the outline with watered-down purple.

It looks different when it dries! (See the next page).

3 While the light purple is still wet, add dark purple on one side & reddish purple on the other.

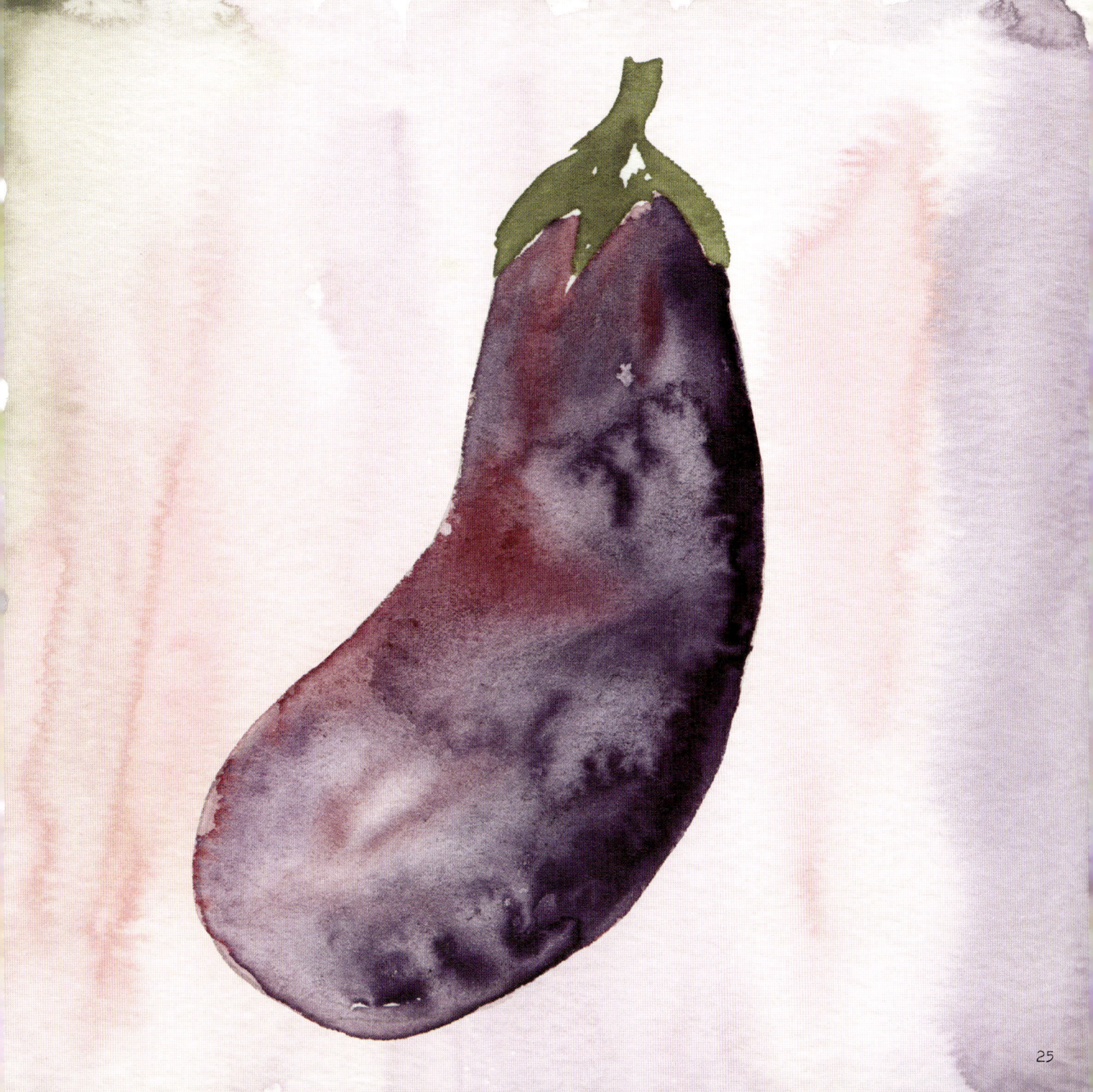

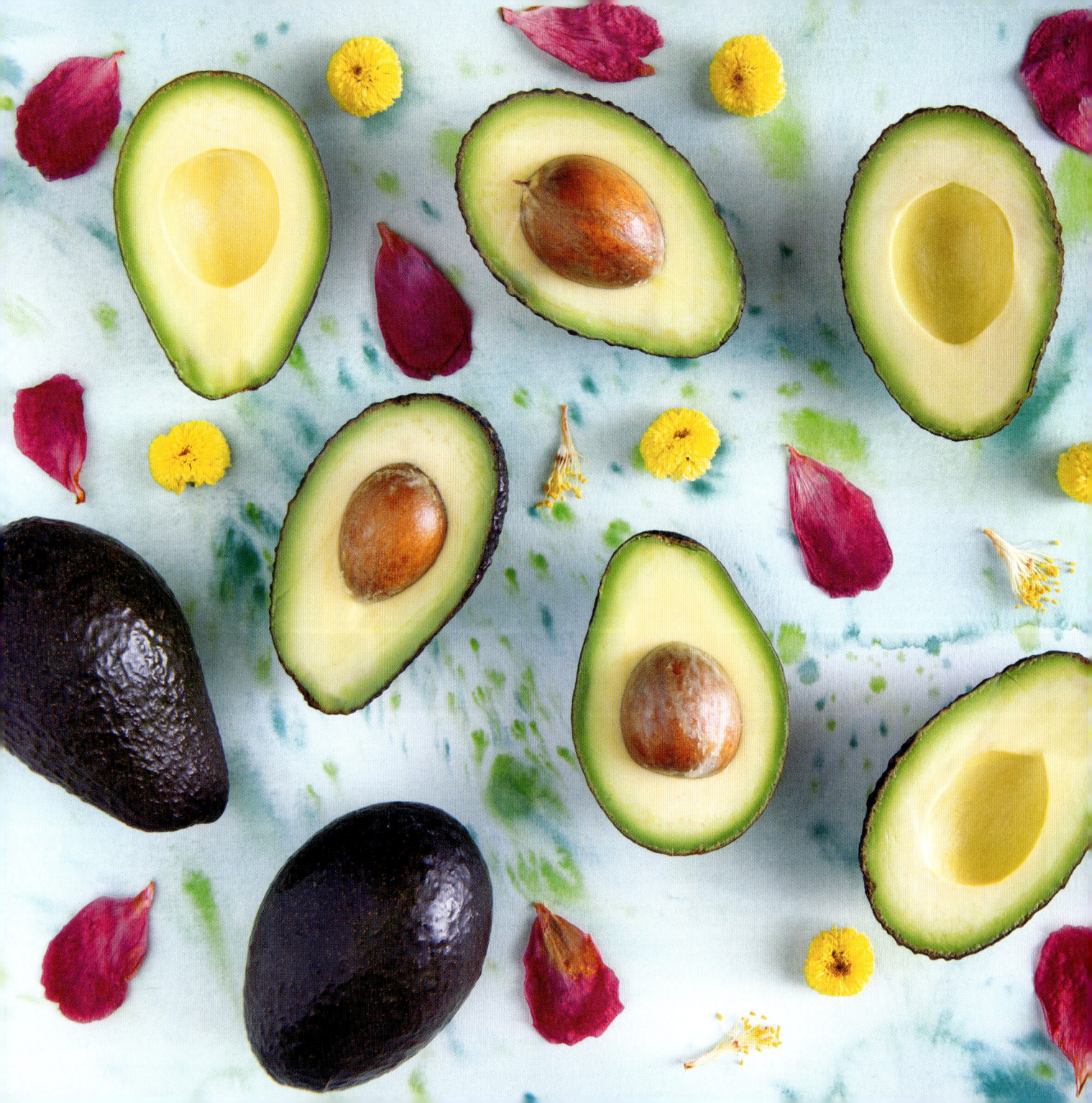

Avocado

Let's try to create 2 distinct areas of color that don't bleed into each other.

↓

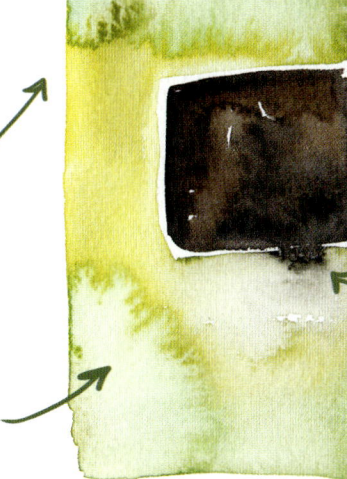

I used a lot of water, which made these "blooms" appear.

Oops! I got too close & they bled, but that's OK!

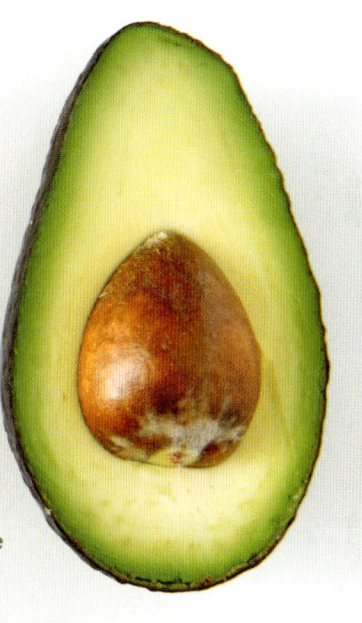

Color Exercise

Start by painting a dark brown box in the middle of your paper. Next, carefully paint light green all around it, leaving a thin white strip between the brown & green so they don't touch & bleed. Add dark green paint over the still-wet light green area & let them bleed together.

Recipe Idea

On a platter, scatter large cubes of ripe-but-firm avocado, quartered strawberries, halved yellow cherry tomatoes, fresh mozzarella balls & chopped basil. Dress with olive oil, salt & pepper.

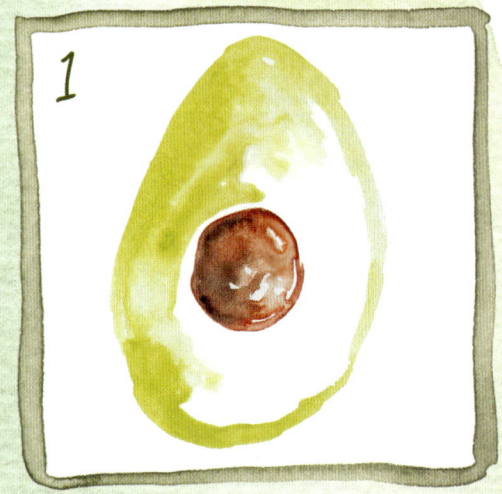

1

Start by painting the pit using 2 shades of brown. Leave some unpainted white bits. If you use a pencil to outline, erase it before you paint.

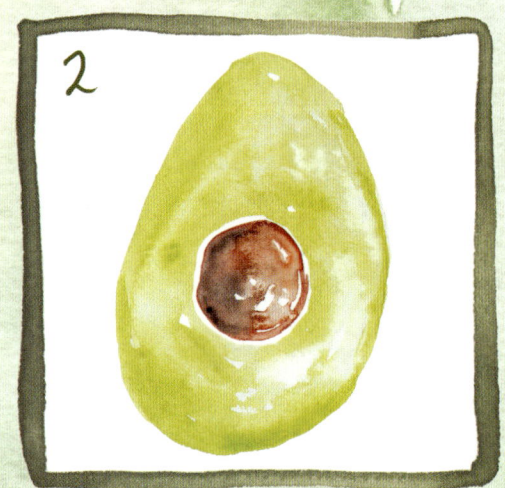

2

My pit is still wet, so I'll leave a bit of unpainted white space around it to keep the colors separate as I add light green (green + yellow).

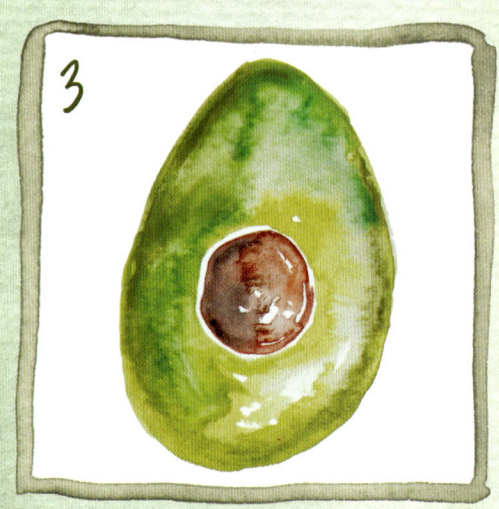

3

While the light green is still wet, add 2 darker shades of green along the edges & allow them to bleed inward. For dark green, try mixing green + a tiny bit of brown or black.

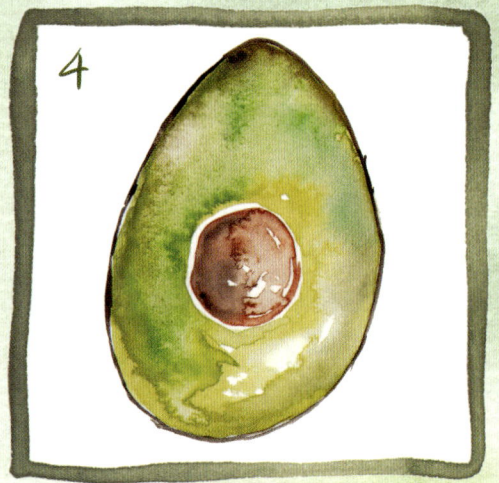

4

When the paint is mostly dry, add a thin blackish-brown line around the outer edge. Mine bled a bit at the top, which I like.

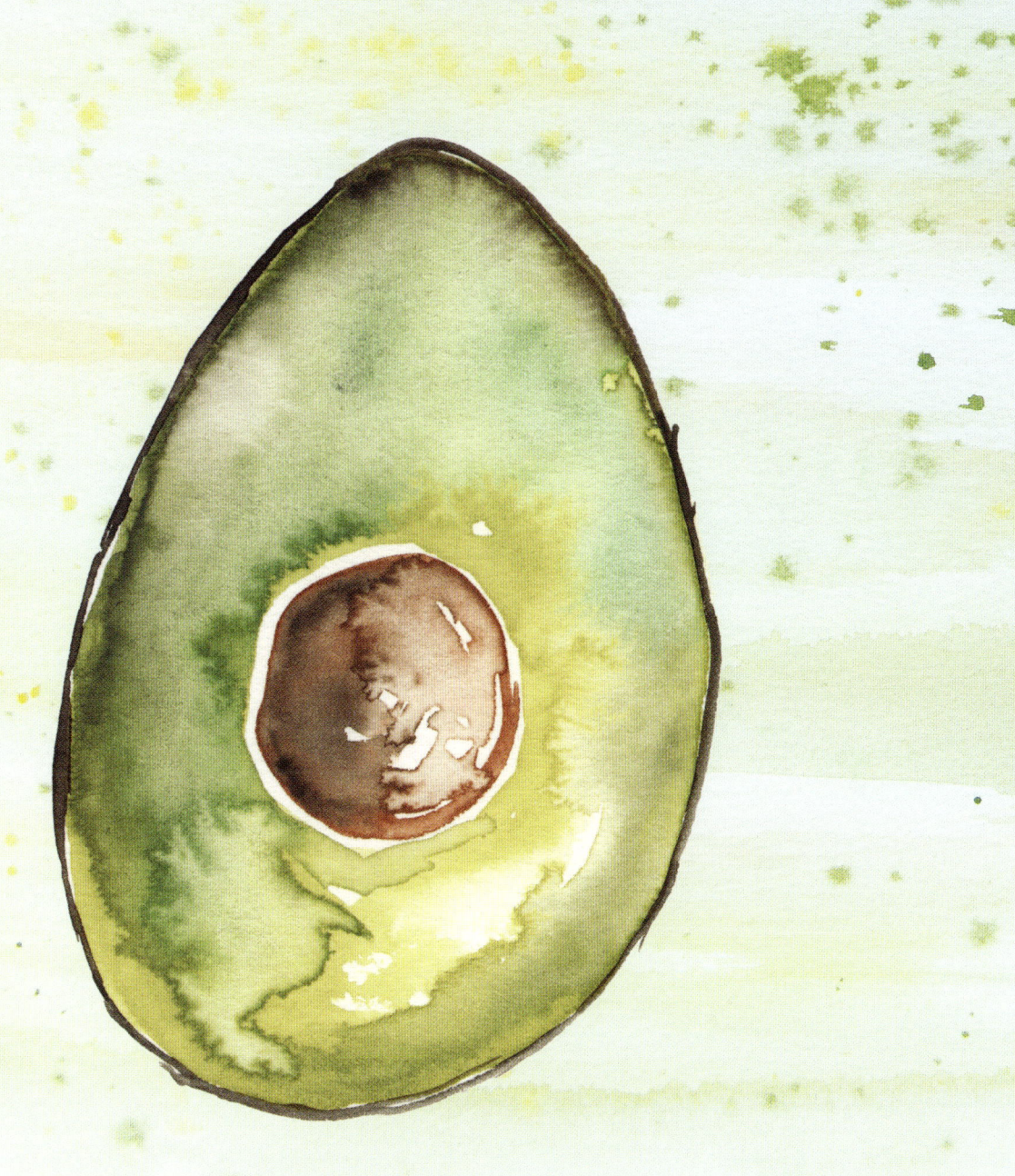

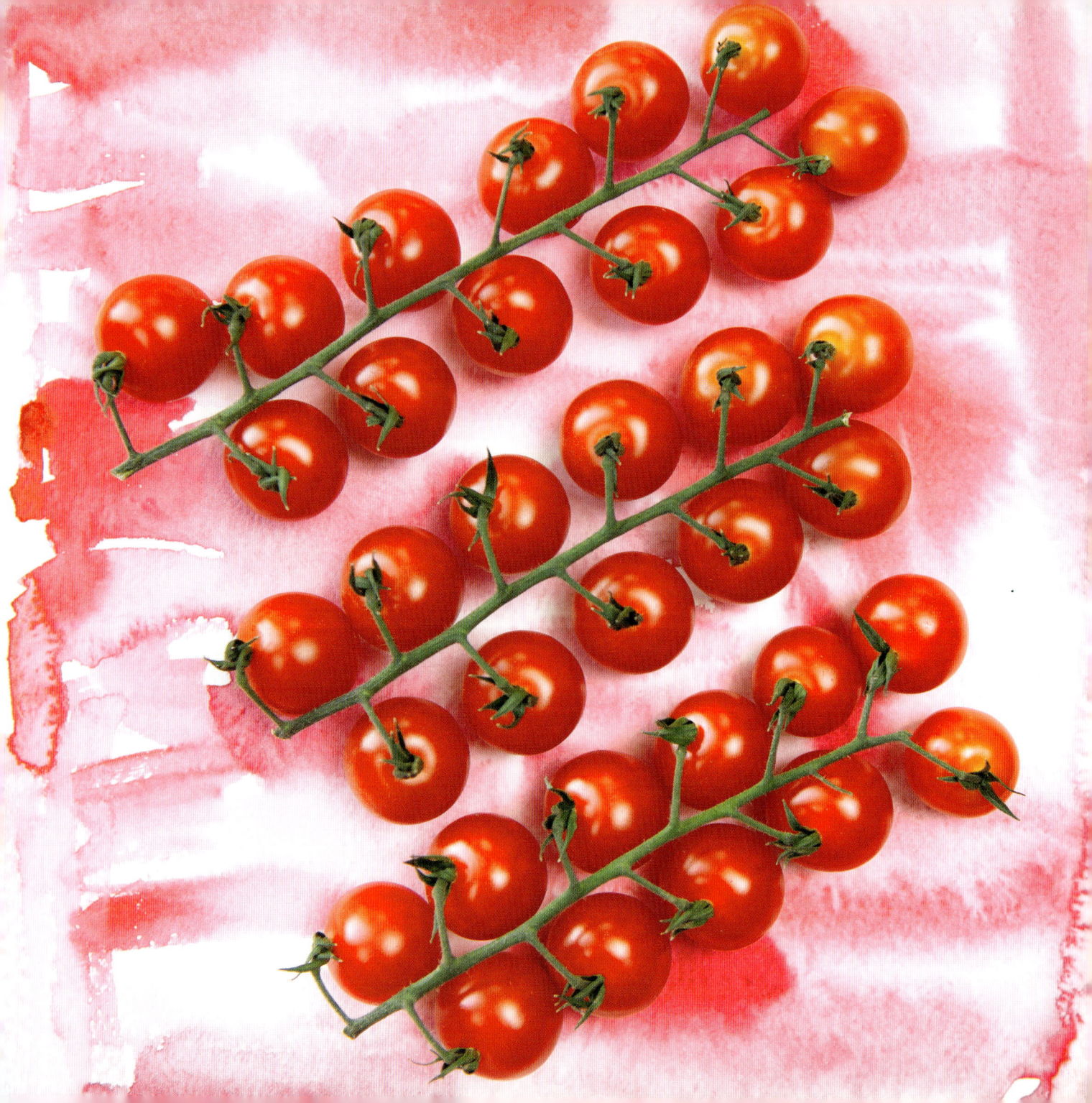

Tomato

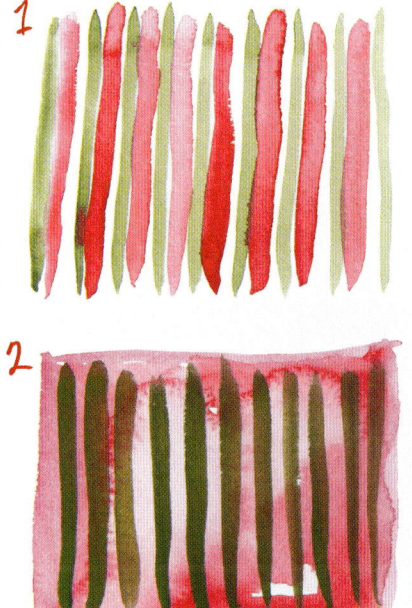

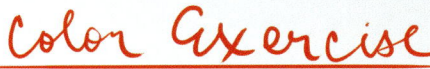

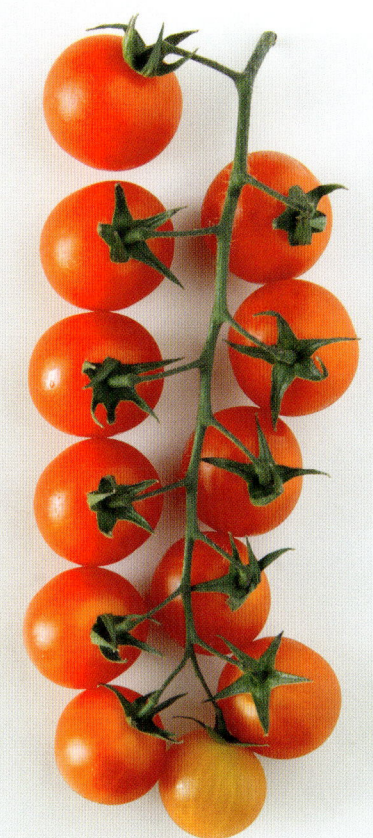

Color Exercise

1) Paint alternating green & red stripes with white space between, but allow them to touch & bleed sometimes.

2) Paint a red rectangle & let it dry. Paint green stripes over it & notice how the green appears a bit darker over the red.

Recipe Idea

Make a salsa by mixing chopped cherry tomatoes, pomegranate seeds, diced red onion, chopped cilantro, lime juice & salt.

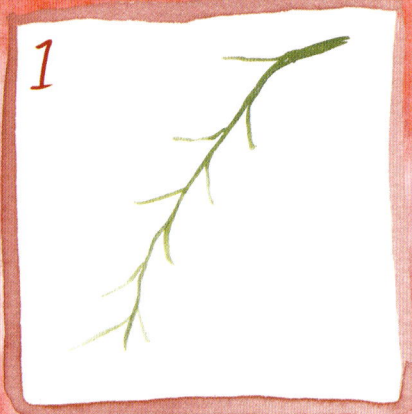

1

Begin by painting a green vine with stems.

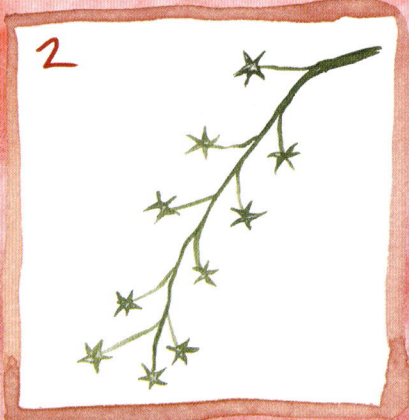

2

Add little star-shaped leaves. Allow the green to dry so it doesn't bleed with the red paint you're about to add.

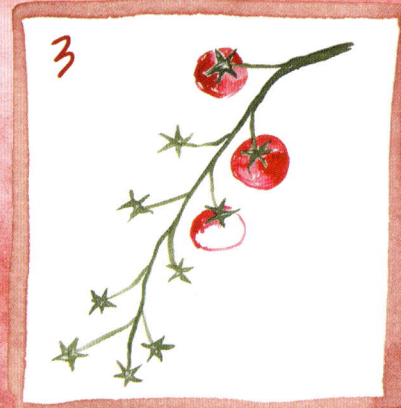

3

Start adding the tomatoes by making a round outline around the leaves, then filling it in. Try not to paint over the green.

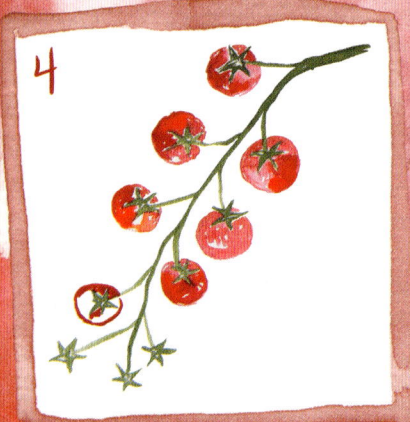

4

I prefer not to fill the tomatoes in completely, because I like the way they look with little specks of unpainted white.

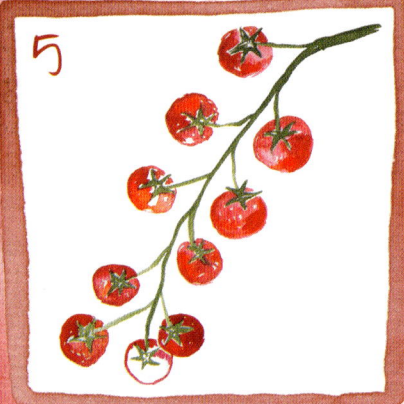

5

I'm using just one shade of red. When I have more water on my brush, the color appears lighter.

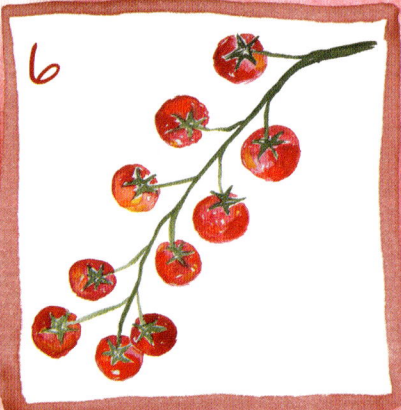

6

While the tomatoes are still wet, dot a few of them with yellow paint.

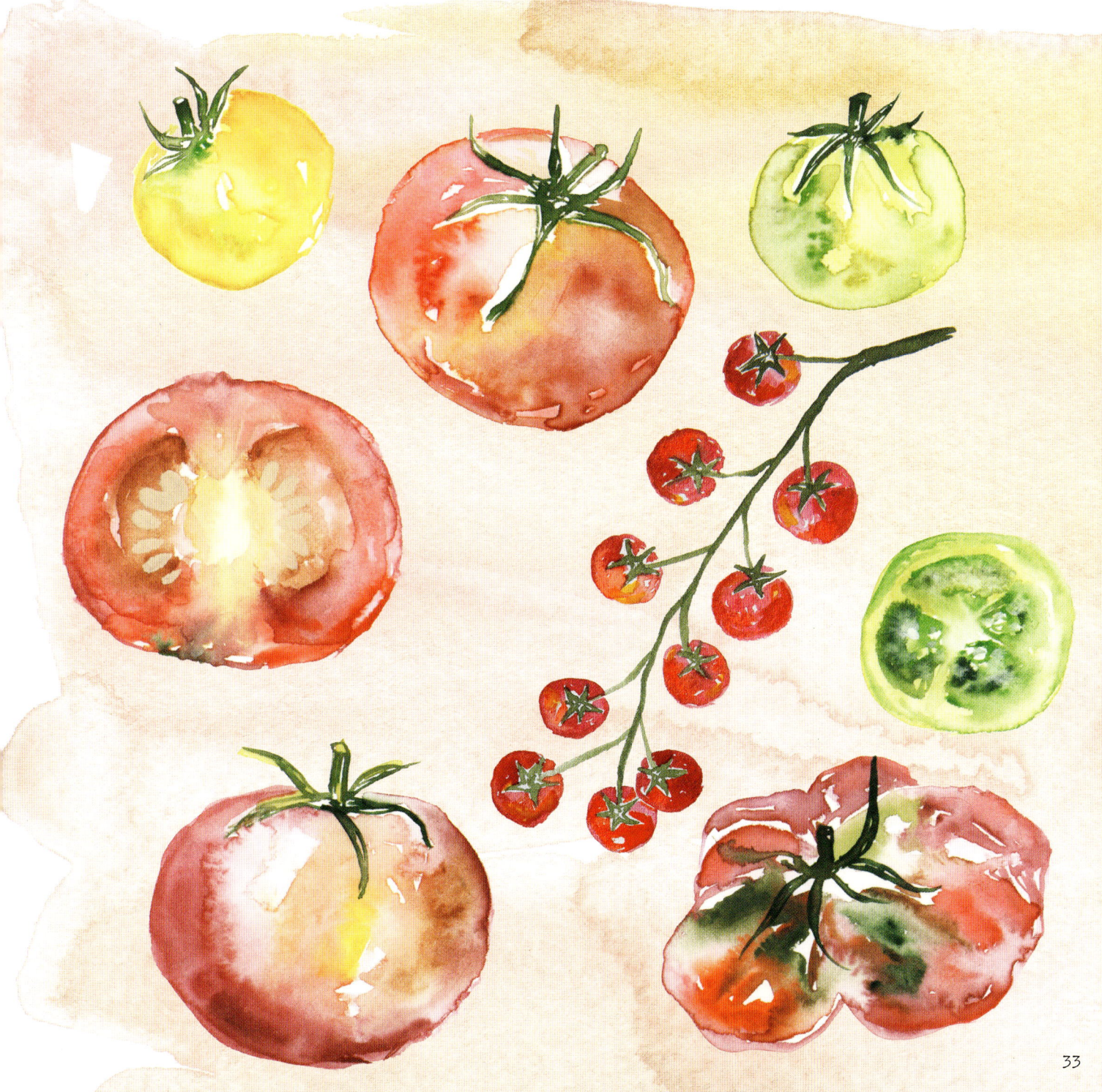

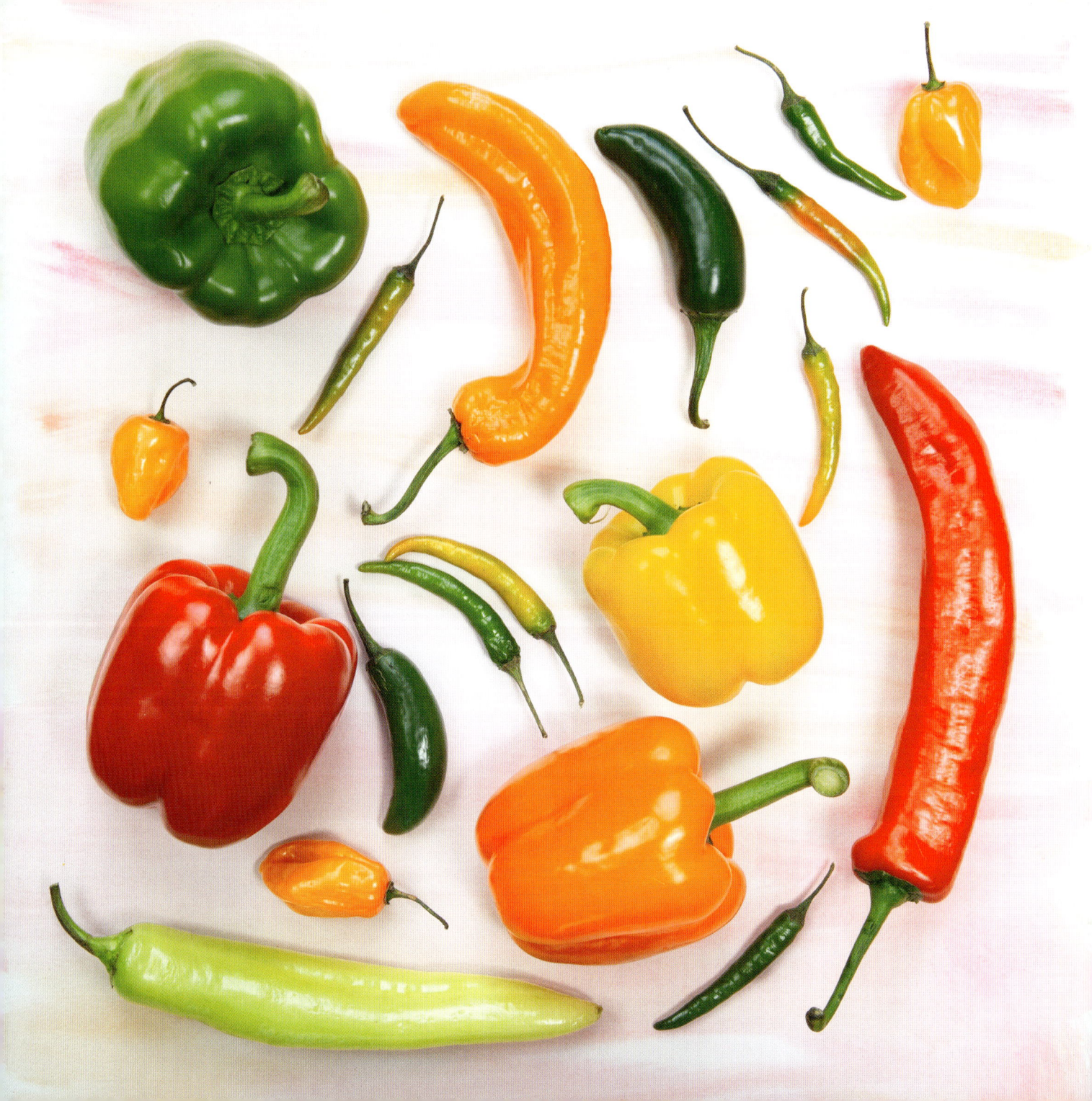

Bell Pepper

On your plate, mix a couple shades of red (try red + orange, or red + brown).
Also mix a couple shades of green (try green + brown, or green + black).
Paint a wash of color using 2 different brushes & varying amounts of water.
Watch how the colors change based on how much water is on your brush.

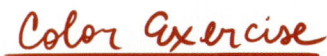

Color Exercise

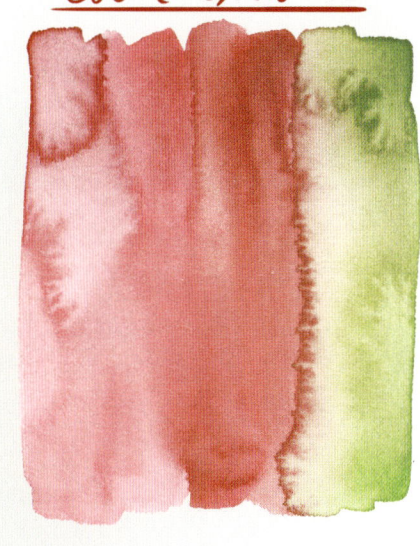

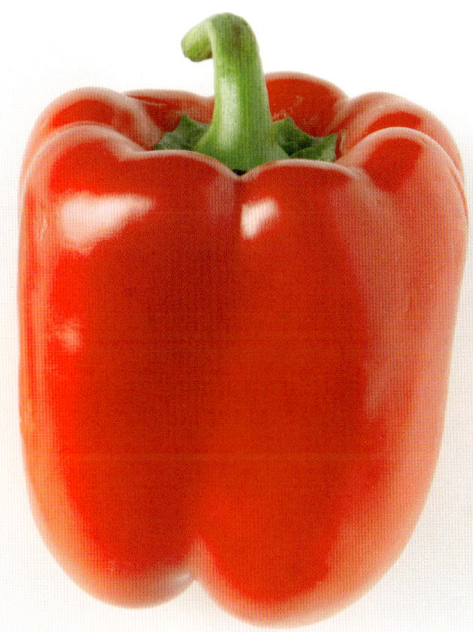

Recipe Idea

Make a Mediterranean-style chopped salad by combining cubed
bell peppers (any & all colors), cucumber, red onion & tomato,
plus crumbled feta, garbanzo beans & mint. Toss with olive oil,
lemon, salt & pepper. Garnish with edible flowers (see page 103).

1

Begin by painting
a green stem.

2

Next, add the red
bumps of the pepper
behind the stem. If
the green is not dry,
it may bleed a bit.

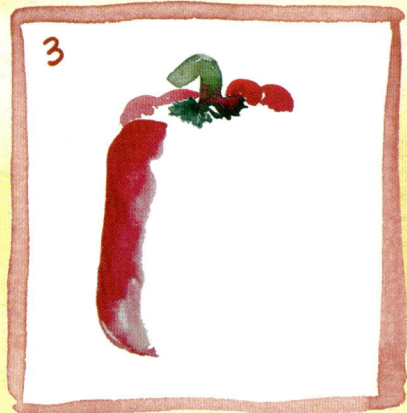

3

Starting on one side, paint
the long sections. As you use
just one shade of red, more
water on your brush will
make it appear lighter.

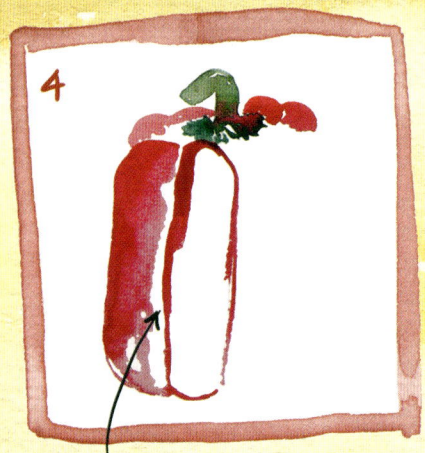

4

Leave a bit of white between
each long section to show
separation. Use a pencil to
draw the sections if easier.

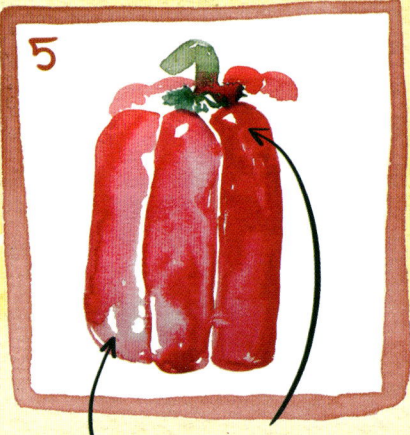

5

Also leave some
unpainted specks
of white instead of
filling it all in.

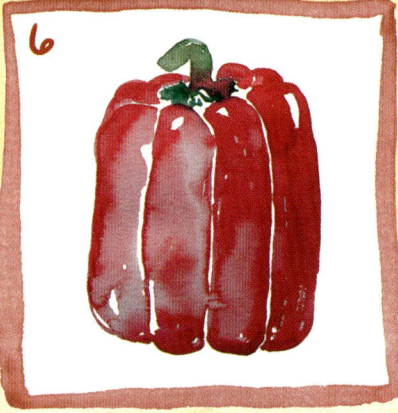

6

Notice how unpainted
white bits & lighter
red areas appear as
highlights.

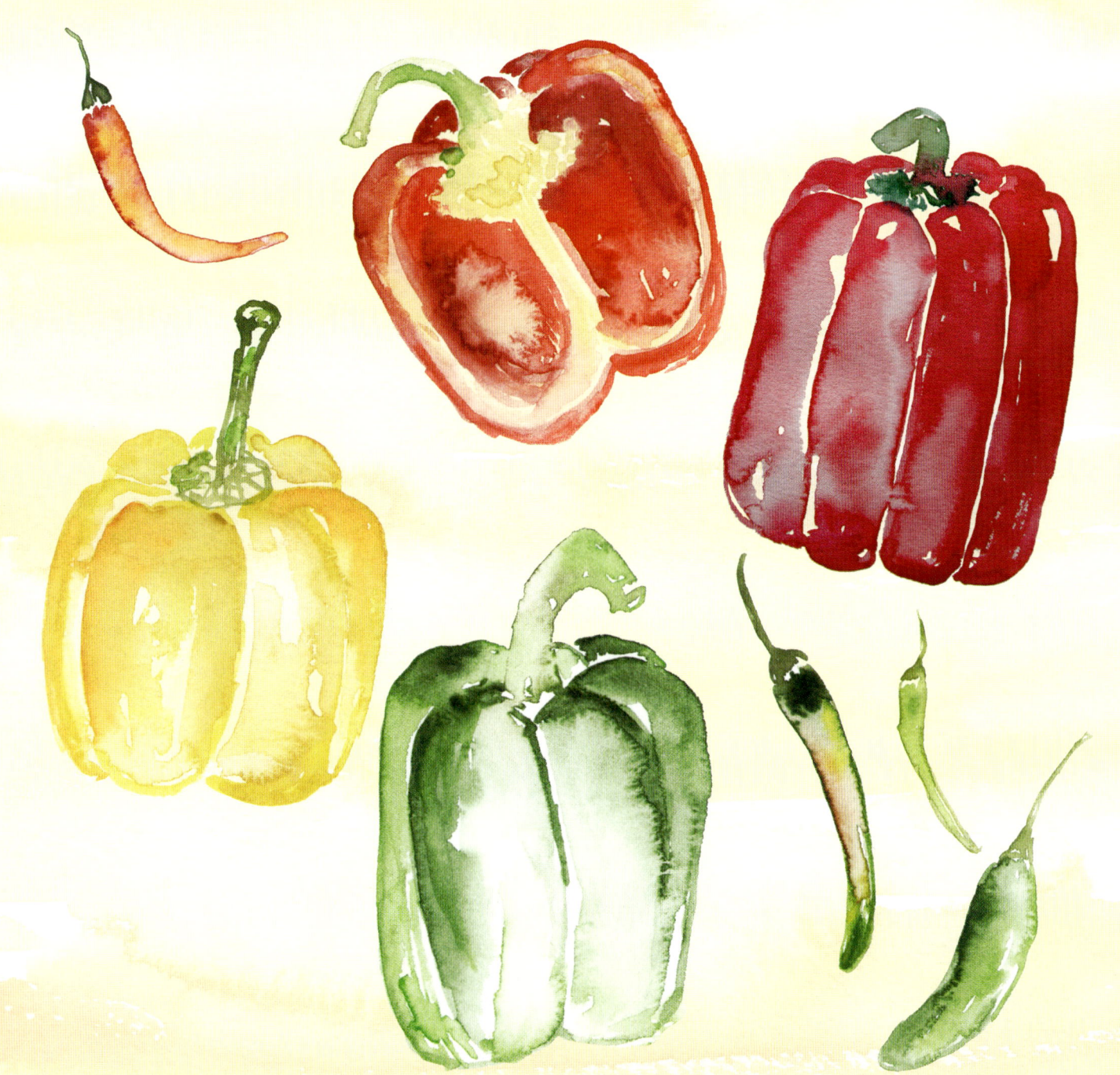

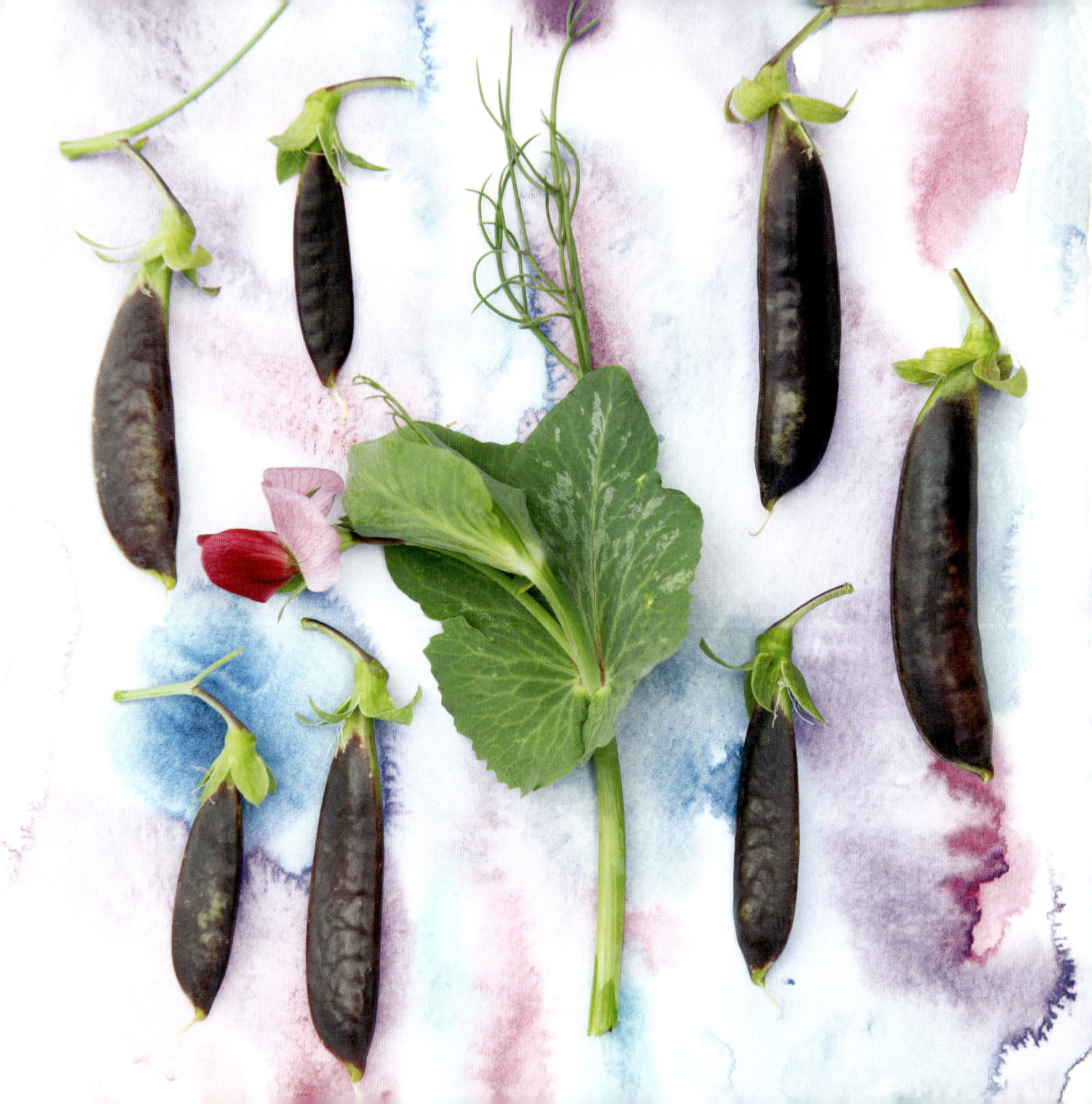

Pea

Did you know peas can be green OR purple? They grow on a vine-like plant & produce beautiful edible flowers. (However, these flowers should not be confused with Sweet Pea blooms, which are poisonous).

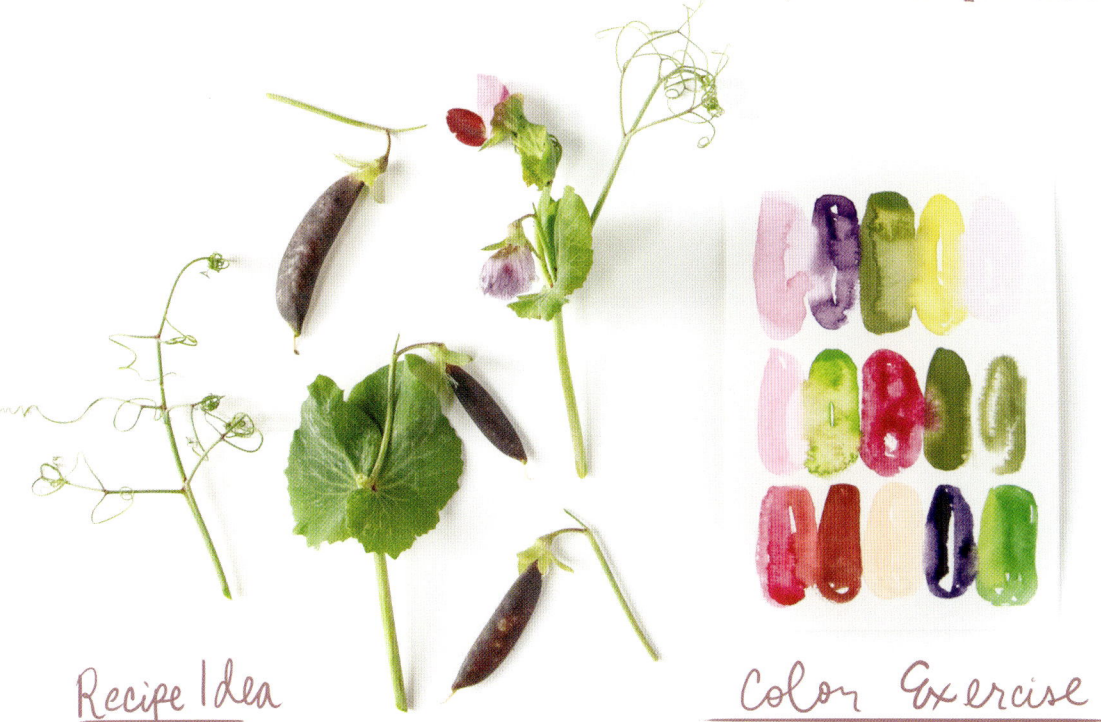

Recipe Idea

Try eating these peas raw (the whole pod!). Or sauté them briefly with butter & toss them with mint, Parmesan, salt, pepper & a squeeze of lemon.

Color Exercise

Take a moment to look at all the colors in this pea plant. I see different shades of purple, green & pink. Make a small, loose painting like the one above, being sure to rinse your brush well between colors. Notice how when the colors touch, they bleed together to form new colors! The wetter your brush, the more they are apt to bleed.

1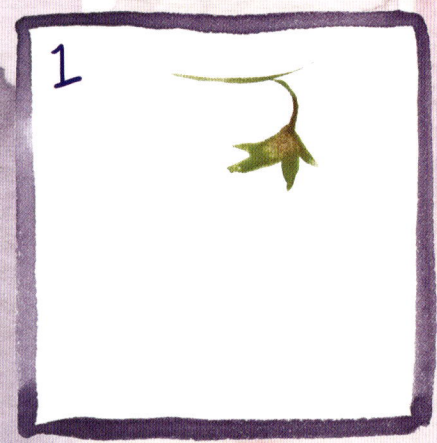

Start by painting a green stem. Then add a dab of brown while it's still wet. Allow to dry.

2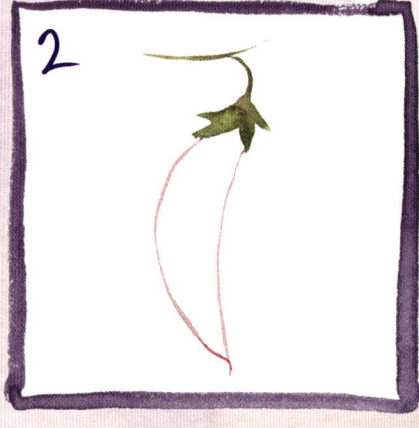

Use a pencil to draw the outline of a pea, then erase it so there's just a faint guide. Mix purple paint with a lot of water to make a light shade. Use that to paint over the pencil.

3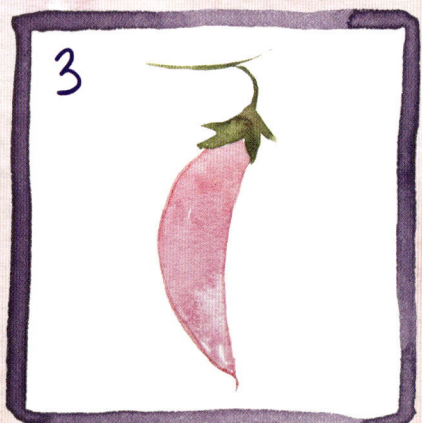

Fill in the pea with light purple. Leave a few unpainted white bits.

4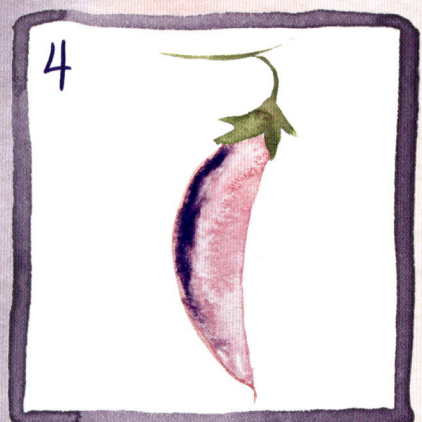

While the pea is still wet, paint with dark purple to add shading & contour on one side.

5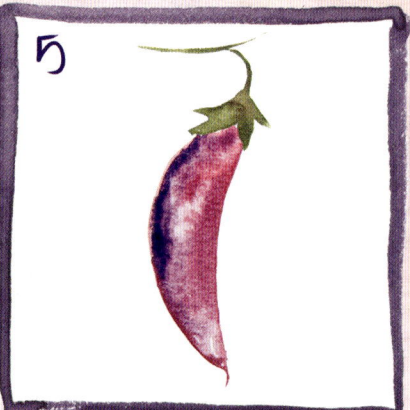

Mix some purple paint with a bit of red to create a different shade & add that to the other side of the pea.

6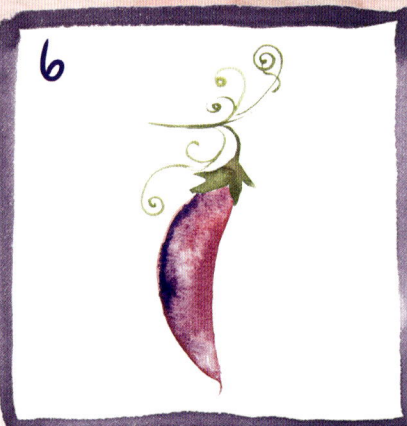

Using green paint (small brush, not too drippy), paint thin little curlicue tendrils.

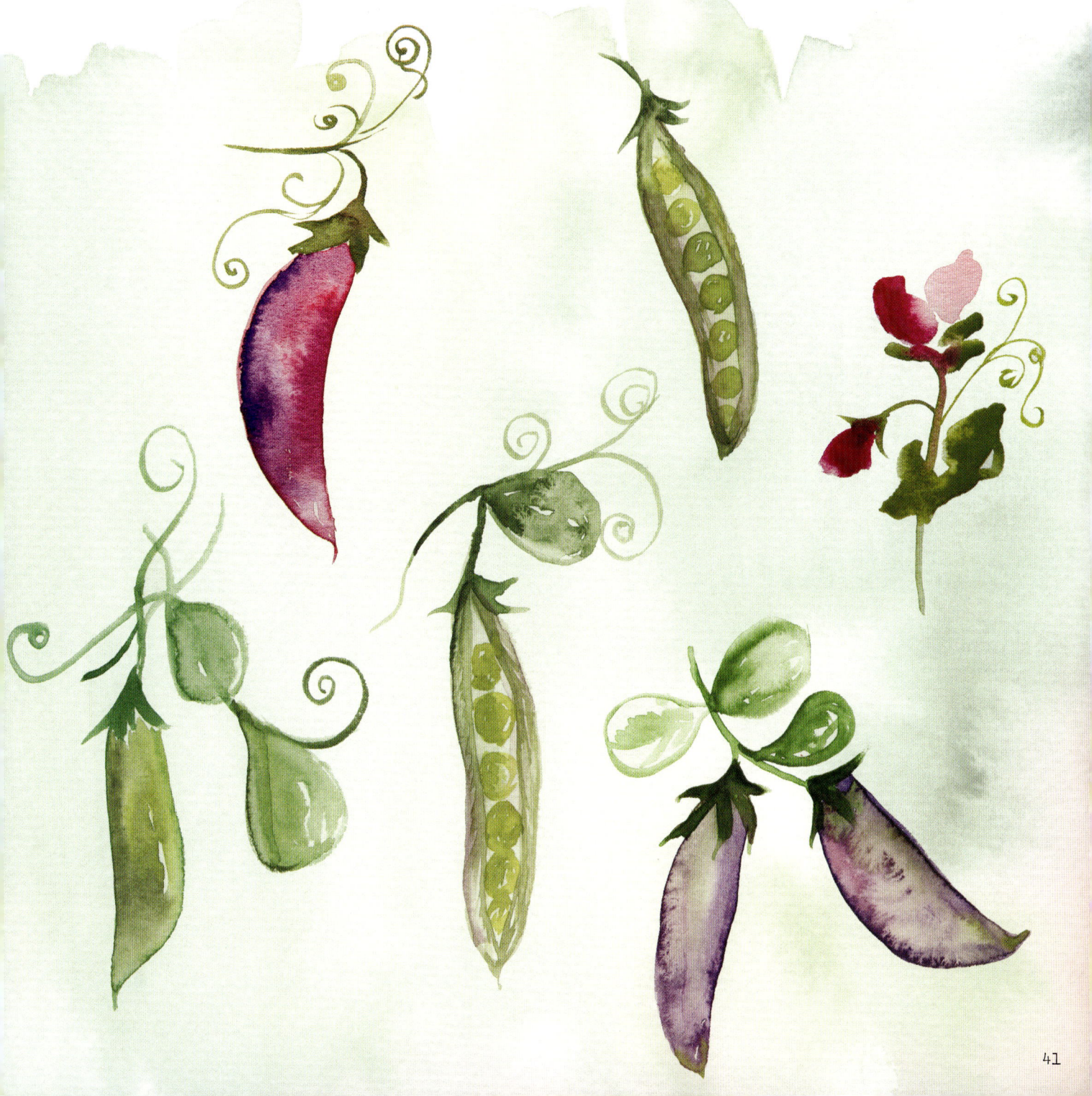

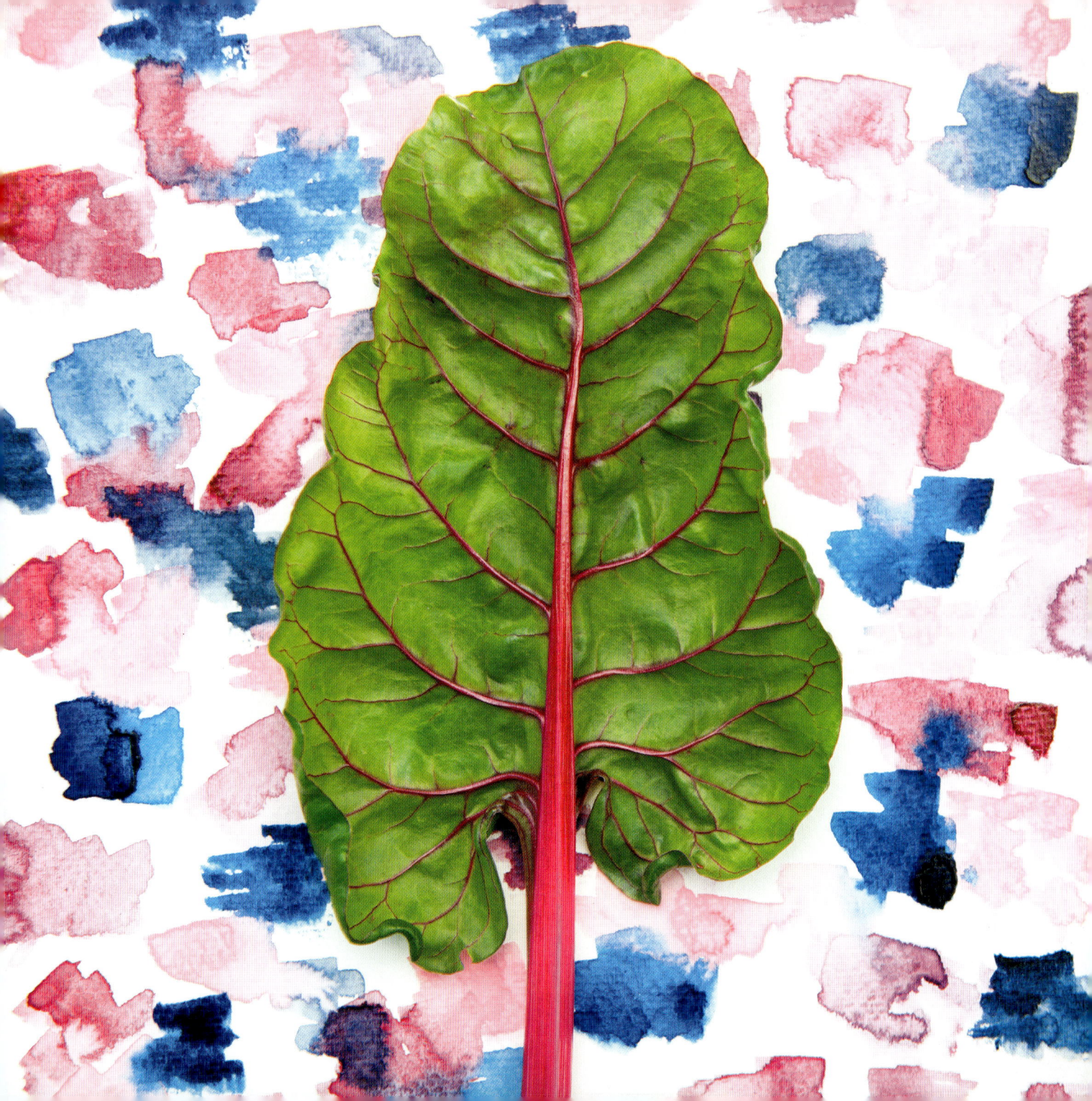

Chard

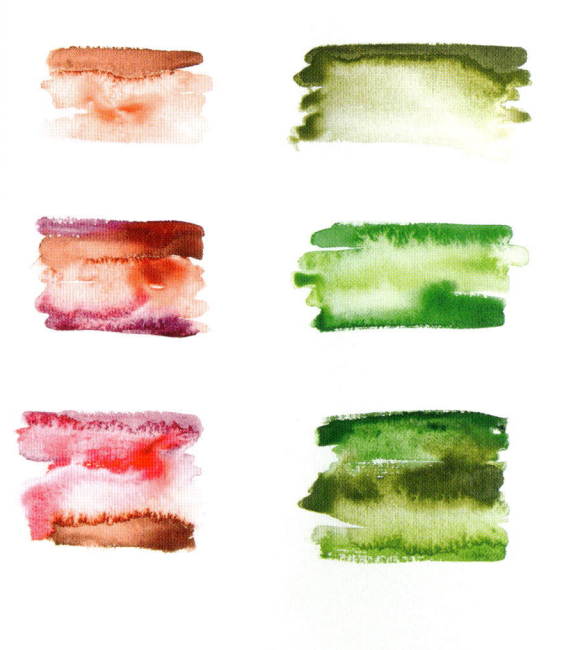

Color Exercise

Chard is so amazing! Explore this vibrant leafy green by painting several small blocks of color. Mix different shades of green together with varying amounts of water. Try mixing your red paint with pink, purple & rusty brown.

Recipe Idea

Chard is delicious when sliced into ribbons & sautéed briefly with butter & garlic. Finely chop & include those beautiful stalks!

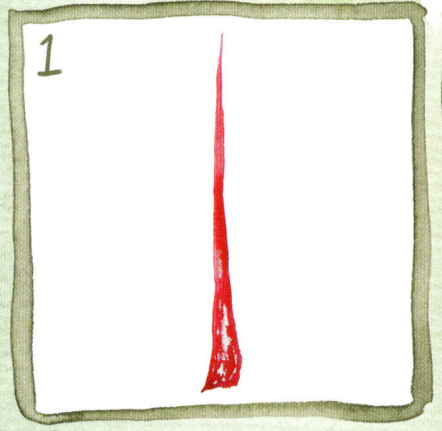

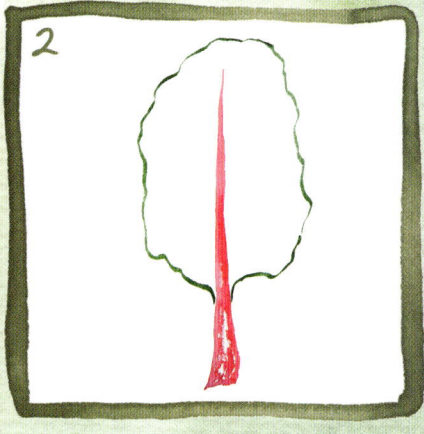

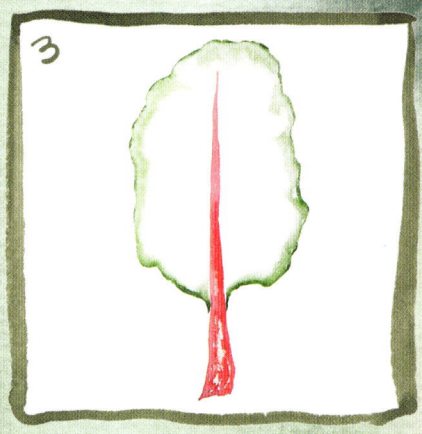

Start by painting a red spine/stalk. Leave a few bits of unpainted white.

Next, add a wavy dark green outline. Quickly rinse your brush & fill it with just water.

Paint with water inside the outline to blur the line. Try not to touch the red spine, but get close.

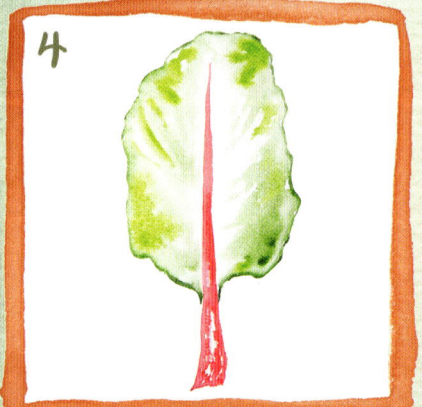

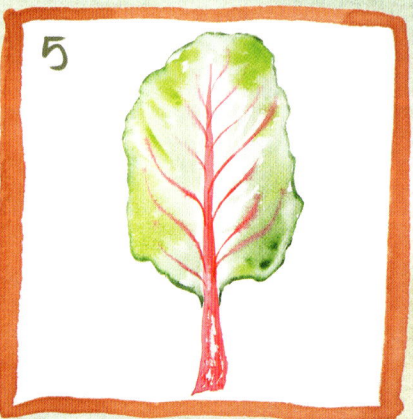

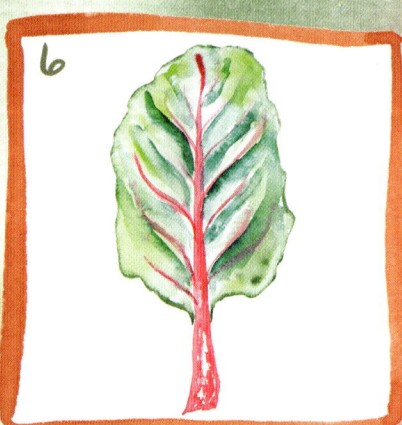

Using 2 shades of green, paint strokes from the outline inward.

Let it dry for a moment or blot lightly with a cloth. Pressing lightly with the tip of your smallest brush, add small thin lines of red for veins. Notice it bleeds more where it's wetter.

Allow it to dry another minute, then add dark green between the veins. Blot areas that bleed too much & repaint.

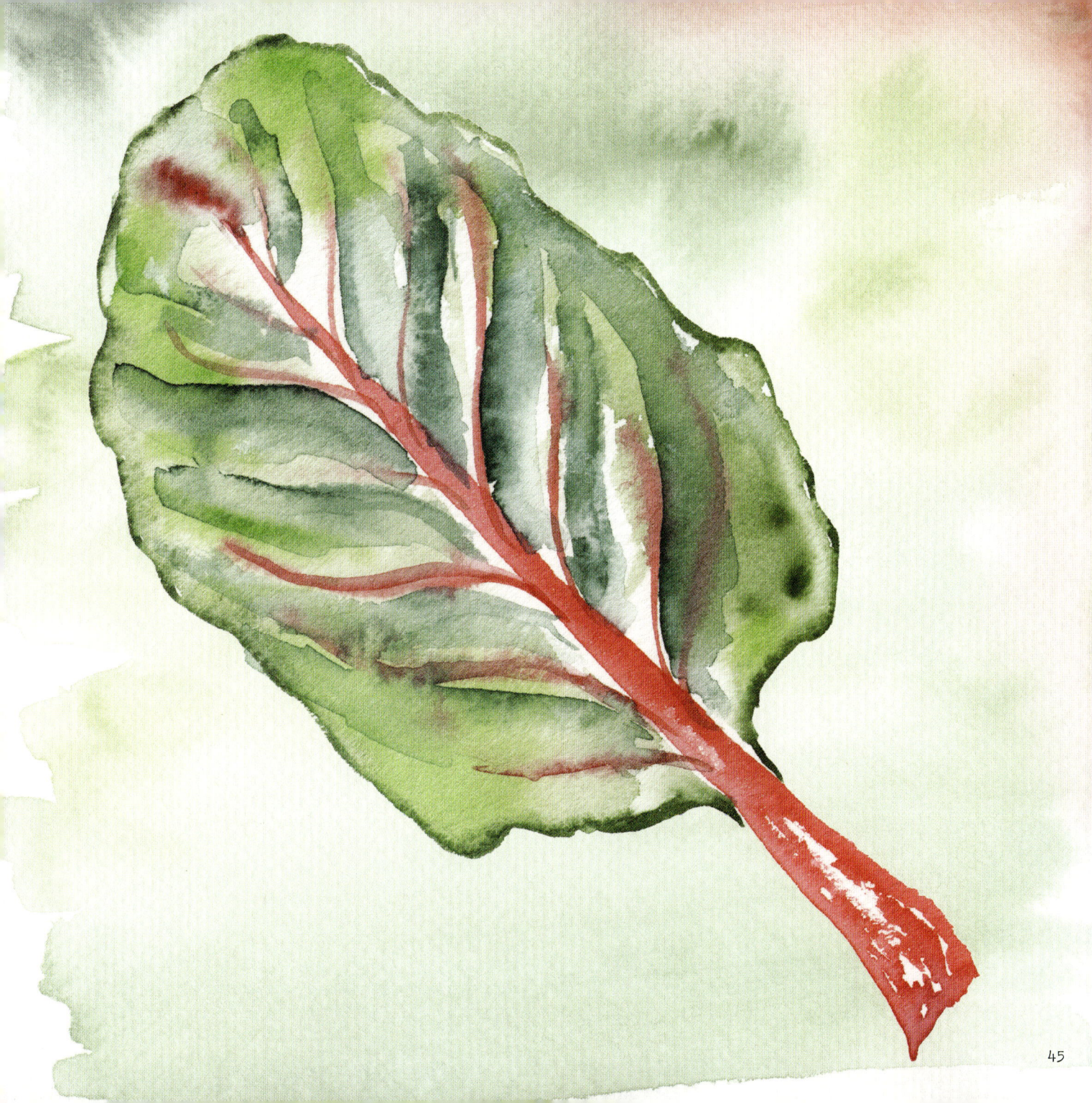

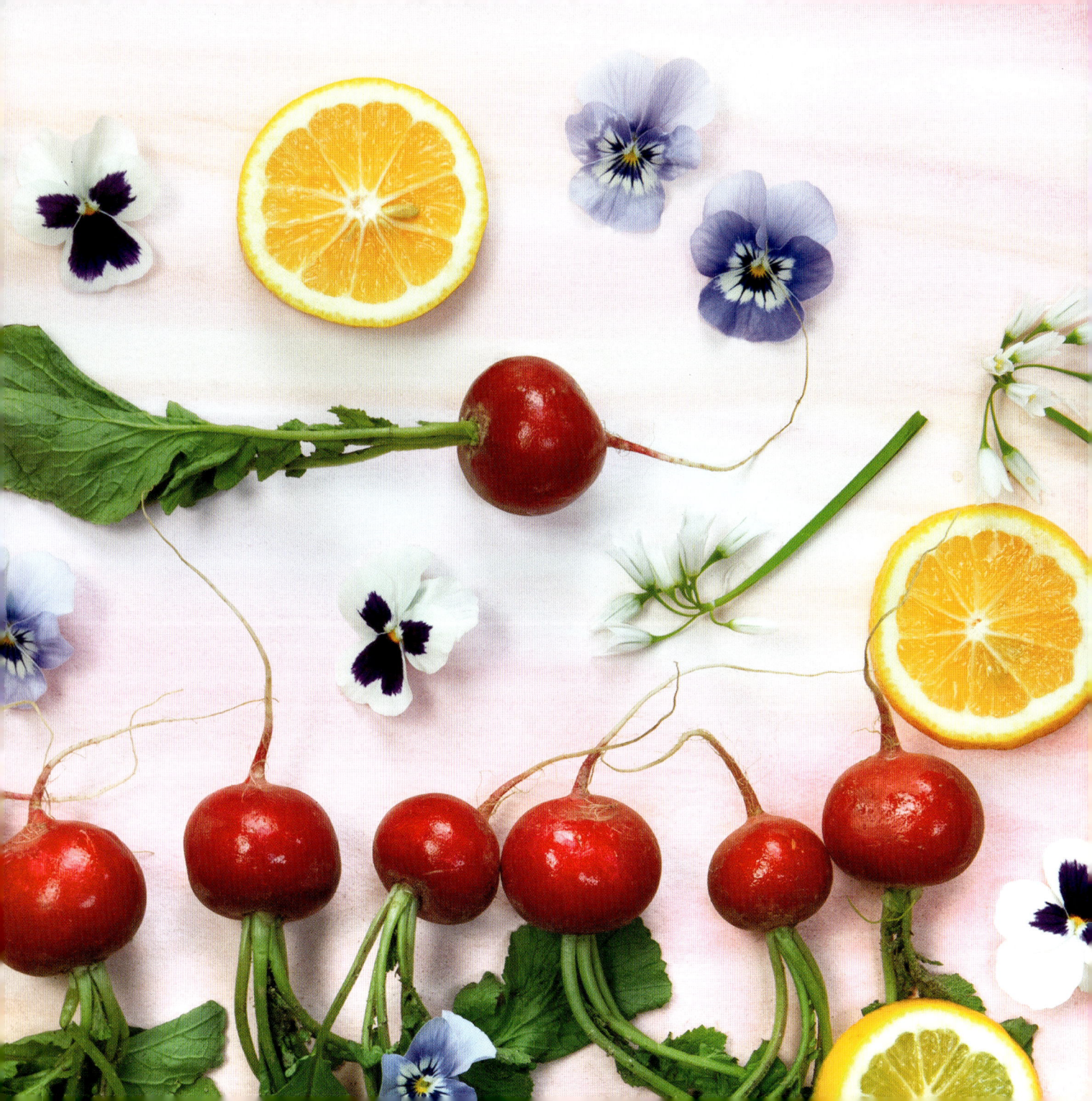

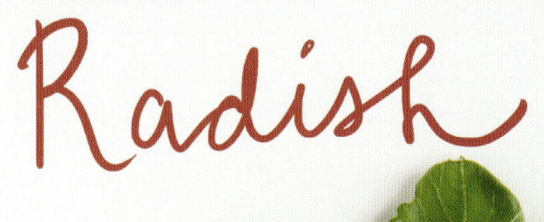

Radish

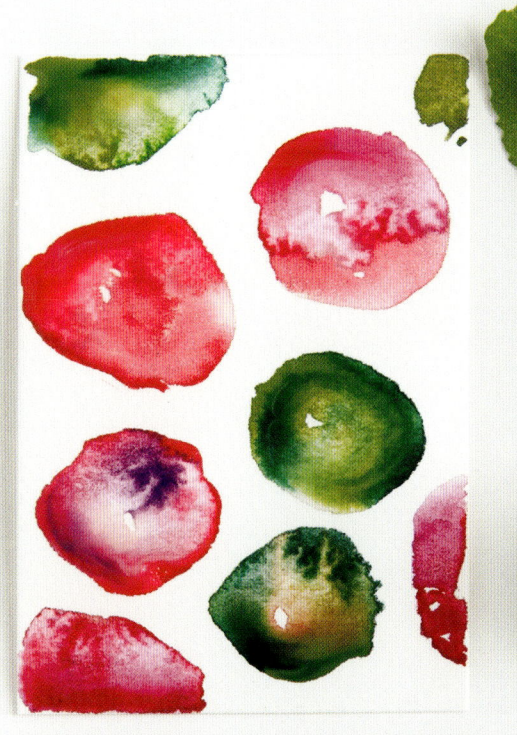

I see shades of green, red, purple, pink & brown. On your plate, try mixing your own shades by combining these colors.

Color Exercise

Using a brush with just water, paint & fill in several circles. Next, dab paint onto each water circle & watch the colors bleed together. I wonder how it will dry!

Recipe Idea

Top halved radishes with butter, flaky salt & chopped chives.

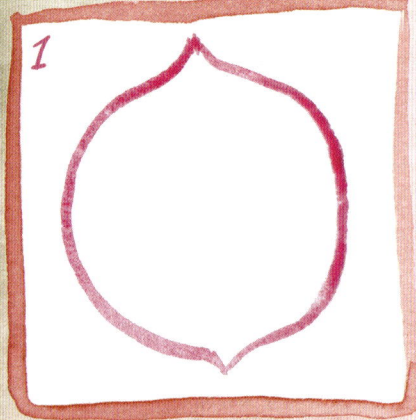

1

Start by painting the outline of the radish. Get a good deal of watery paint on your brush so the outline is quite wet.

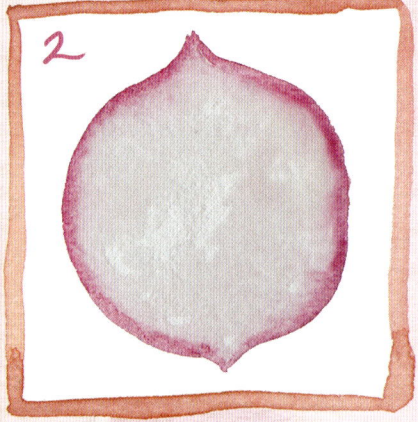

2

Working quickly before the outline dries, rinse your brush & using just water, pull the color toward the middle, leaving a few dry spots.

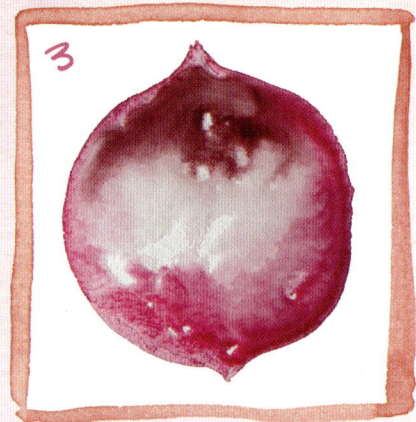

3

Next, dip your brush in shades of purple, red & brown. Paint on the wet areas, mostly around the edges. Let the colors bleed into each other.

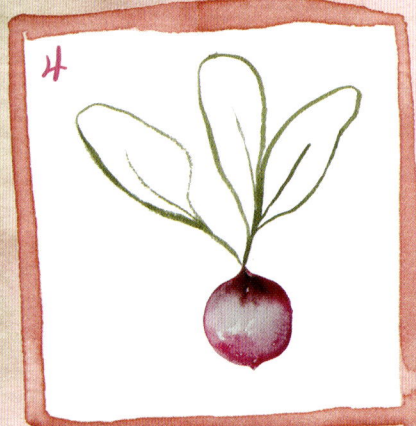

4

Now let's add leaves. Paint leaf outlines using 1 or 2 shades of green.

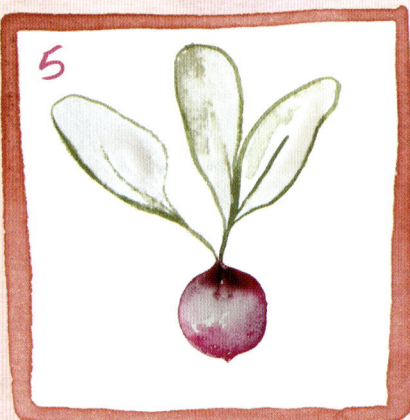

5

As in step 2, rinse your brush & pull the paint inward with just water. Add light green paint over the wet areas.

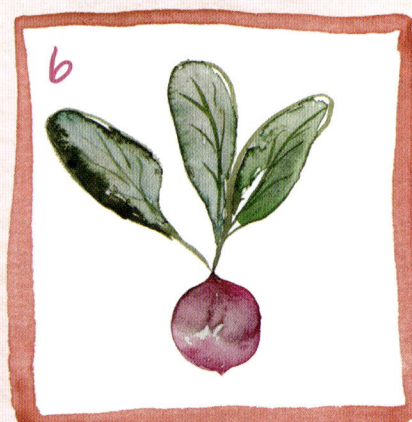

6

Add dark green around the edges. Let it dry. Paint veins on the leaves & notice how the line stays crisp over dry areas.

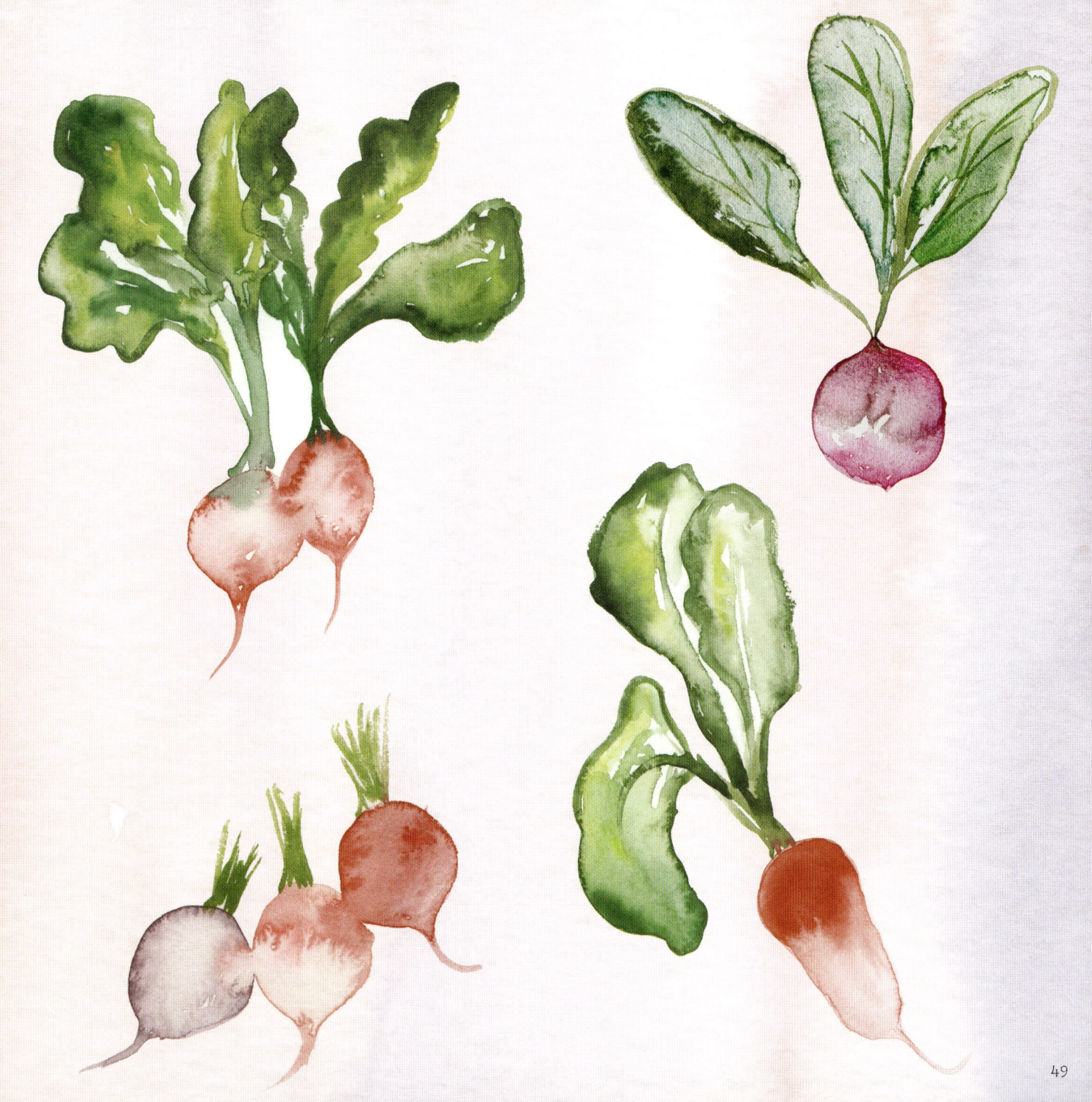

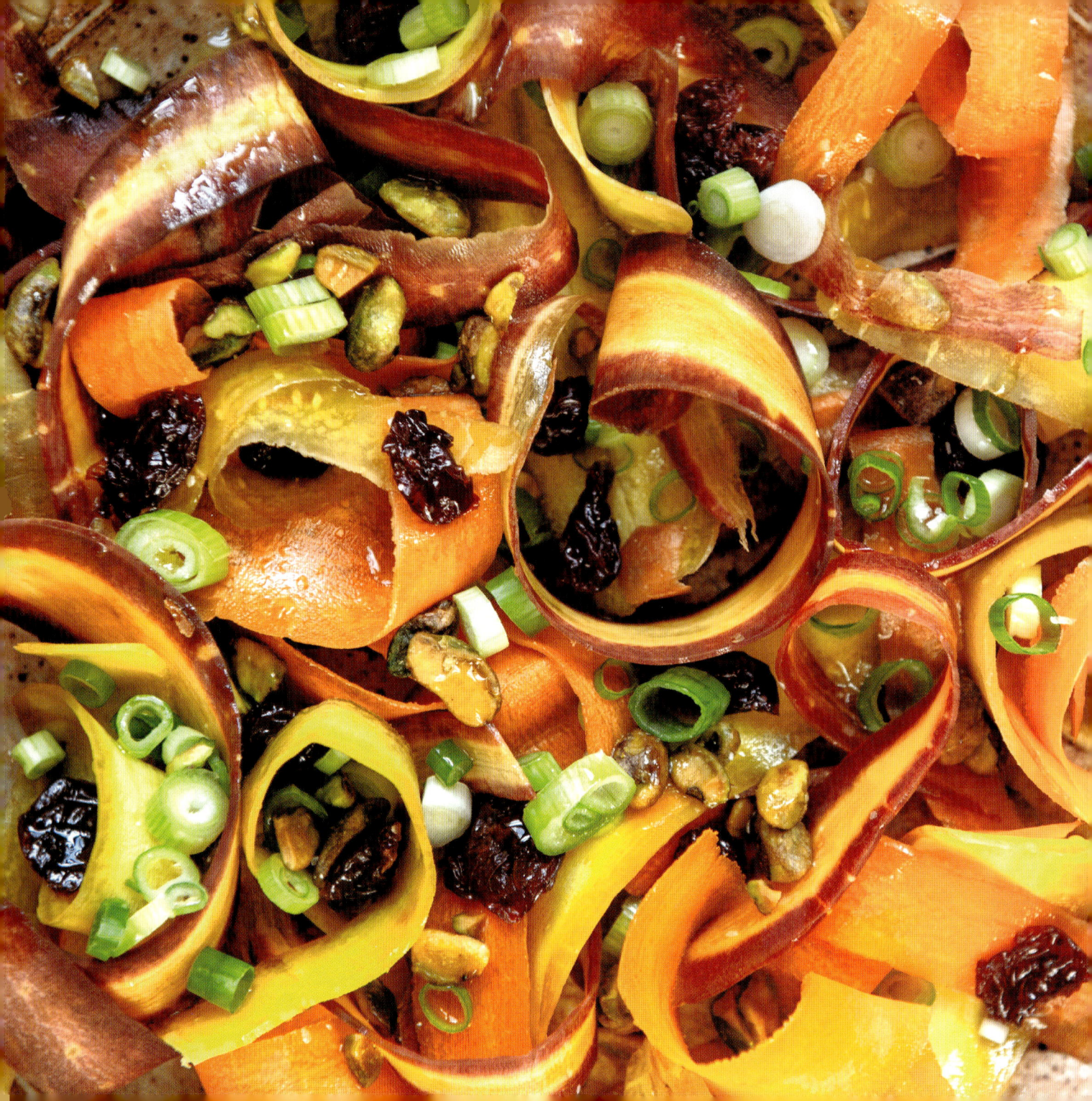

Rainbow Carrot

Rainbow carrots come in many sunset shades. I love how the purple ones are sometimes orange in the middle.

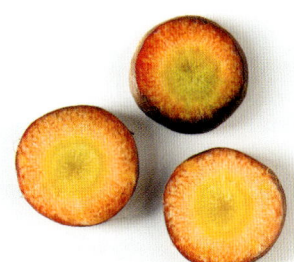

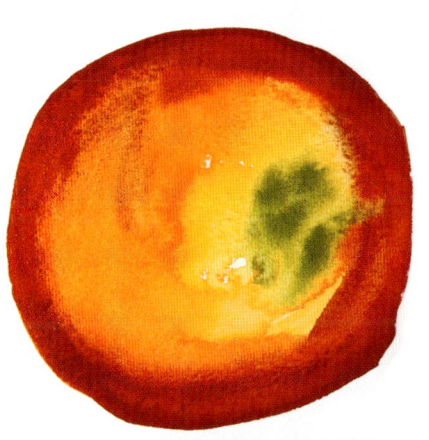

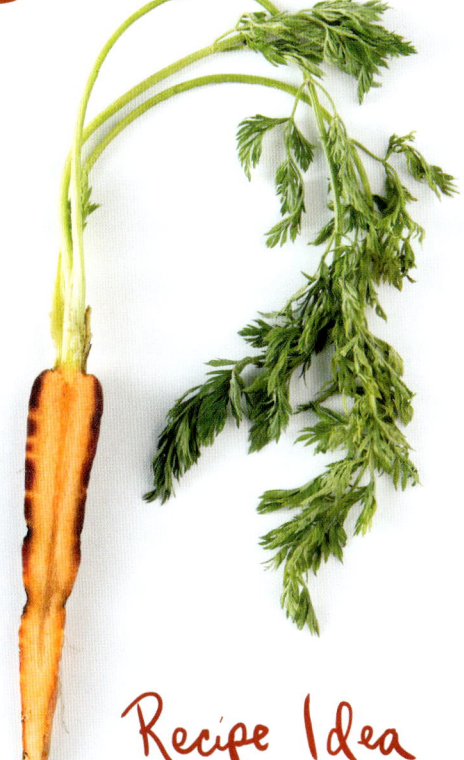

Color Exercise

Paint a yellow & orange circle, then add a dark maroon rim. If it's just damp, the dark paint won't reach the center of the circle. Add a couple dots of green & notice how it changes as it dries.

Recipe Idea

Use a peeler to shave long ribbons of carrot. Pile the ribbons on a plate & top with dried cherries, green onion, pistachios, olive oil, lemon & salt.

1

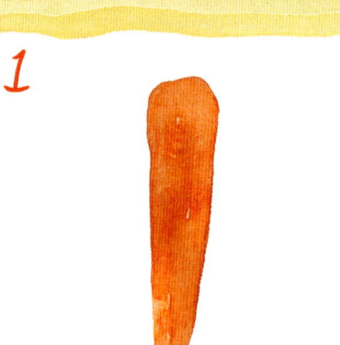

With not too much water, create an even, orange carrot shape.

2

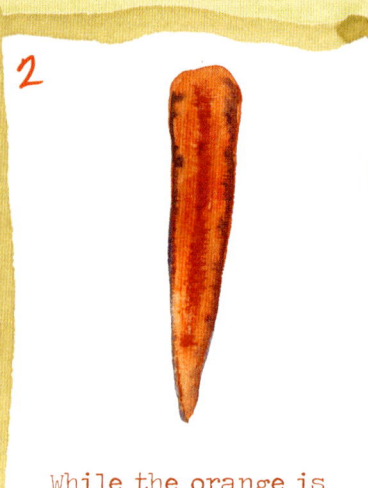

While the orange is damp, add a small amount of purple along the edges & center.

3

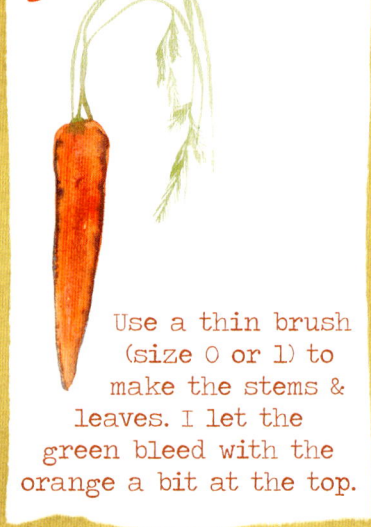

Use a thin brush (size 0 or 1) to make the stems & leaves. I let the green bleed with the orange a bit at the top.

4

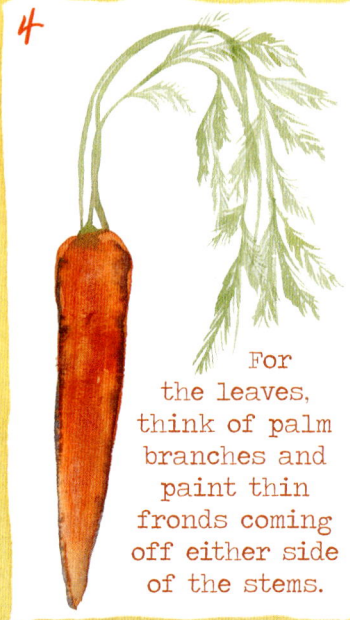

For the leaves, think of palm branches and paint thin fronds coming off either side of the stems.

5

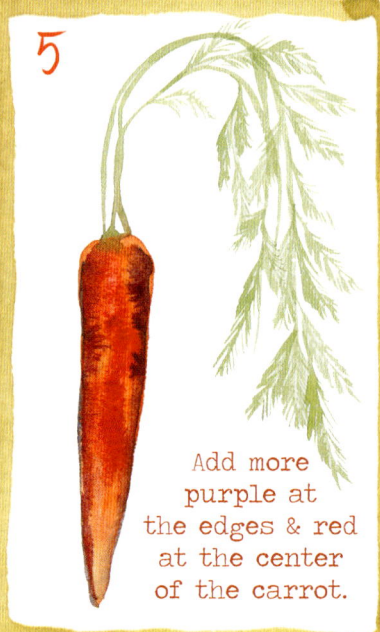

Add more purple at the edges & red at the center of the carrot.

6

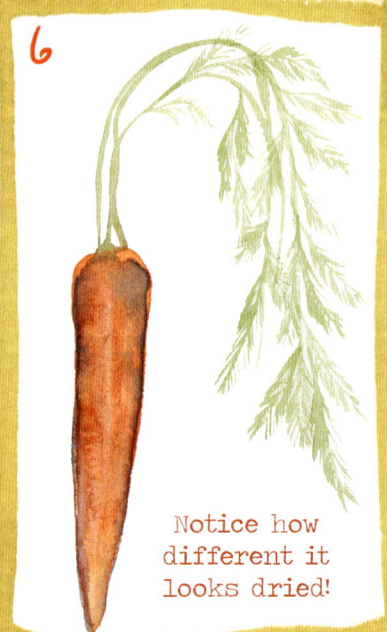

Notice how different it looks dried!

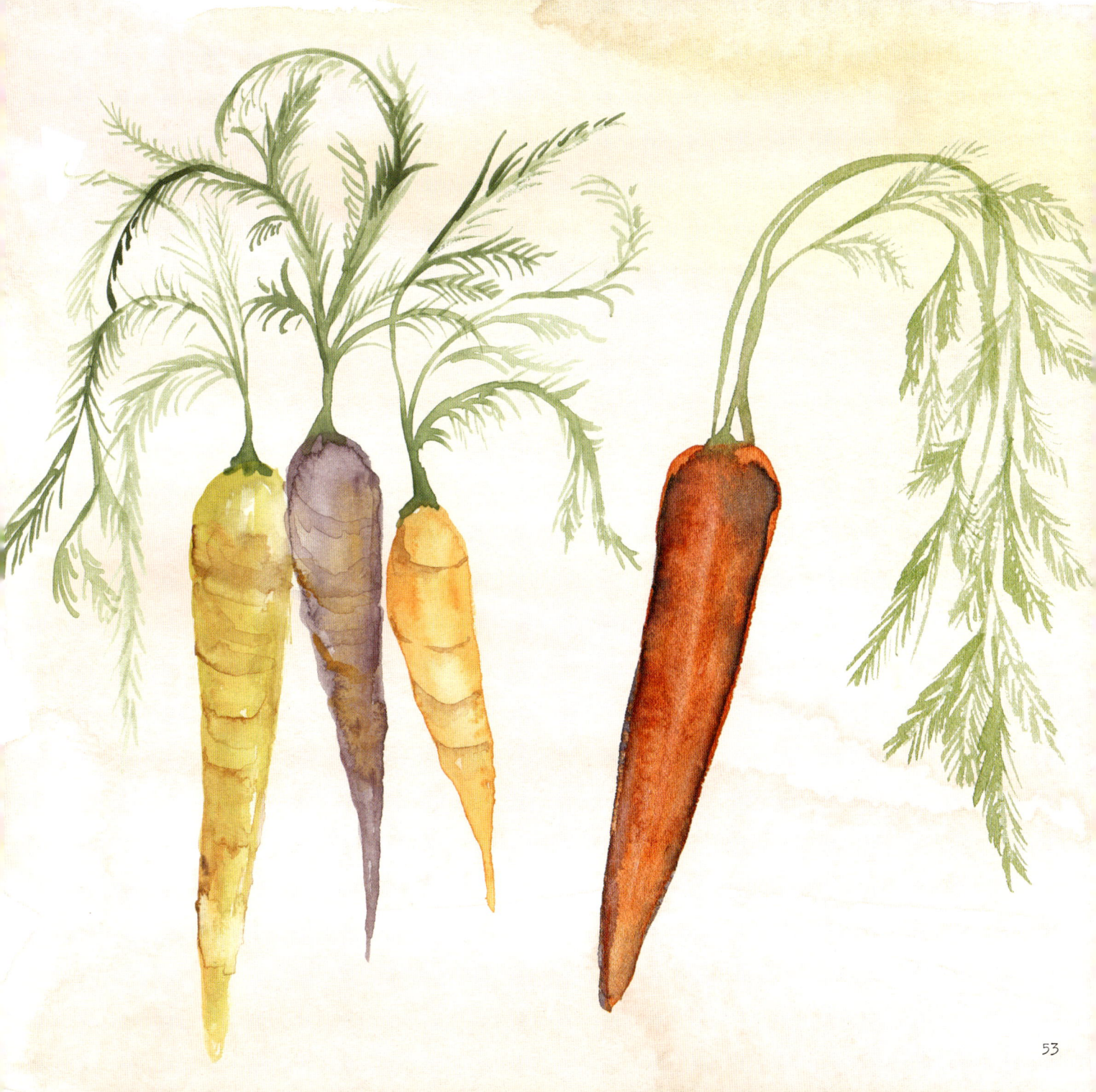

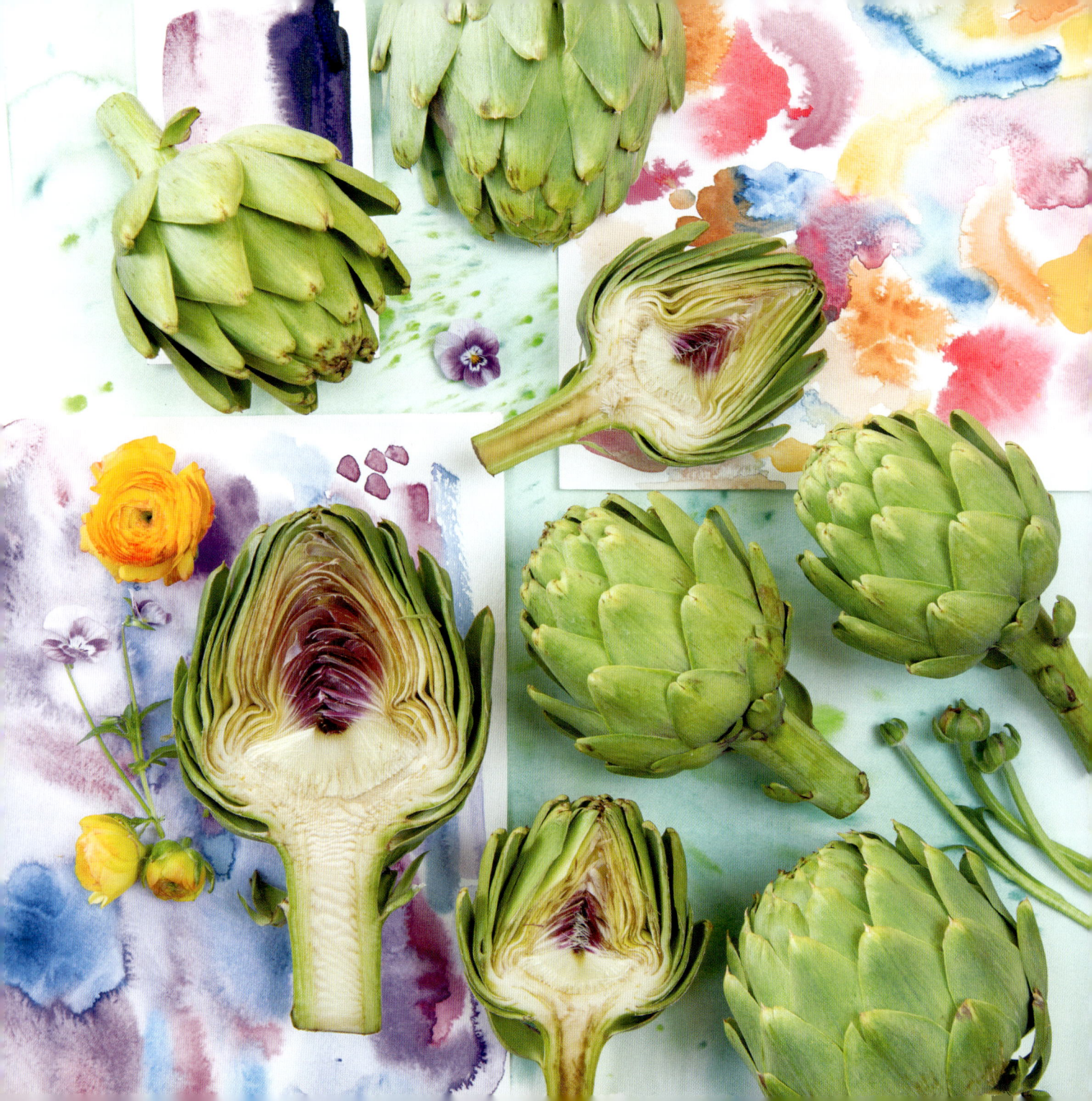

Artichoke

While artichokes are usually green, I love it when I find a purple one at the farmer's market. After you paint a whole artichoke, try slicing it in half to paint the interior.

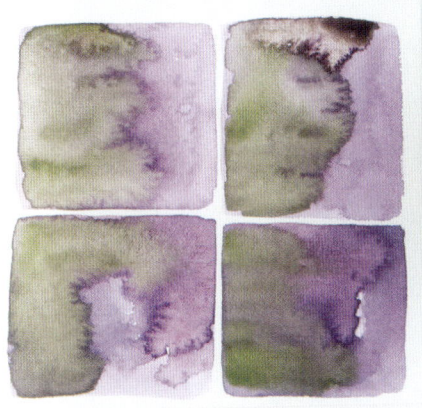

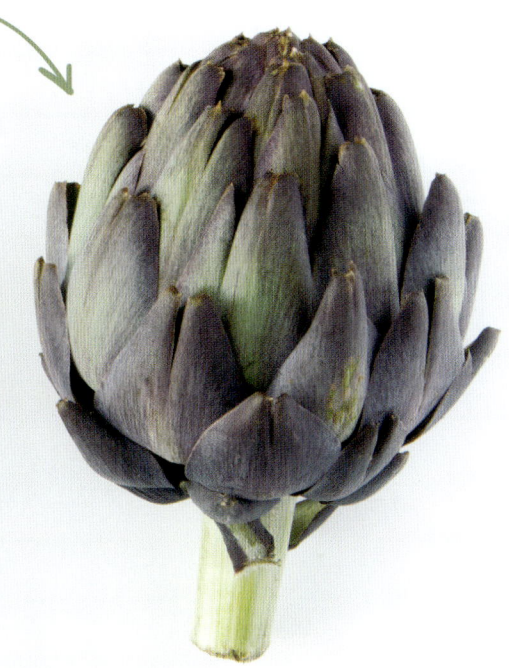

Color Exercise

Create a small color study by painting 4 purple squares. While they're still wet, add a bit of green to each. With enough water, distinct rippled "blooms" will appear as the paint dries.

Recipe Idea

I like to make an edible table runner by placing artichokes, lemons & carnations down the middle of a table. Afterward, I steam the artichokes & enjoy them the classic way, with melted garlic butter.

Testers found this to be one of the more challenging tutorials in this book.
But I know you can do it! Practice makes perfect.

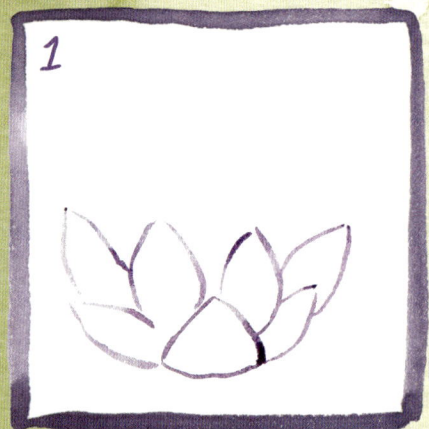

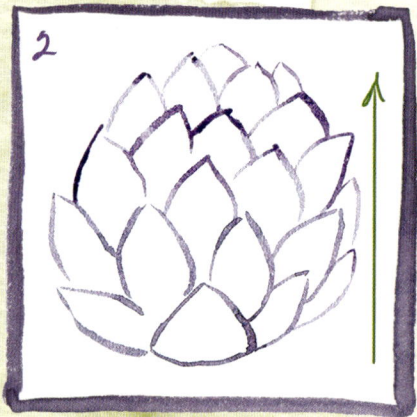

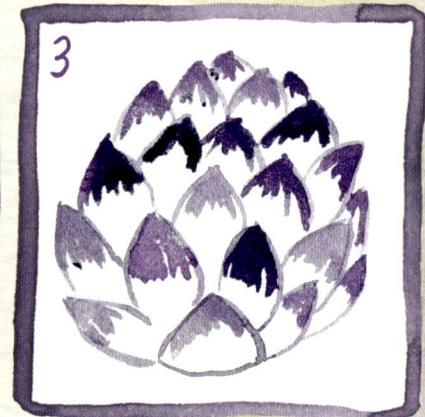

Start by painting thin purple lines for the outlines of the leaves. If the overall shape feels tricky, try using a pencil first.

Begin at the bottom with larger leaves & work your way up, making smaller leaves at the top.

Using 1 shade of purple & varying amounts of water, paint the top portion of each leaf, using small strokes.

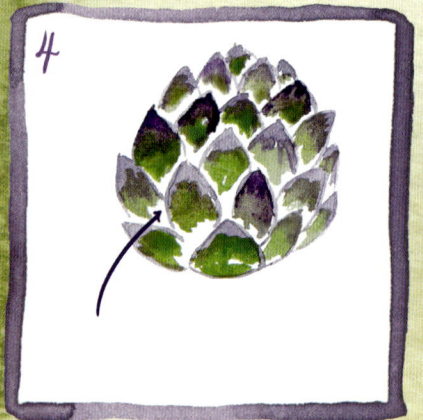

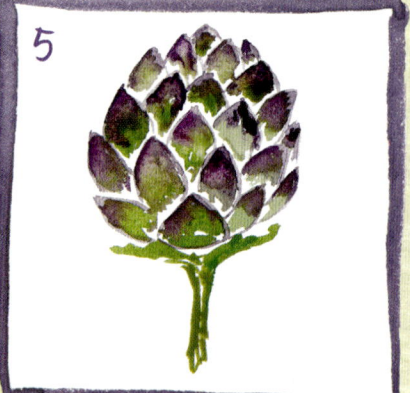

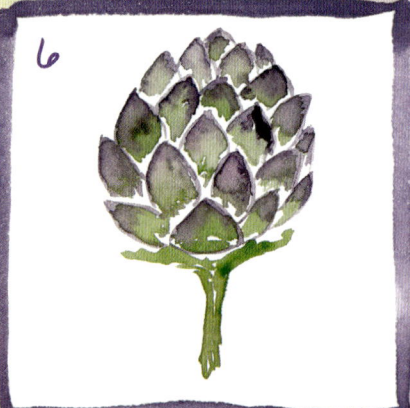

While the purple is still wet, add green to each leaf. Leave a bit of unpainted white between the leaves.

Next, add some reddish purple to the tips, plus a green stem. It will lighten as it dries.

Notice how the unpainted white spaces between the leaves keep the artichoke from looking like a ball.

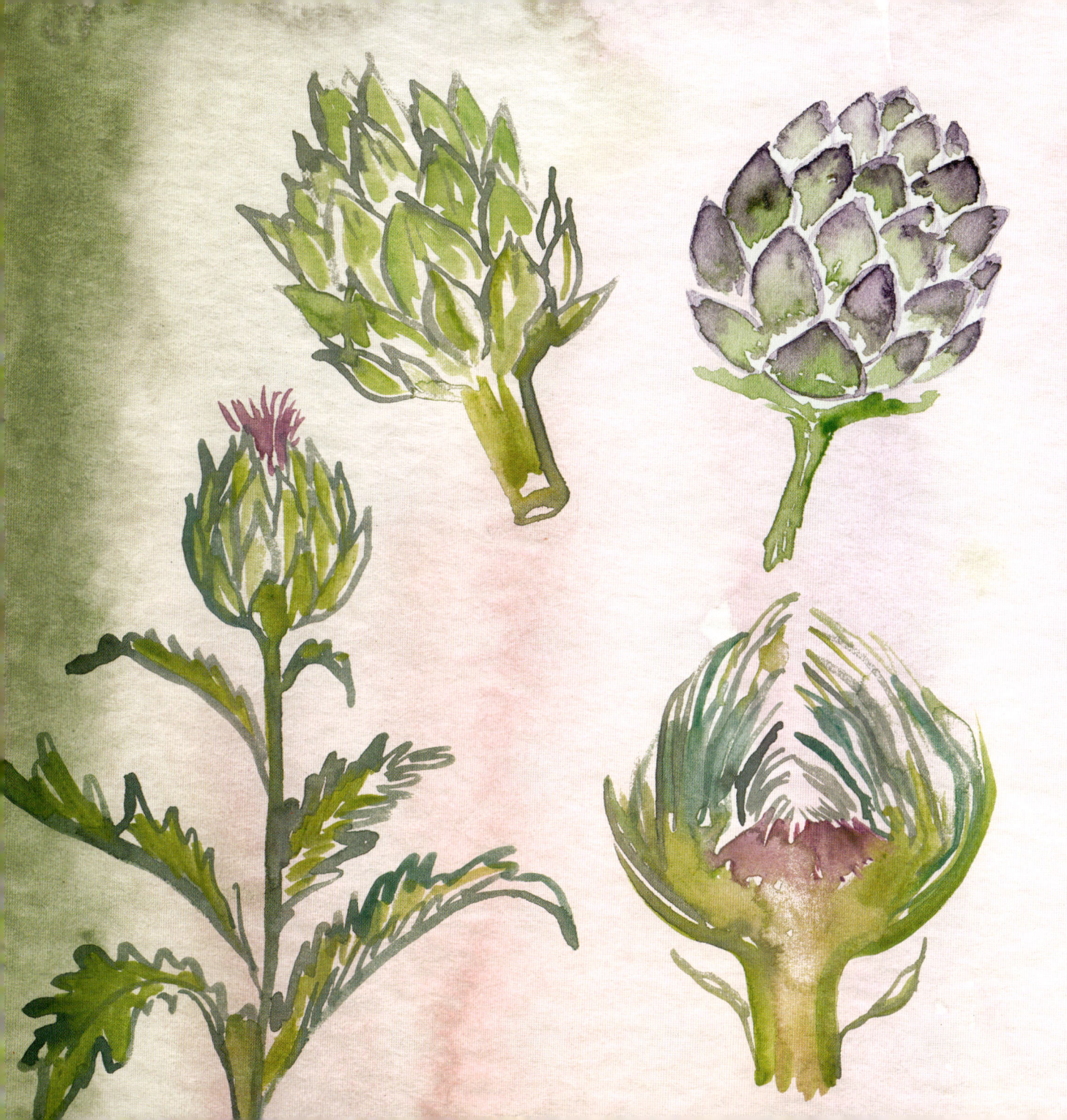

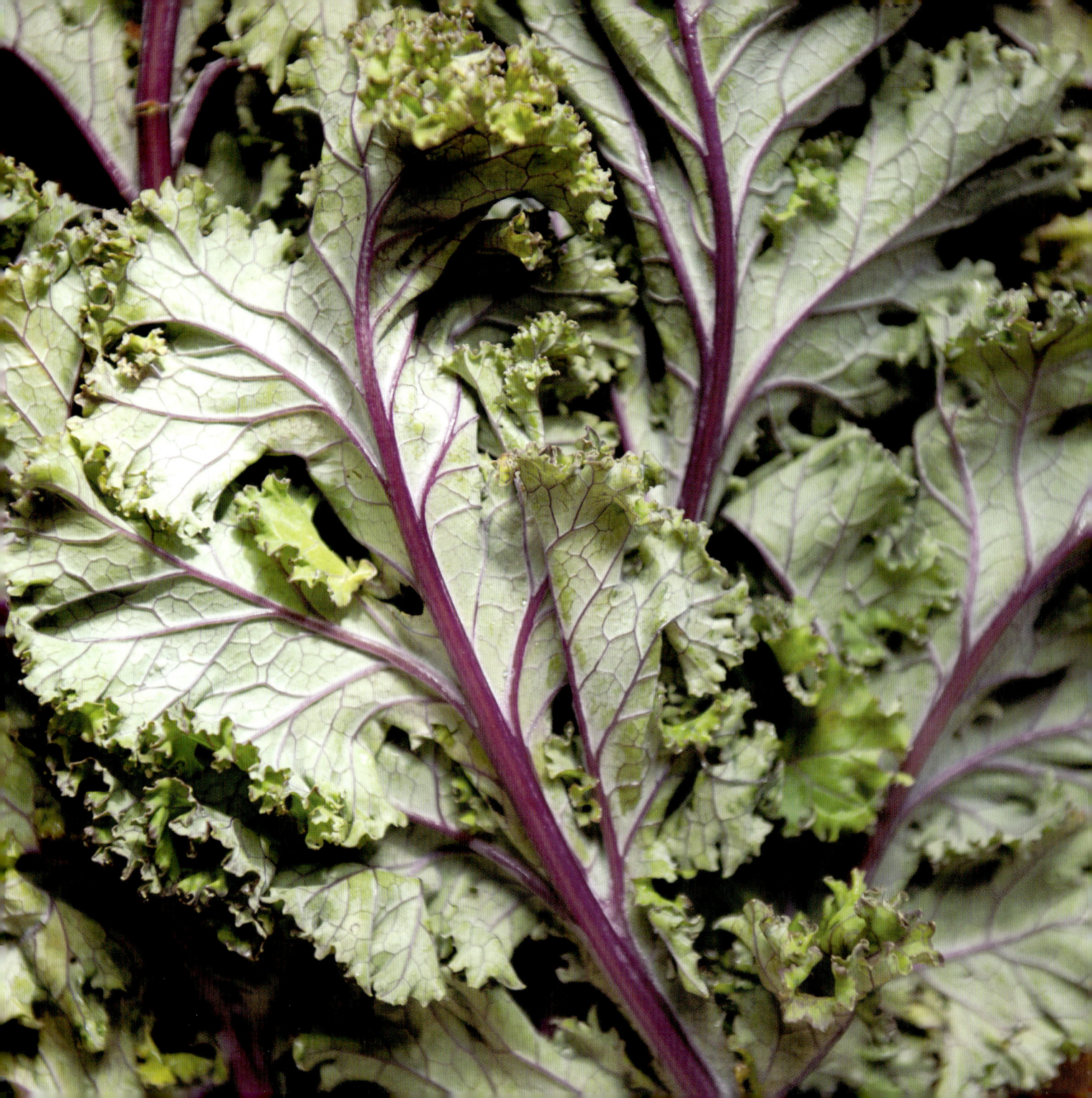

Kale

Recipe Idea

My favorite way to cook kale is to sauté ripped leaves quickly with butter, salt & pepper (thick stems removed). I love it alongside scrambled eggs & toast.

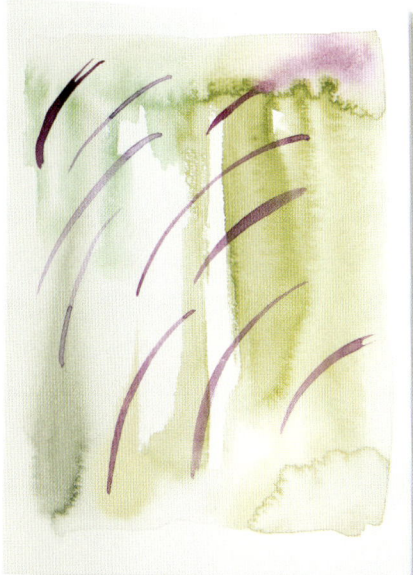

Color Exercise

On your plate, mix a couple shades of green & a couple shades of purple. Try mixing green + brown or yellow. Try adding red or brown to purple. Do a watery wash of green over your paper, then let it dry. Paint strokes of purple on top & notice how it doesn't bleed.

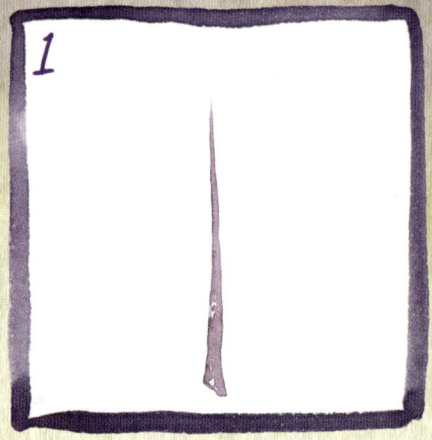

1

Begin by painting a purple stalk.

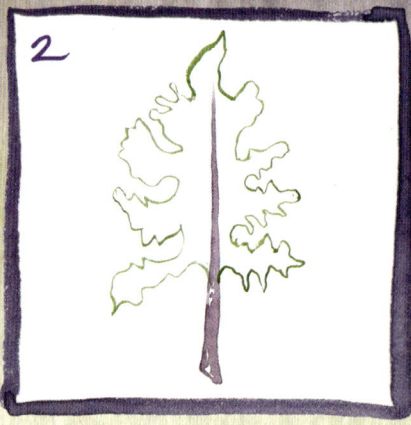

2

Next, add the wavy green outline of the leaf. (Optional: Use a pencil to draw the leaf outline first, but erase before painting.)

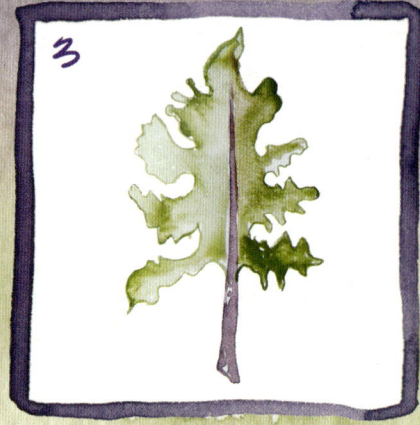

3

Fill in the outline with a watery olive or light green. Leave a few unpainted dry spots.

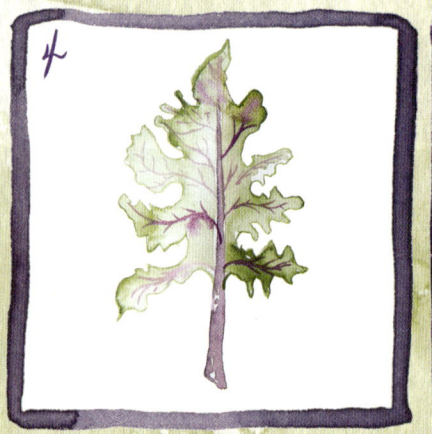

4

When the green is mostly dry, add some purple veins. Notice how mine was still a bit damp in some spots & it bled. (I don't mind!)

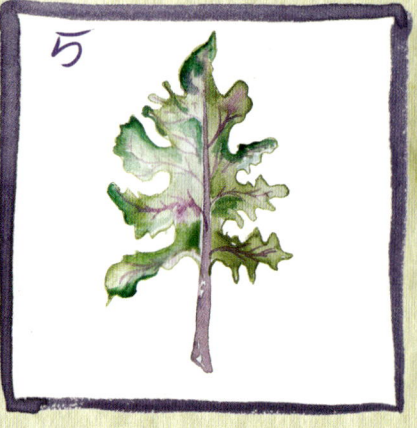

5

Sometimes paintings fade when they dry, which makes me want to add more color. But colors may not mix well if the layer below is already dry. I added dark green here, with extra water to blend it with the olive green below.

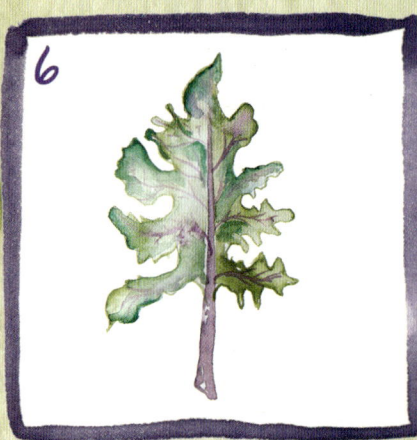

6

As I added dark green, I avoided the veins so they wouldn't bleed. You can also go over any faded veins with more purple if needed.

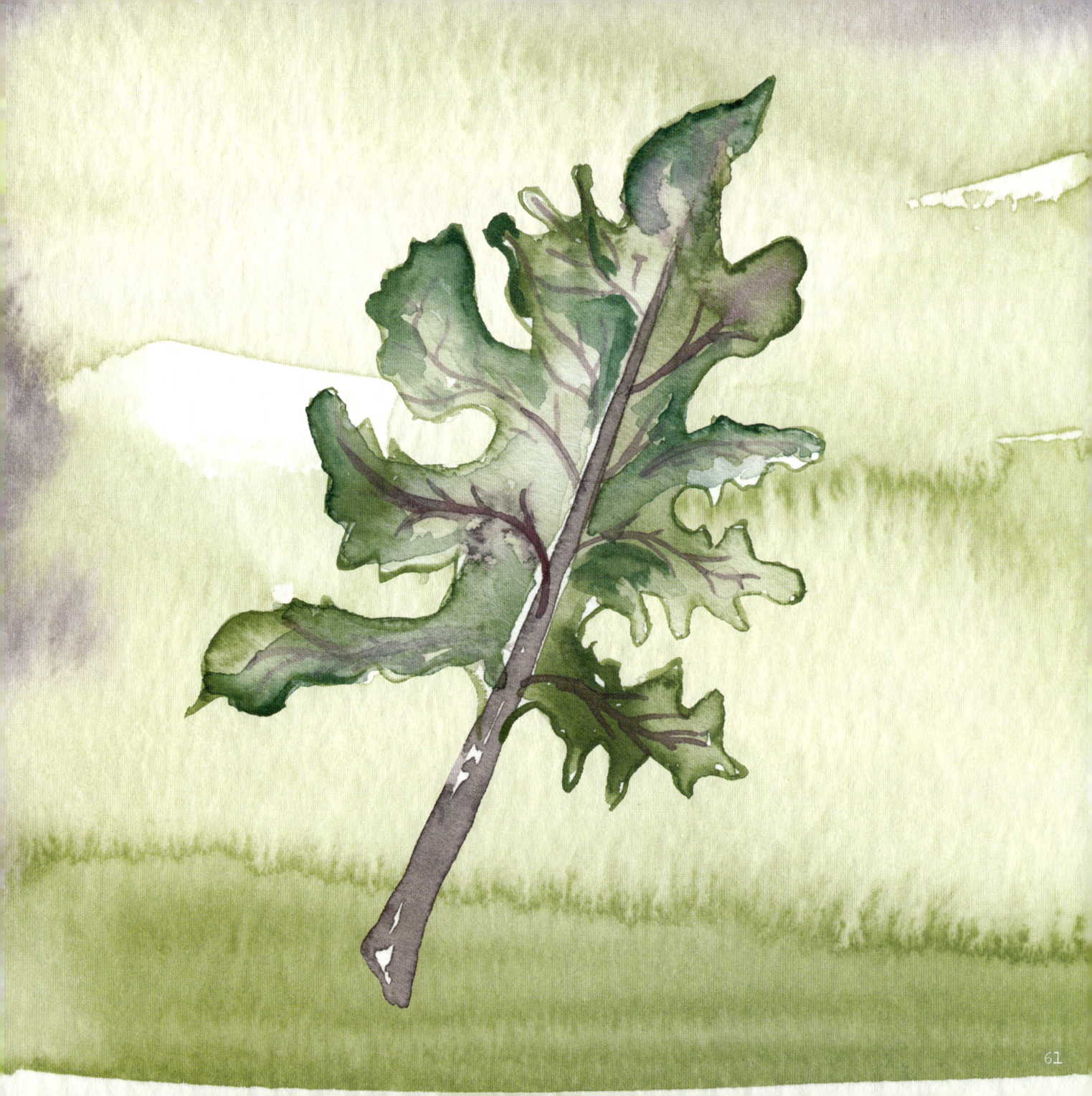

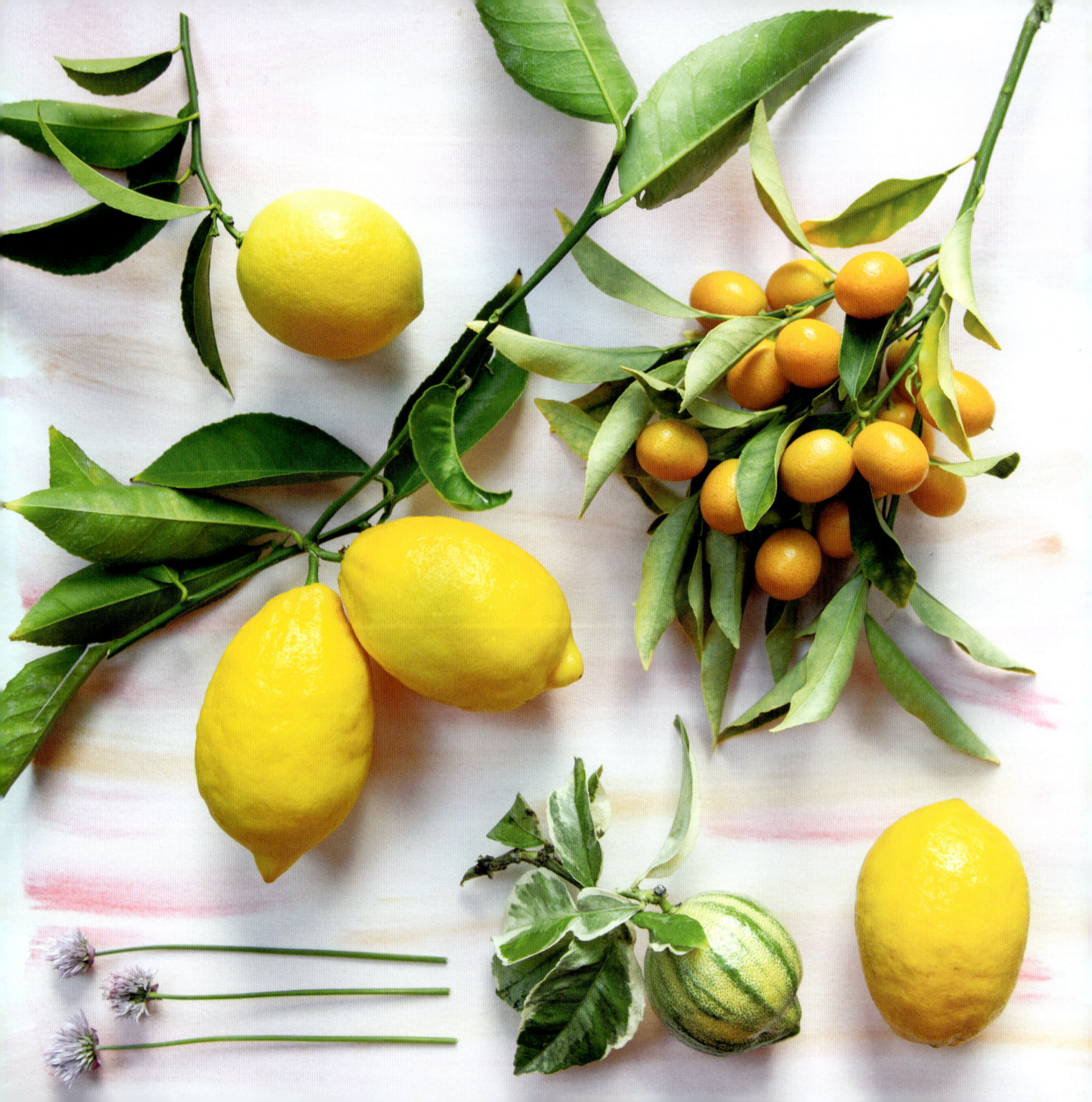

Lemon

What colors do you see in the lemon? I see yellow, beige, orange, green & brown. On your plate, mix a drop of orange with yellow to create a richer yellow tone. Try adding a bit of brown to your green to create an olive tone. And try adding lots of water to your yellow to create a very light shade.

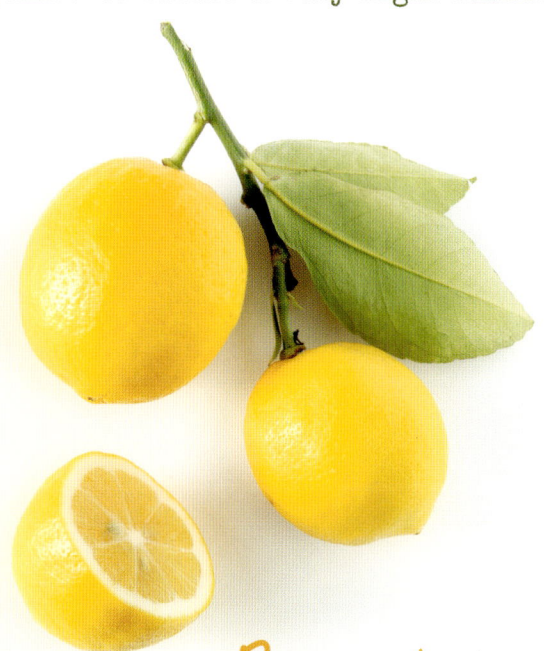

Color Exercise

Using your newly mixed colors, paint a series of stripes close together. Leave a few spots of unpainted white paper. Notice how the colors bleed together more when your brush is wetter.

Recipe Idea

Grate a little lemon zest into hot buttered pasta along with Parmesan, salt & pepper for a simple, flavorful dish.

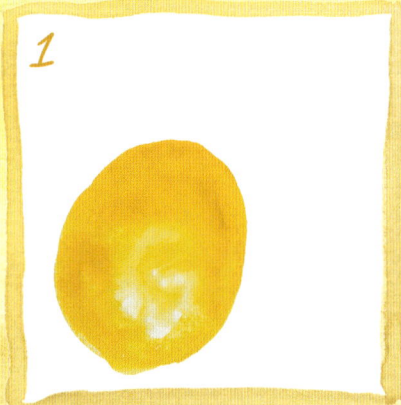

1

Paint a yellow lemon shape. Leave a bit of unpainted white.

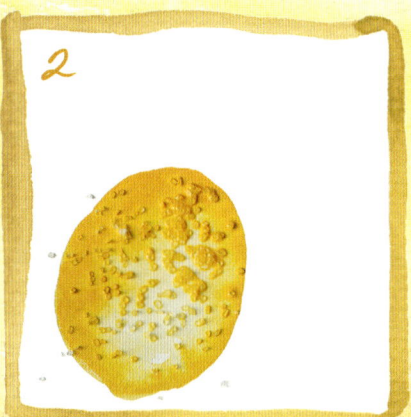

2

While it's still wet, sprinkle your painting with coarse kosher or sea salt.

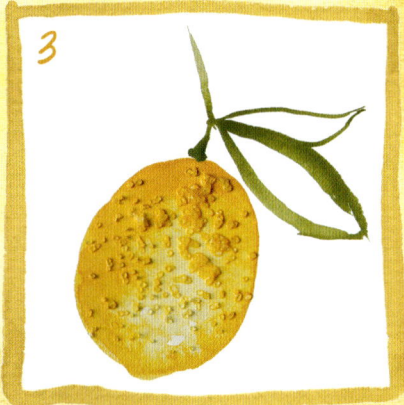

3

While the yellow is drying, paint the stem & an outline of the leaves with a dark olive green (green + a bit of brown).

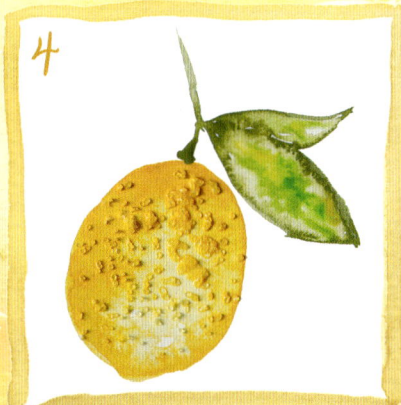

4

While the leaf outlines are still wet, fill them in with a watery light green, plus a little yellow.

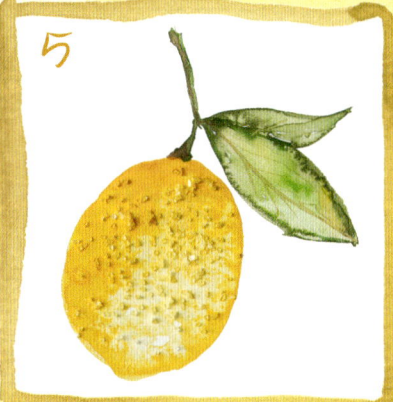

5

When the leaves are dry, add olive-green veins. Define the stem with some brown.

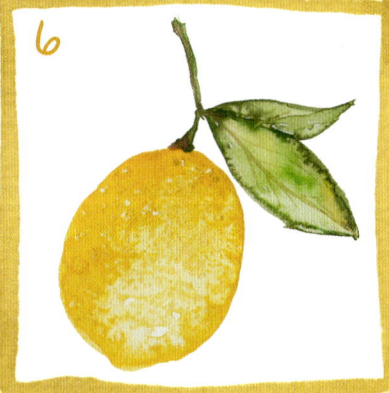

6

When the entire painting is dry, use your fingers to rub the salt off to reveal a dimpled lemon peel texture.

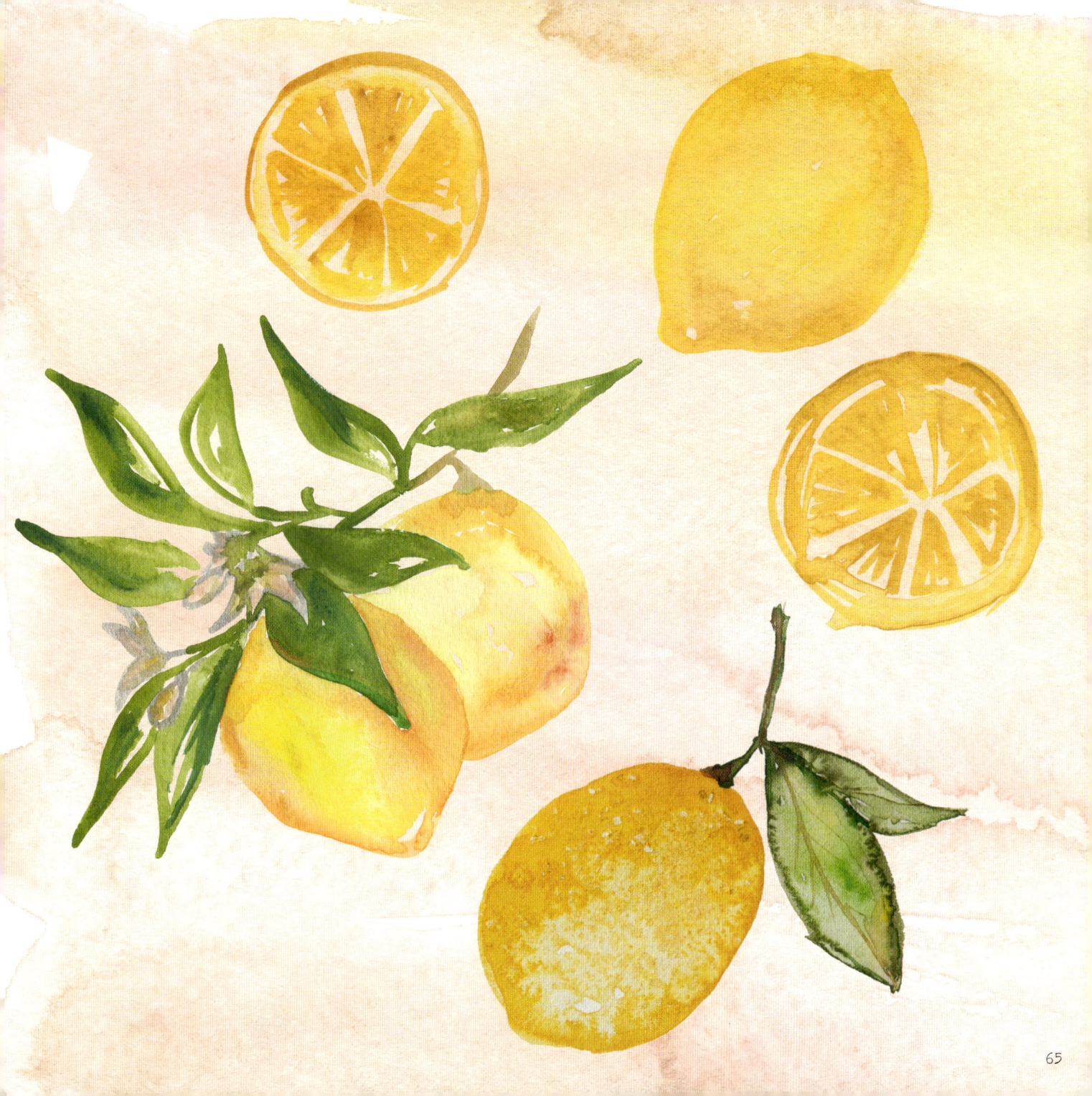

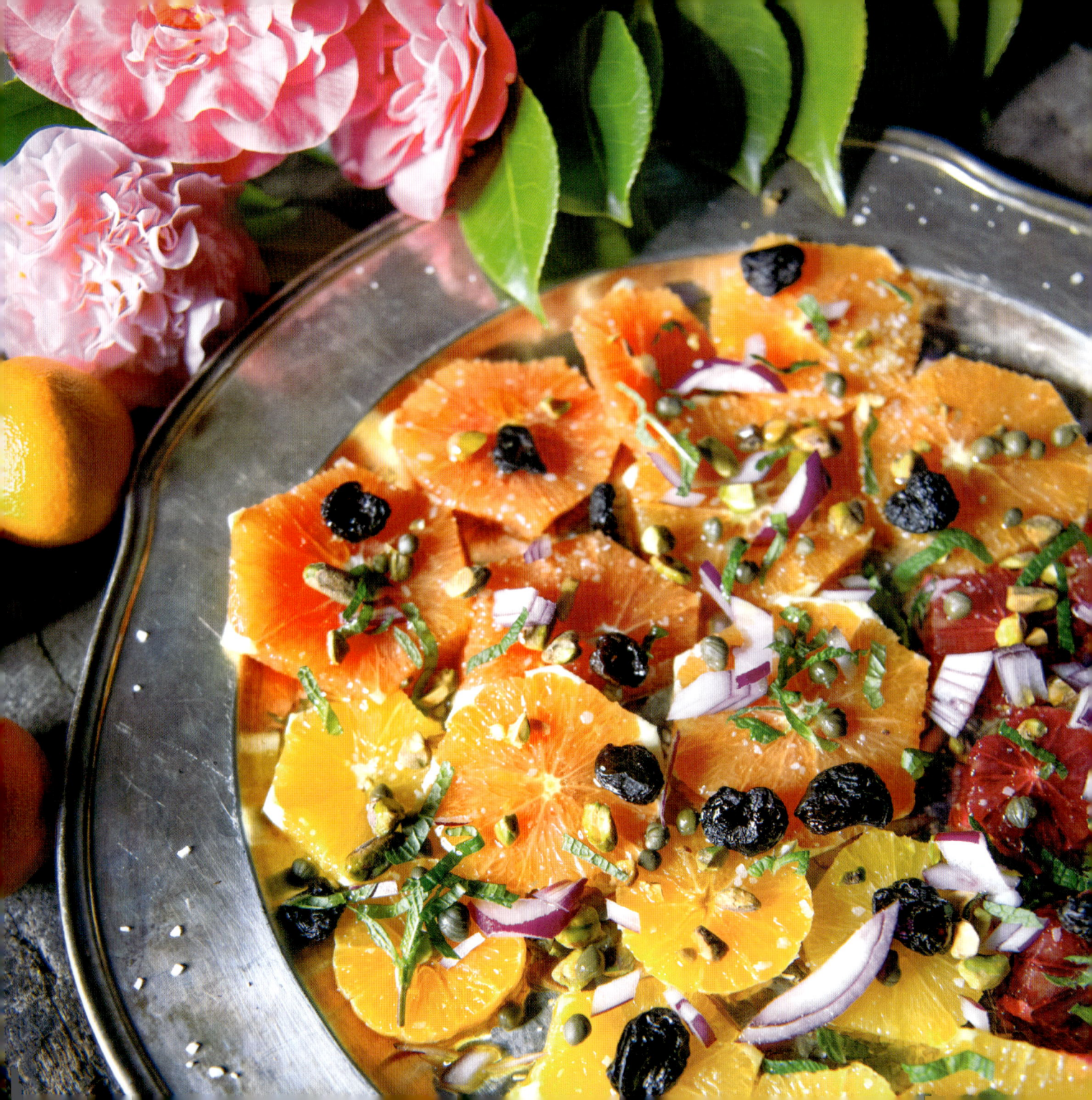

Orange

As I look at the whole orange below, I notice how the direction of light adds a shadow, making the left side a darker color. I can achieve this in watercolor by using just one shade of orange paint. I'll use a lot of paint on my brush (not too watered-down) for the darker side & I'll add lots of water to my paint for the lighter side.

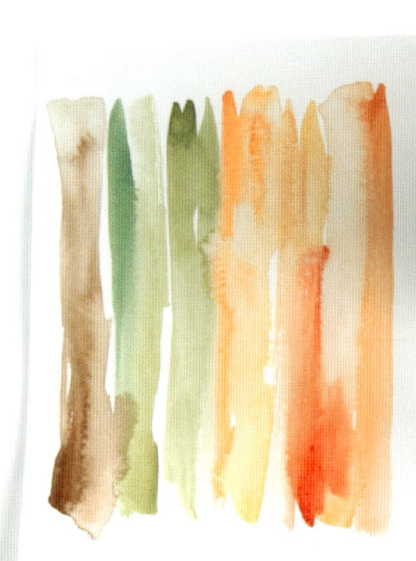

Do you want to paint the whole orange or just a slice of it?

Color Exercise

What **colors** do you see in this fruit? Paint a series of stripes that bleed into each other.

Recipe Idea

Make a salad on a platter by topping peeled slices of orange with dried cherries, capers, red onion, mint, pistachios, olive oil, salt & pepper.

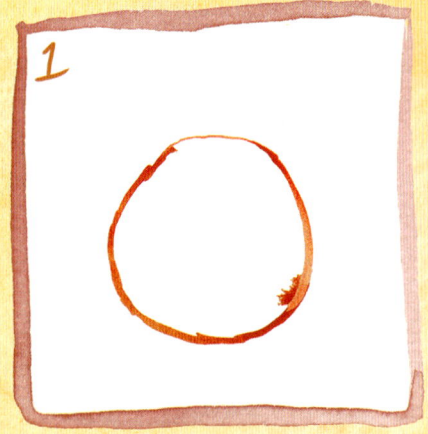

1

Start by painting an outline of the orange with a good amount of wet orange paint on your brush.

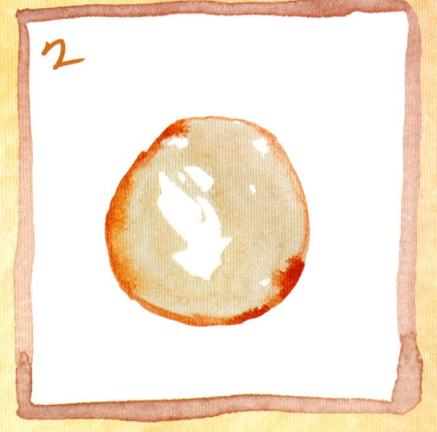

2

Rinse your brush, then using only water, pull the paint from the edges inward. Leave a little dry white space.

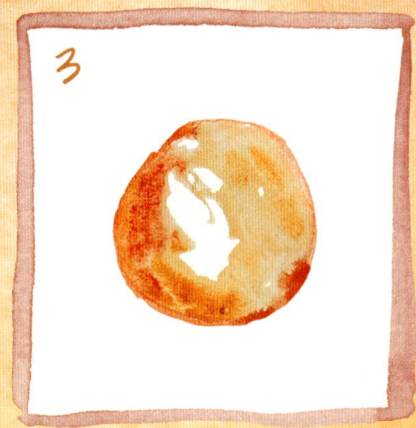

3

Now fill your brush with orange paint again & dab over the wet areas. Watch it bleed! More paint on your brush makes the color darker.

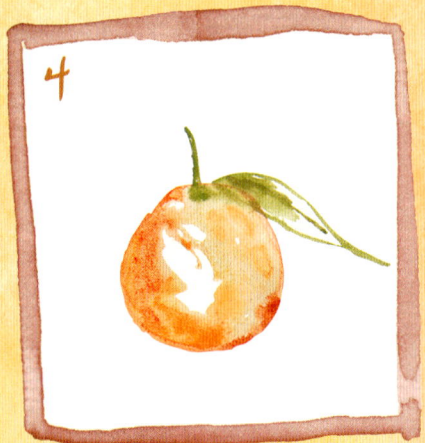

4

Using green paint, draw a stem & the outline of a leaf. Don't worry if the orange & green bleed a bit. Use water to pull green in from the edges & fill in the leaf.

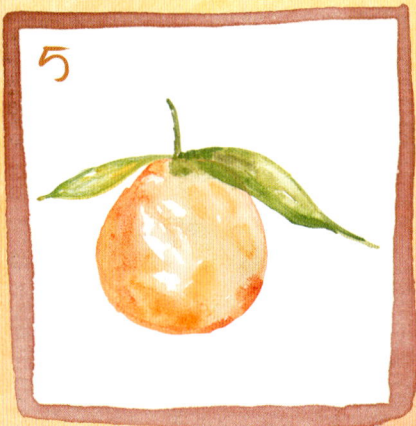

5

Add another leaf. On your plate, create a new shade of green for the leaves. Also add a bit of brown & yellow to the leaves.

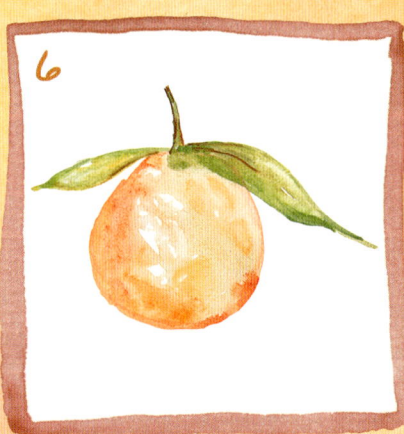

6

Let it dry, then add dark brown on the stem & leaves. The lines will be more defined if your brush is not too wet & the green is dry.

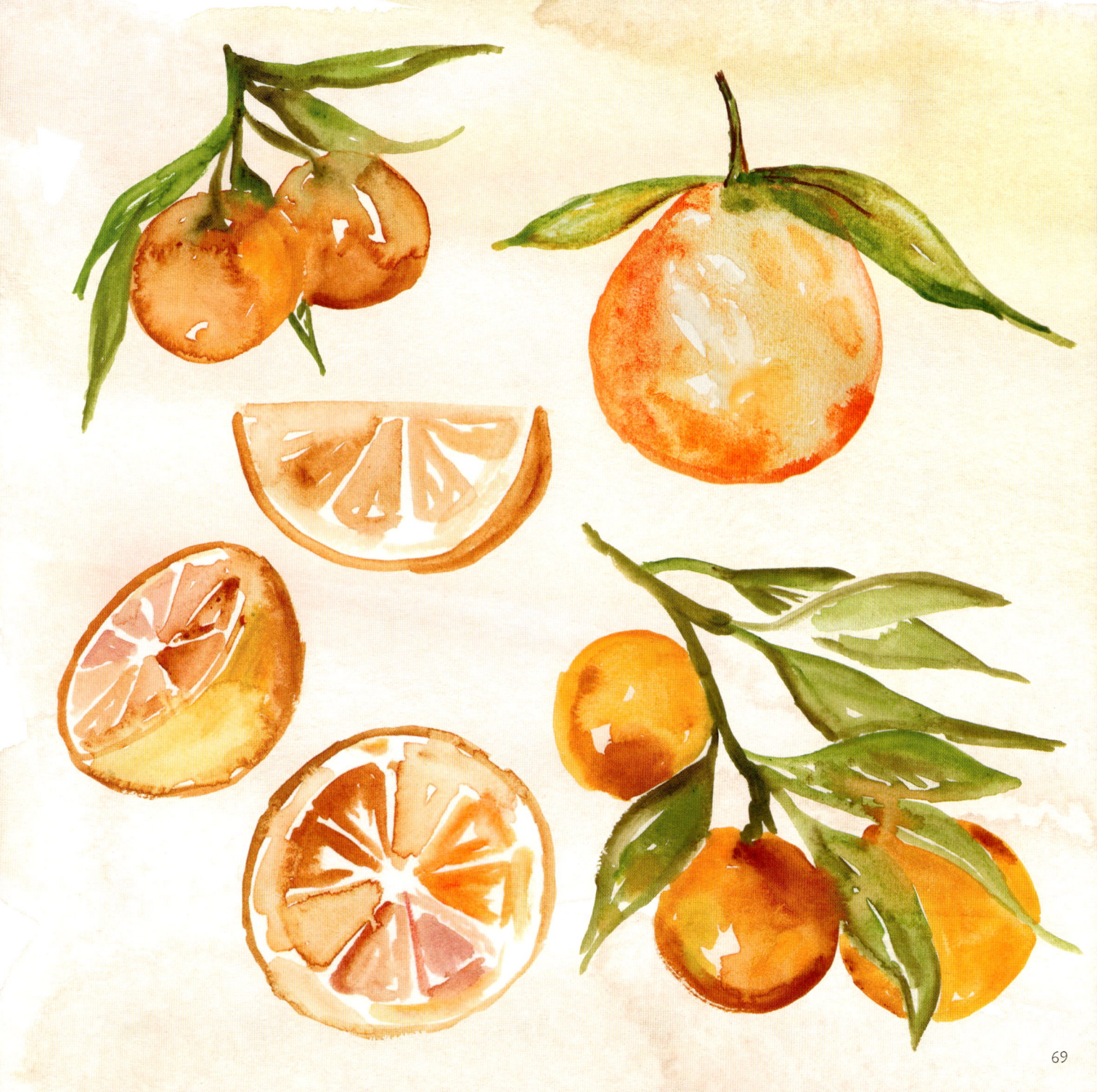

69

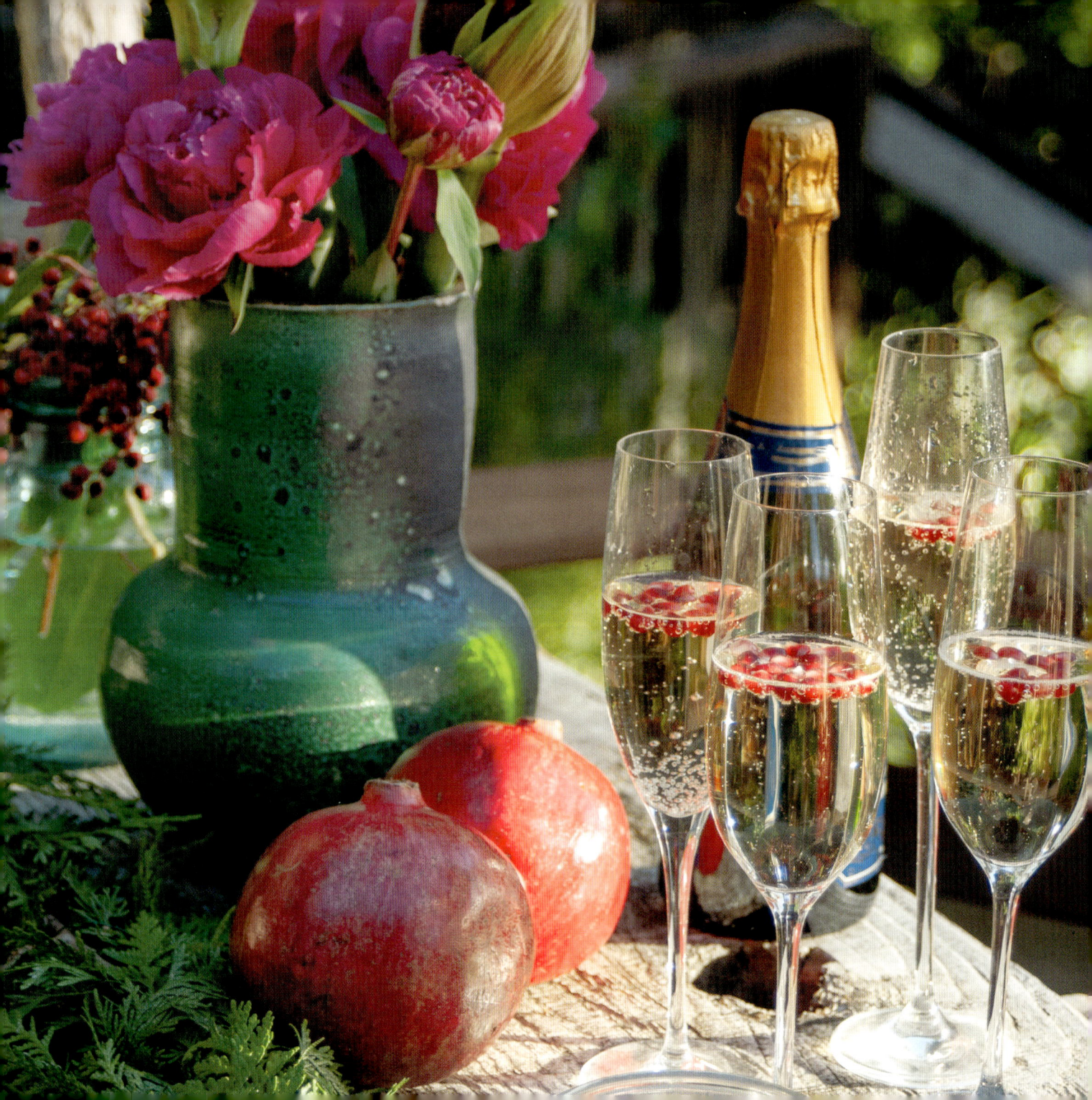

Pomegranate

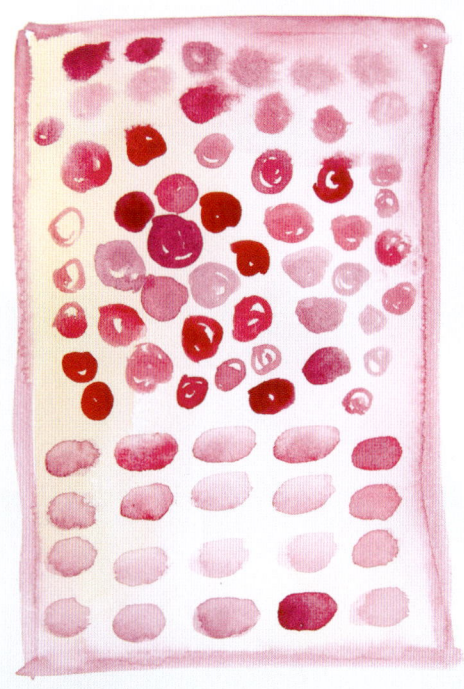

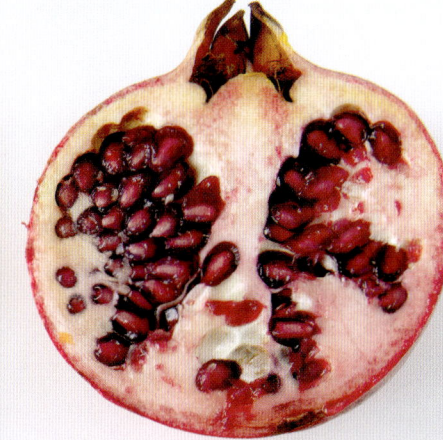

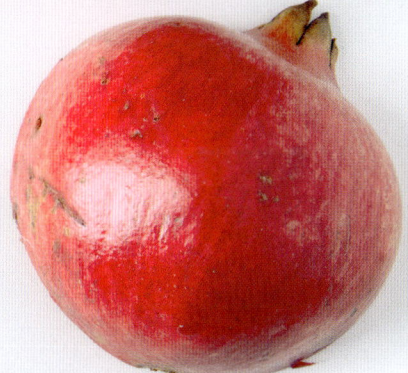

Color Exercise

Paint a creamy light yellow base. Allow it to dry, then paint a red border & red circles over it using different brushes. If there are areas where the base is still damp, the colors may bleed (see top right).

Recipe Idea

Pop pomegranate seeds into your bubbly drink!

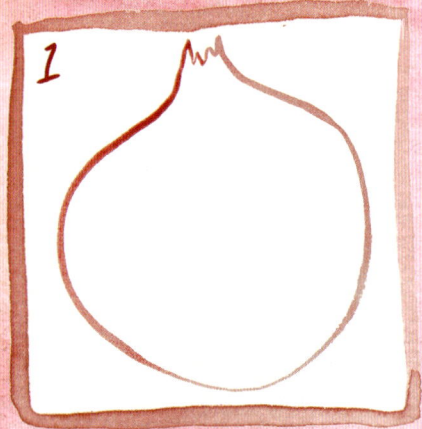

1

Begin by painting a thin outline. Use a pencil if you wish, but erase before painting so it guides you but doesn't show up in the end.

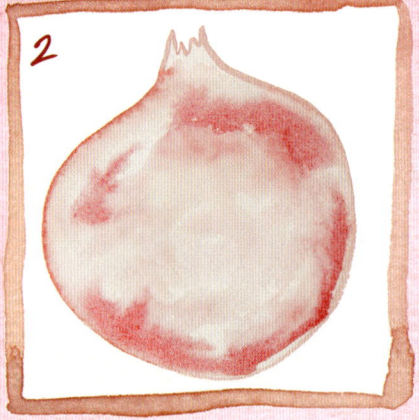

2

Using only water, paint the interior. Pull the paint from the wet outline inward. Then add a couple strokes of red, mostly around the edges.

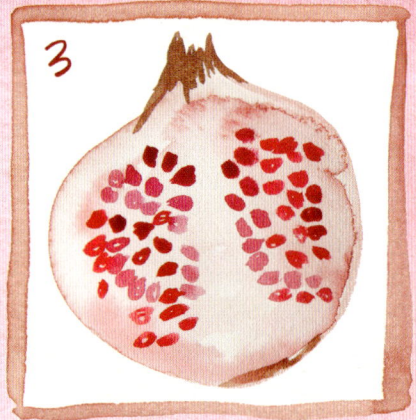

3

Let it dry, then add brown at the top. For the seeds, mix custom colors like red + purple or red + brown. They can be varying shades & sizes. Scatter them with space between, avoiding perfect rows.

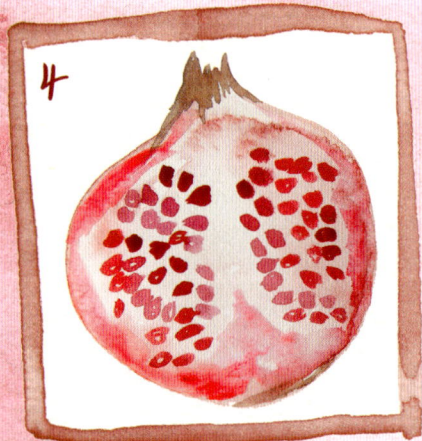

4

Add a bit more watery red around the edges of the fruit.

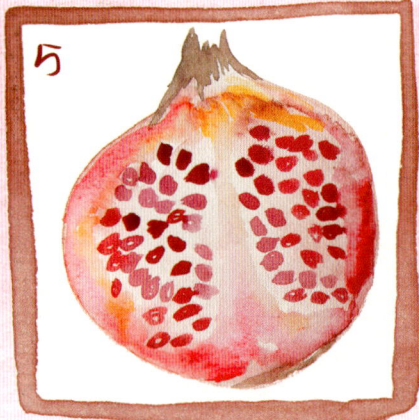

5

Add some yellow while the red is still wet.

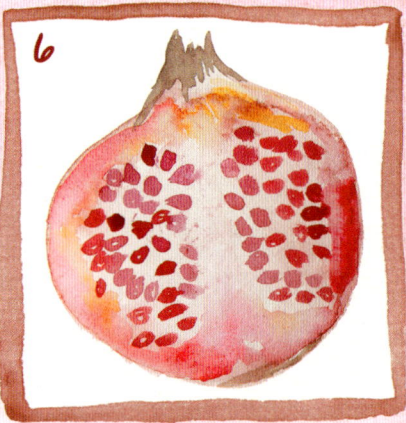

6

Optional: blot your painting with a cloth to create a subtle speckled effect.

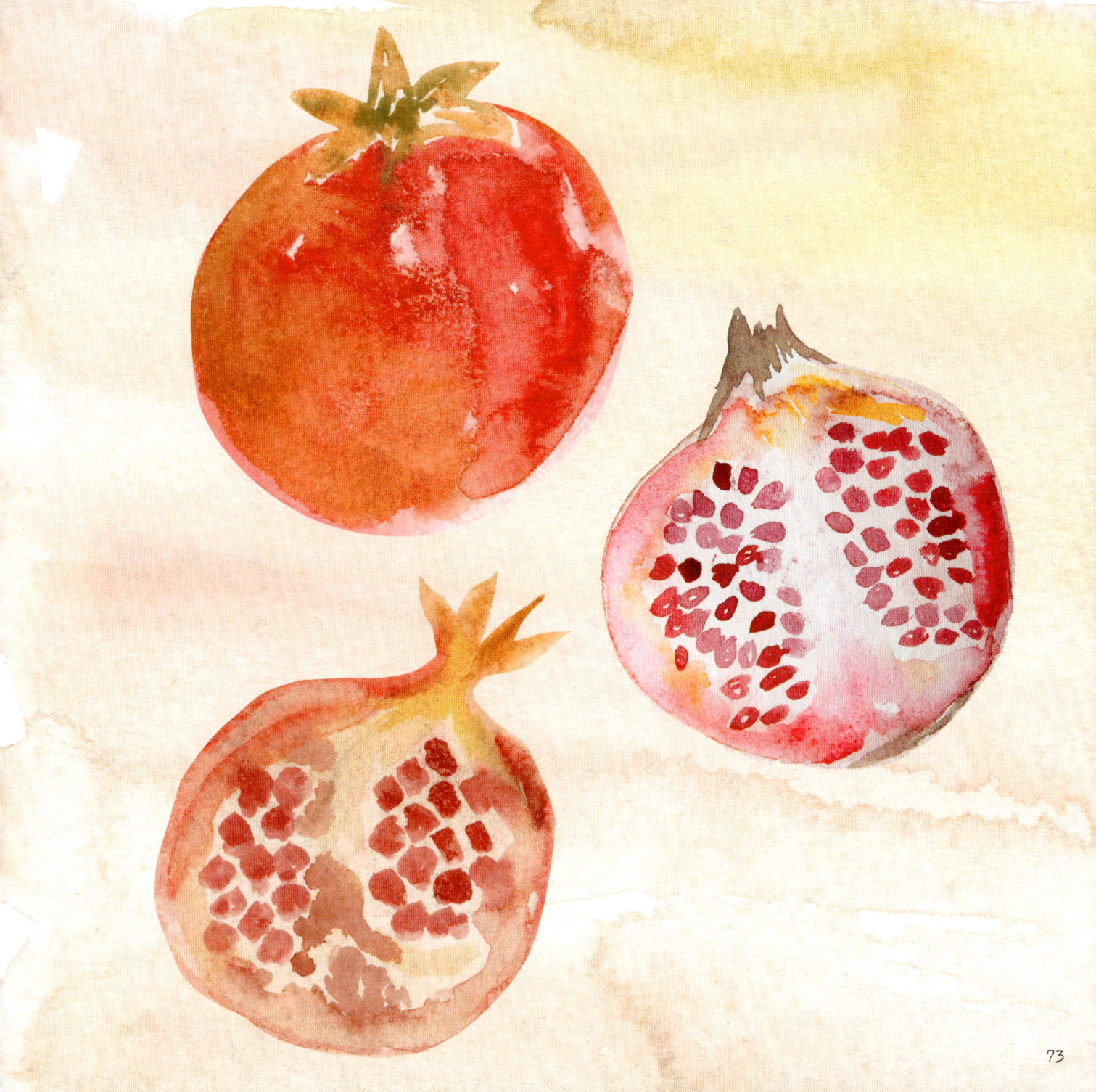

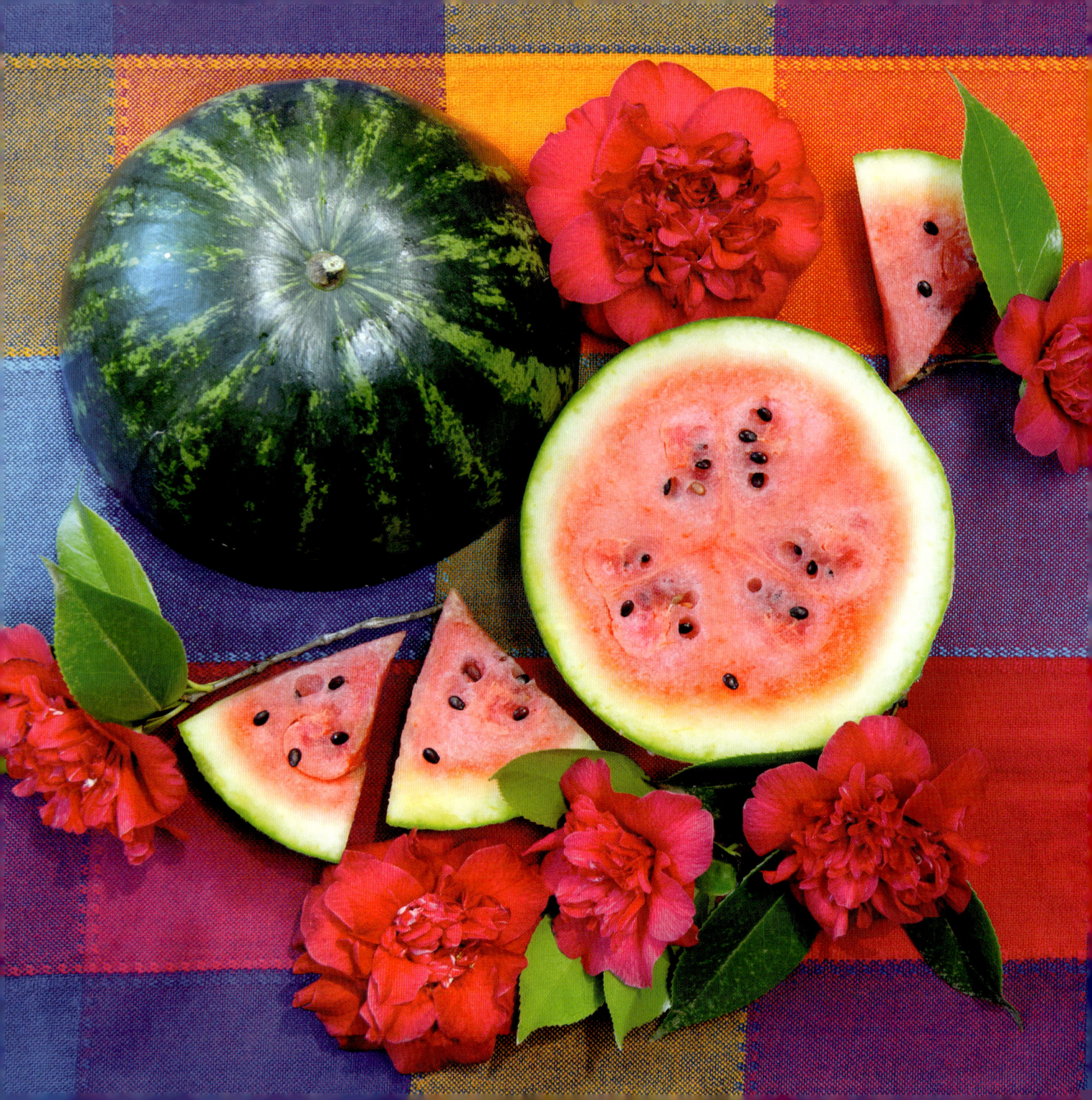

Watermelon

Tip: In this painting, it's important to let the red area dry completely before adding the black seeds so they don't bleed.

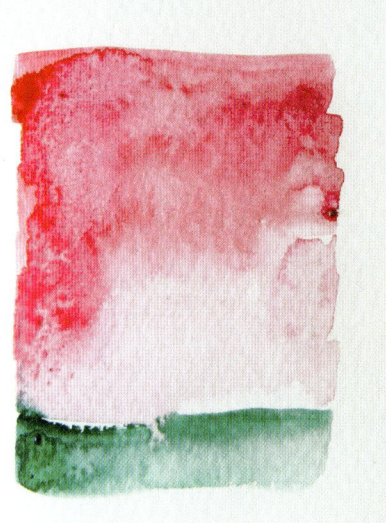

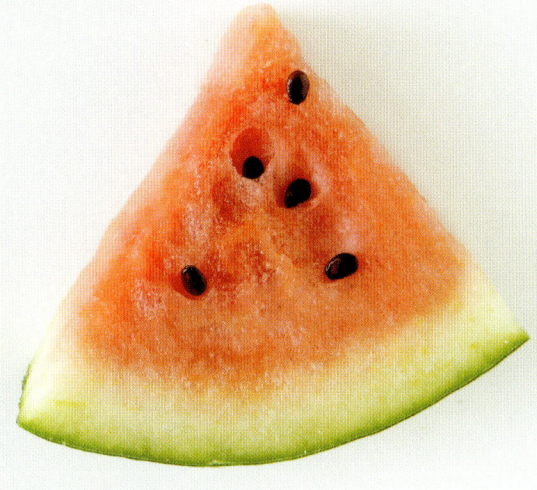

Color Exercise

Paint the top of your paper with a single shade of red, then rinse your brush & use water to pull the color down. Add a green stripe at the bottom & notice how it bleeds if it touches the wet red part. Try this with any color combo you'd like!

Recipe Idea

Lay watermelon cubes out on a platter & sprinkle with crumbled feta, chili crisp oil & chopped mint.

1

Starting with red, paint the top of a triangle. When you've painted about this much, rinse your brush.

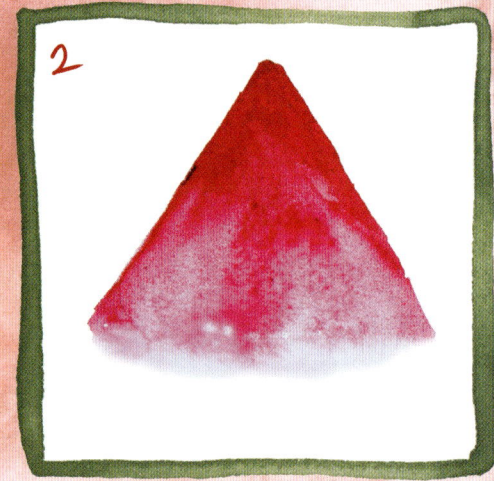

2

Using just water, pull the red paint downward, making the bottom a bit lighter.

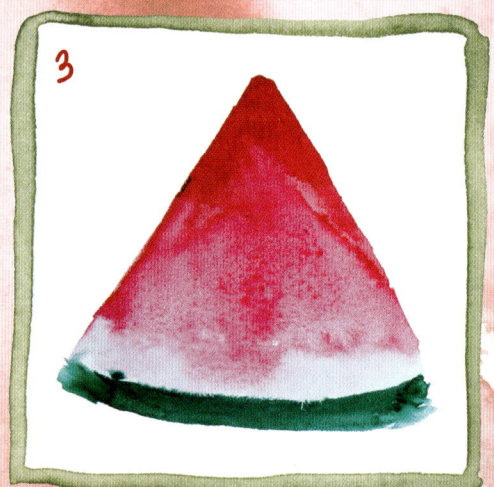

3

Leaving a little space below the wet red area, add a green curved stripe for the rind. If it's not too wet & the colors don't touch, it won't bleed much.

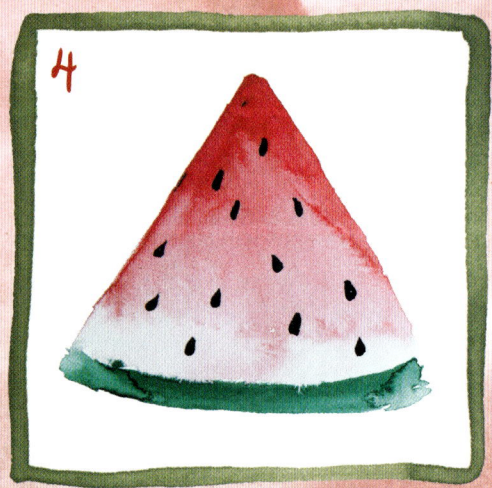

4

Let it dry, then use your smallest brush to add tear-shaped black seeds.

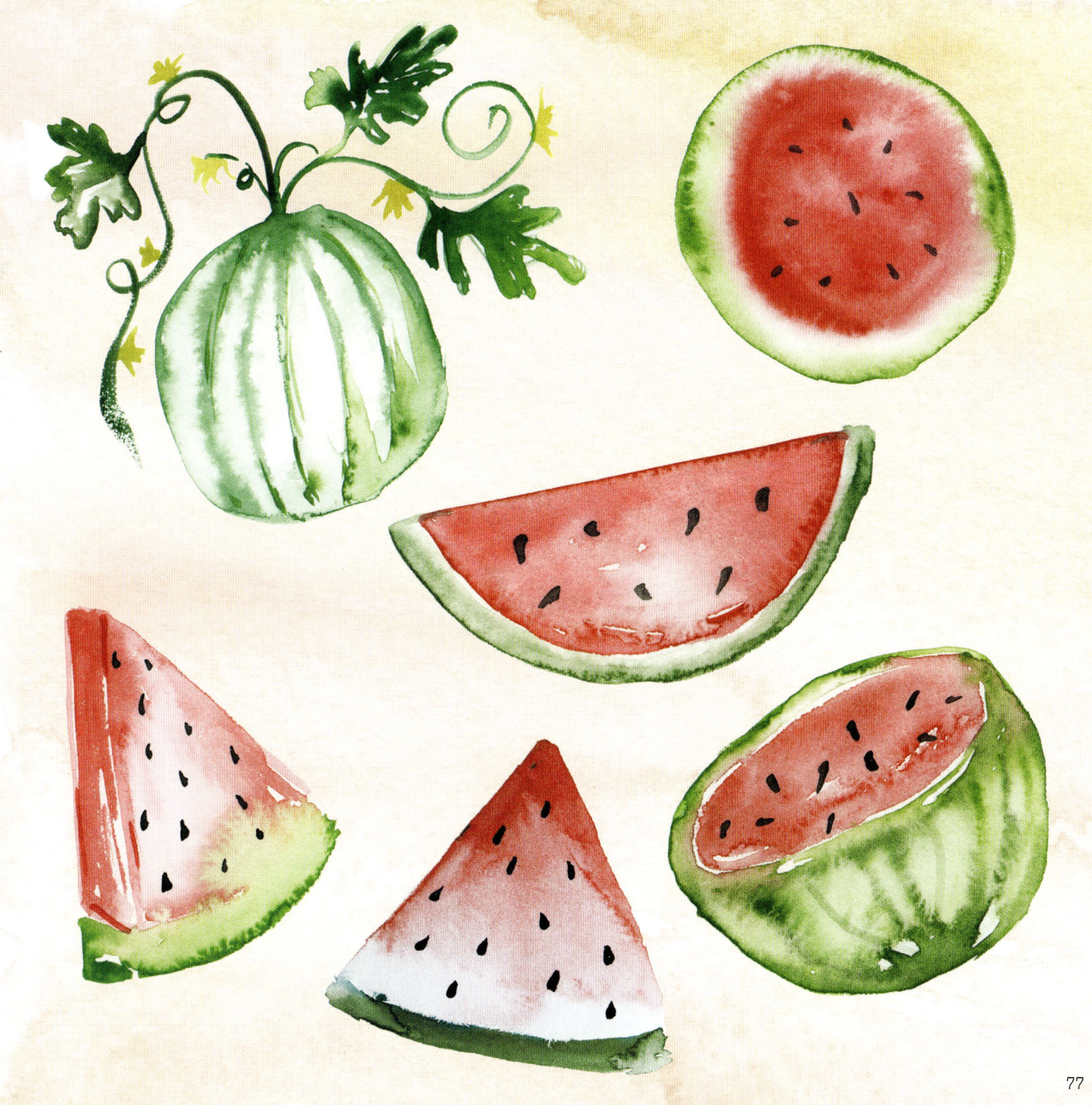

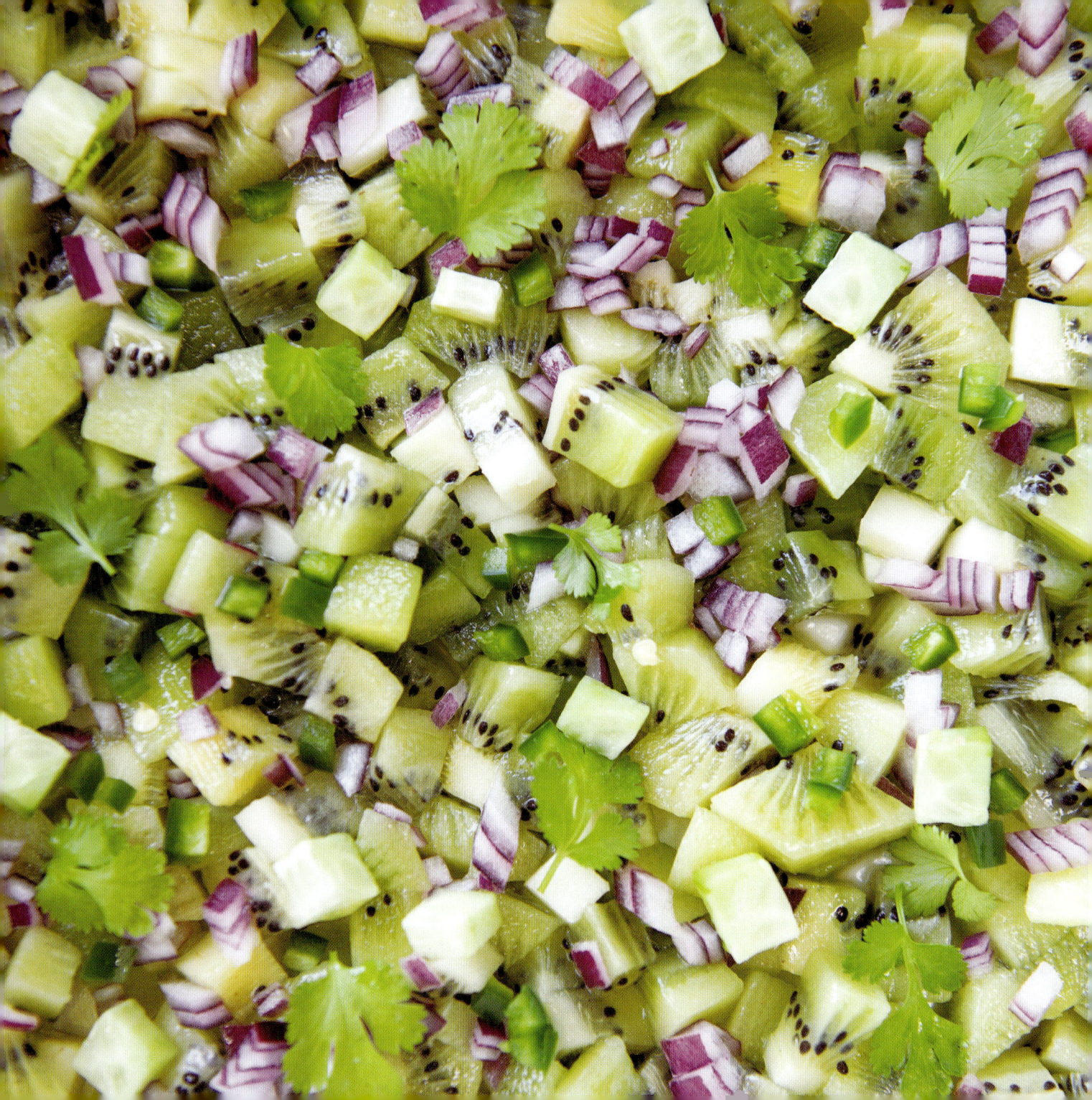

Kiwi

How many colors do you see in this kiwi? On your plate, try mixing 3 shades of green for the fruit, 3 shades of brown for the skin & 3 shades of black for the seeds.

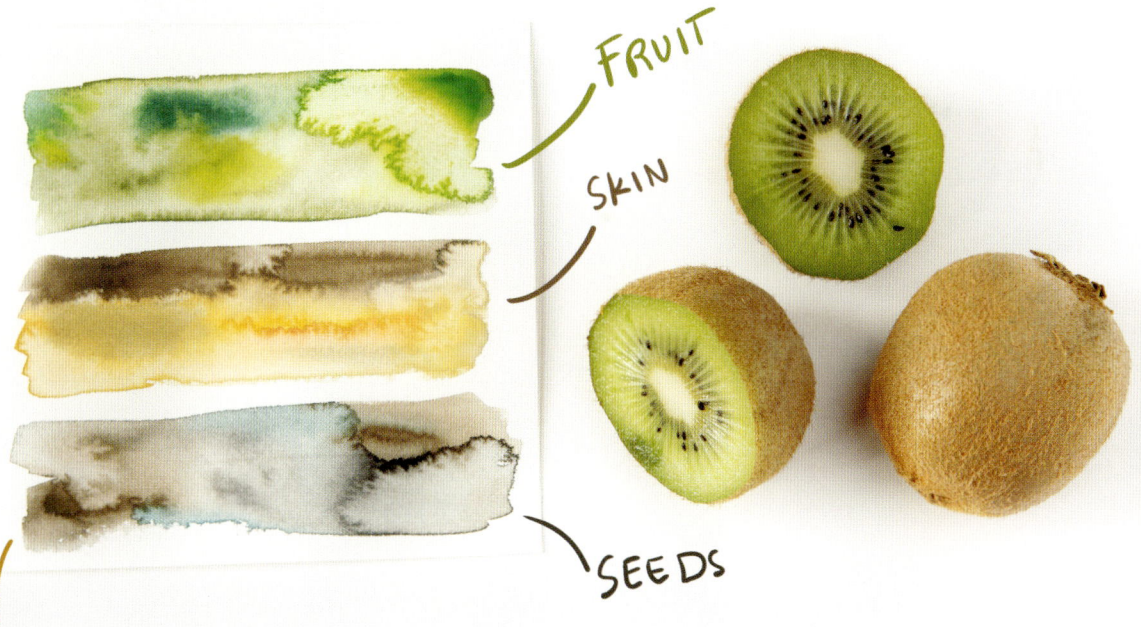

FRUIT

SKIN

SEEDS

Color Exercise

Make a wide stripe that represents each element of a kiwi & explore a couple shades within each. Also, use your imagination! Could there be a touch of blue in those black seeds?

Recipe Idea

Kiwi salsa! Finely dice firm kiwi, red onion, jalapeño & cucumber. Combine with cilantro, lime juice & salt. Stir & serve with chips or on tacos.

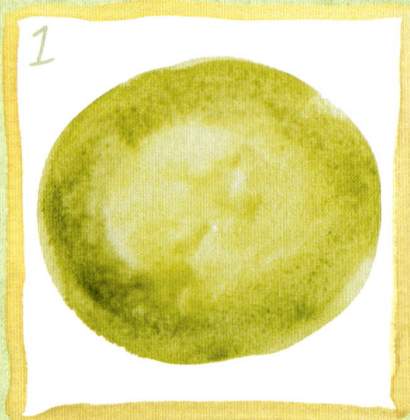

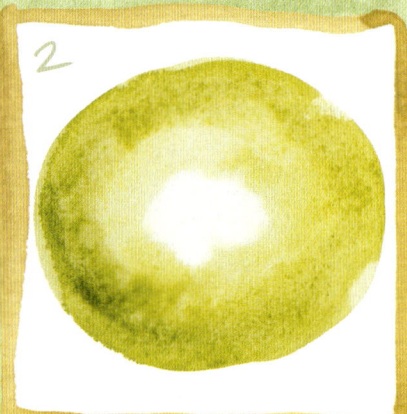

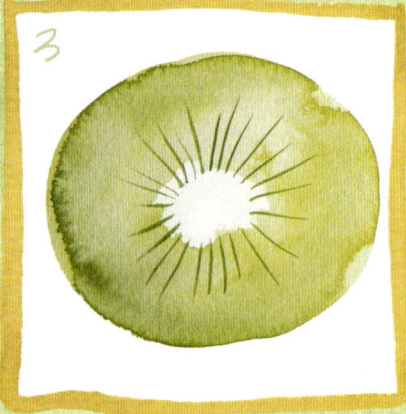

Paint a light green circle. Apply most of the paint around the edges & use water to pull it inward.

Use a cloth to blot the middle, removing some of the paint & water, making the circle lighter in the center.

Allow the circle to dry (the dried color may look different), then paint thin darker-green lines coming out from the center.

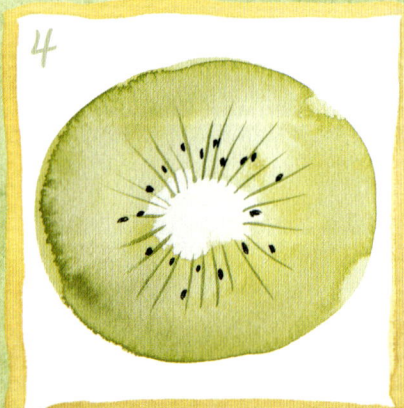

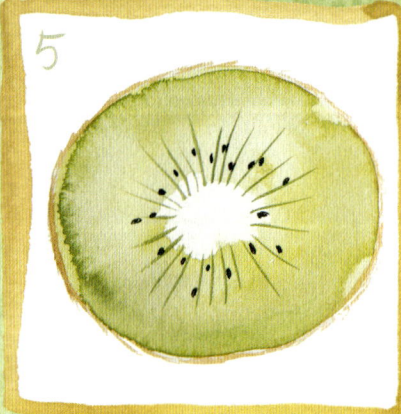

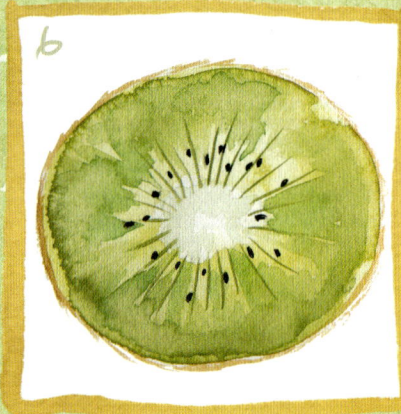

Next add some small black oval seeds using the tip of your smallest brush & very little water. Let the green dry completely before painting the black seeds, so they don't bleed.

Using a somewhat dry brush with a small amount of light brown, paint quick, short strokes around the edges to create fuzzy skin. You could stop here, or . . .

If yours doesn't feel green enough (like mine), you could add an overall wash of green in a darker shade. I painted carefully around the seeds to avoid bleeding.

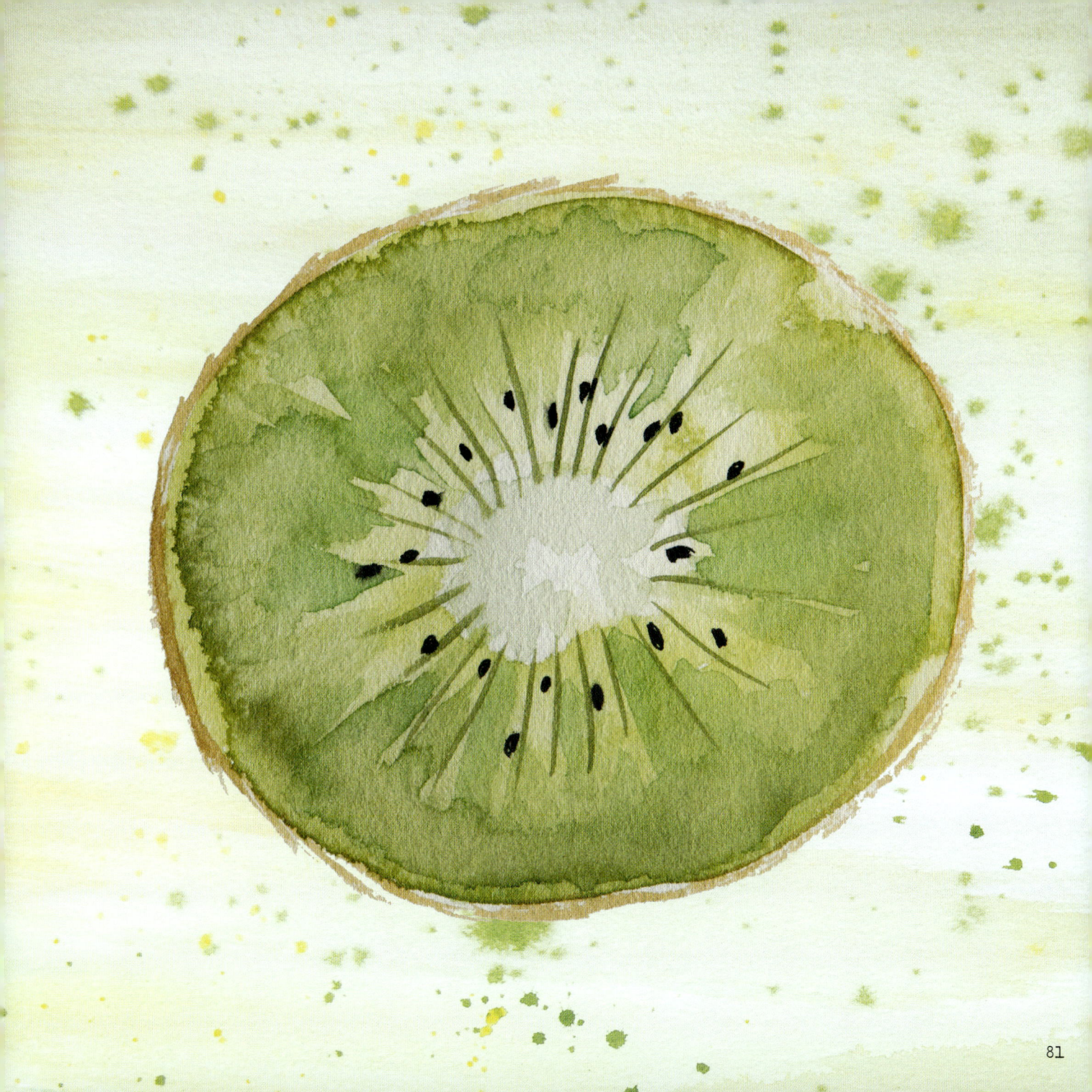

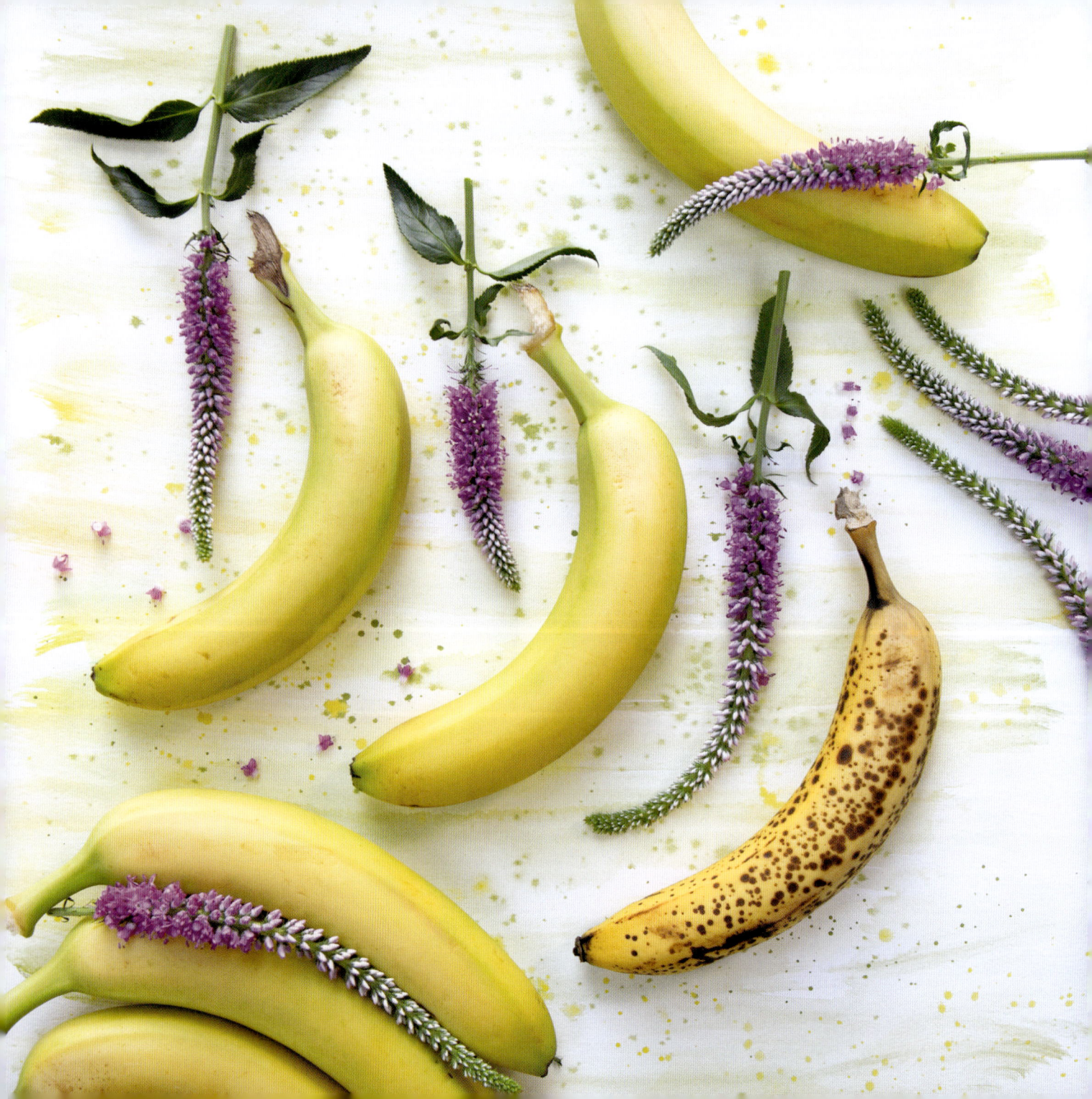

Banana

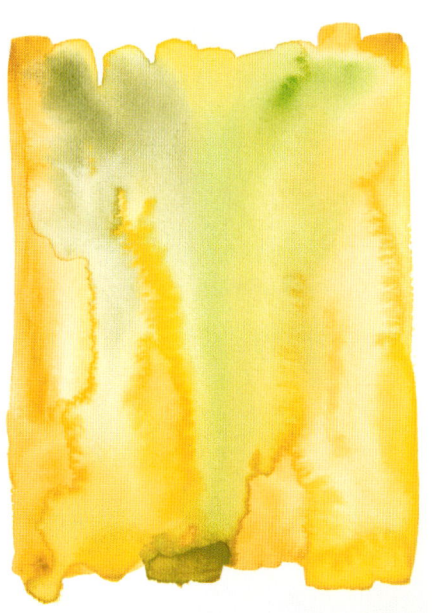

Color Exercise

Look at how beautifully the green
& yellow blend together at this
banana's stem! Try painting a watery
wash of yellow, then add green.

Recipe Idea

Halve a banana lengthwise & fry
the pieces cut side down in butter
until golden. Drizzle with honey,
sprinkle with sea salt & enjoy warm.

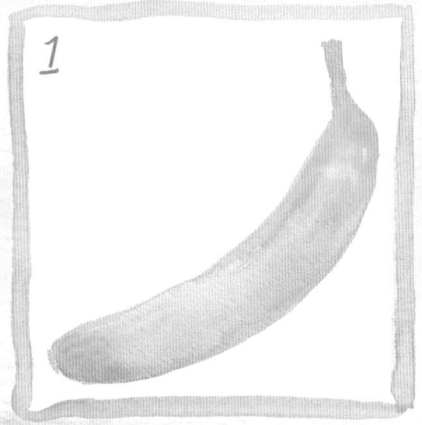

1

Begin by painting the
yellow base of the entire
banana. Make it a bit
darker around the edges.

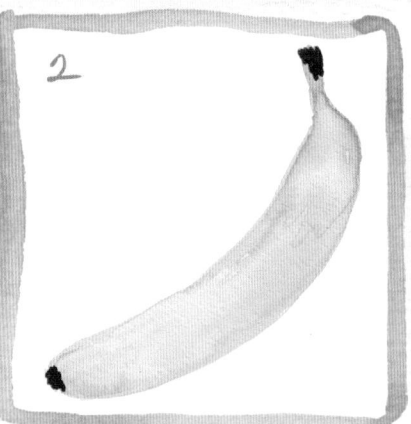

2

Let it dry, then add
dark brown to each end.

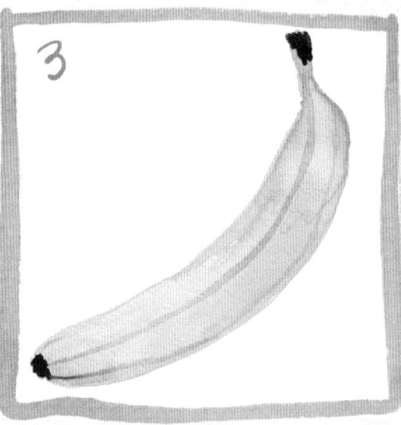

3

Use light brown to add
lengthwise lines.

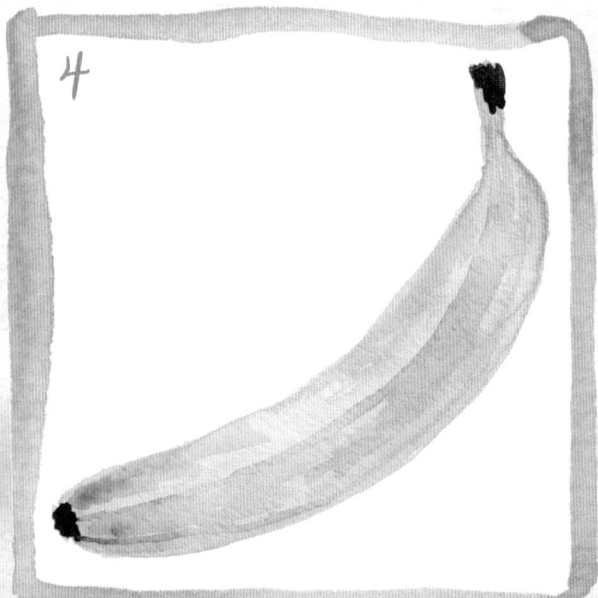

4

Using watered-down brown, fill
in the lengthwise sections a bit.

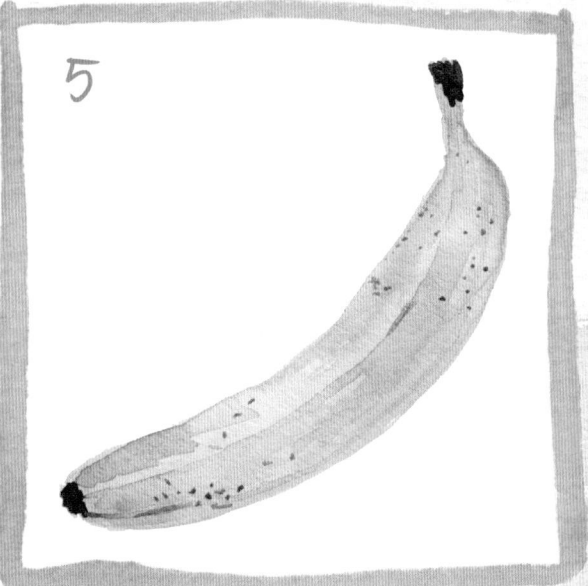

5

Allow it to dry, then add some
small brown dots with your
smallest brush (I used size 0).

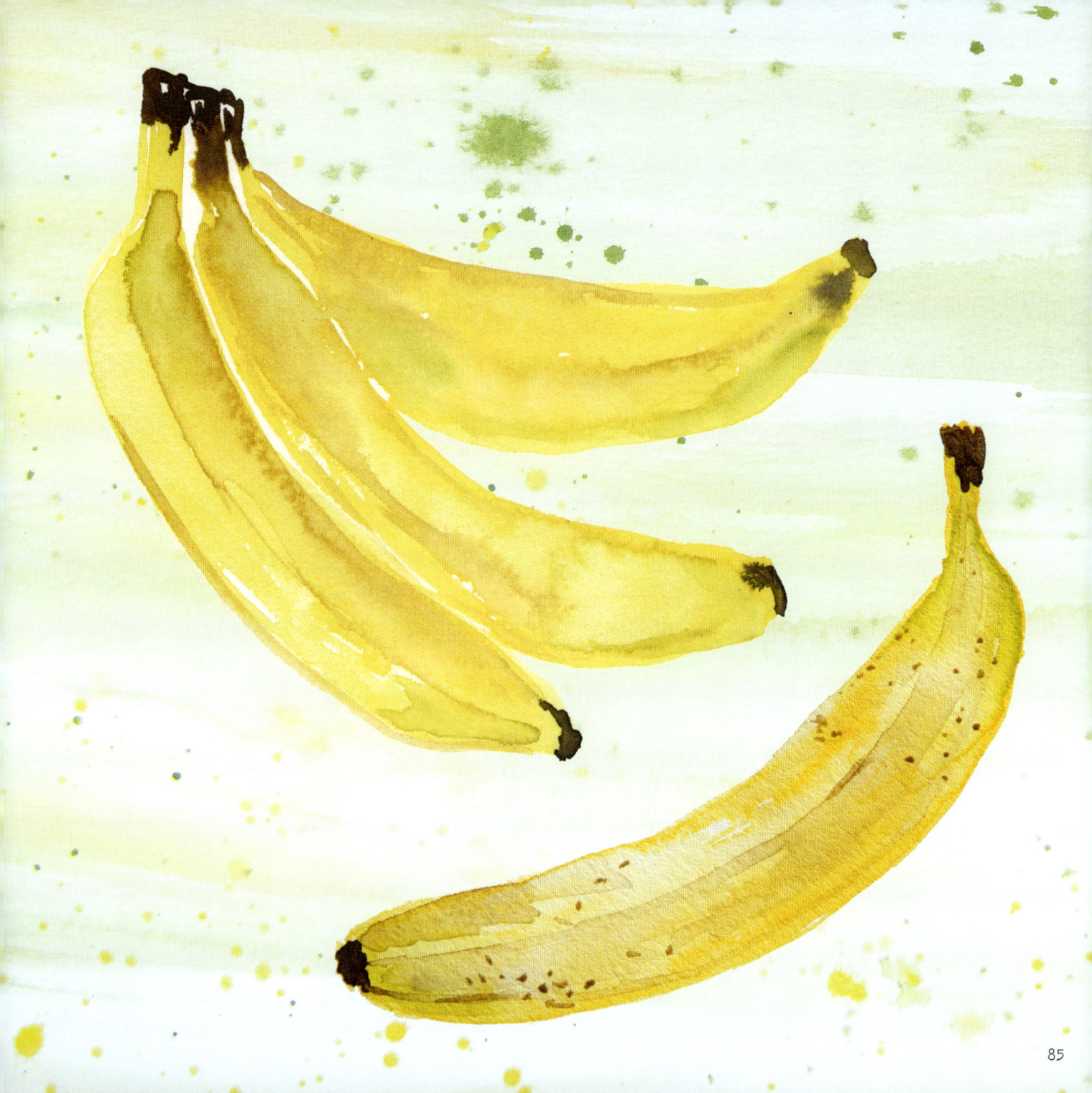

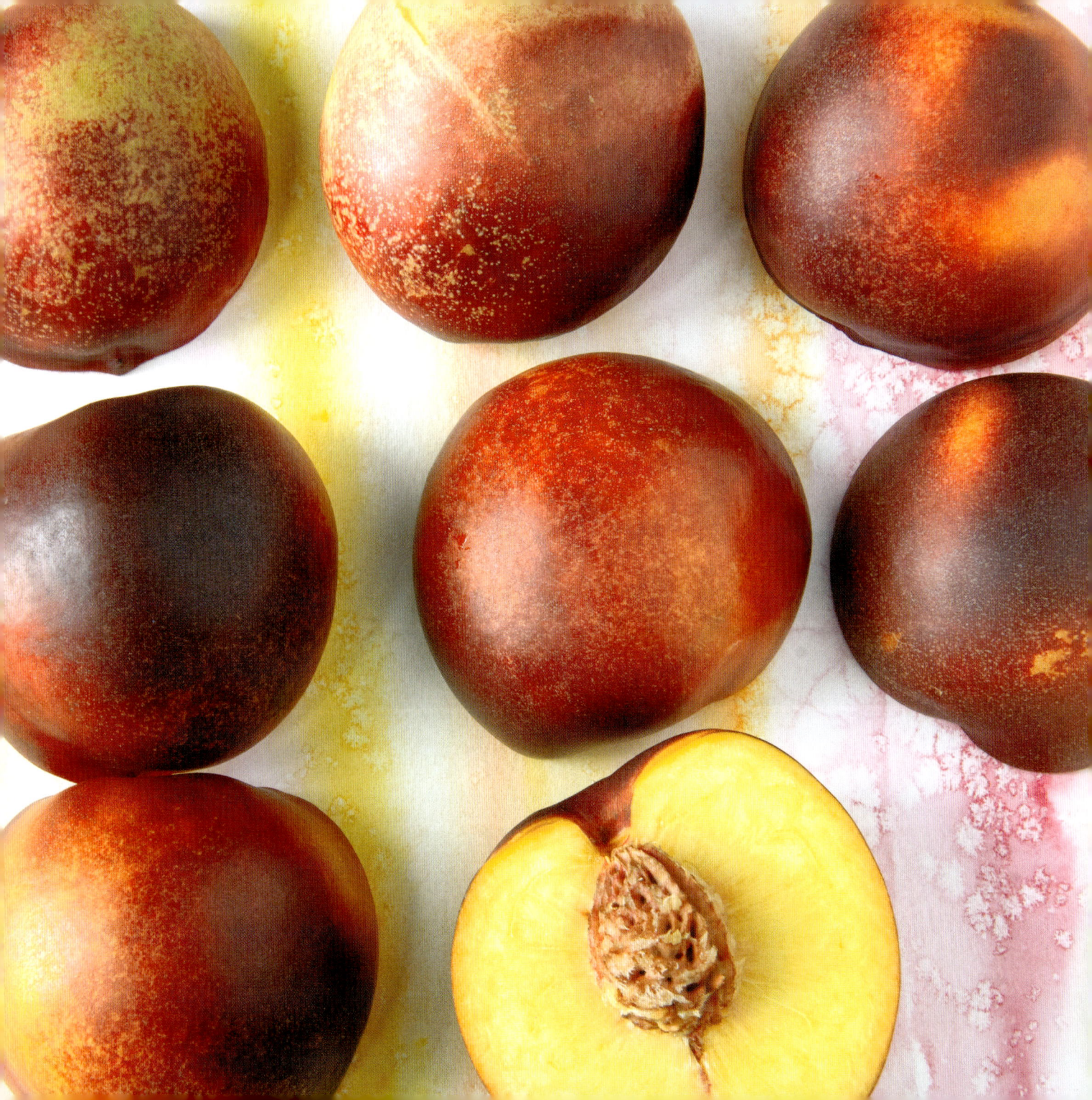

Nectarine

Recipe Idea

Nectarine caprese! Layer slices of nectarine, tomato & fresh mozzarella on a platter. Sprinkle with fresh basil, salt, pepper & olive oil.

red + a tiny bit of purple = magenta

watery yellow + white = light yellow

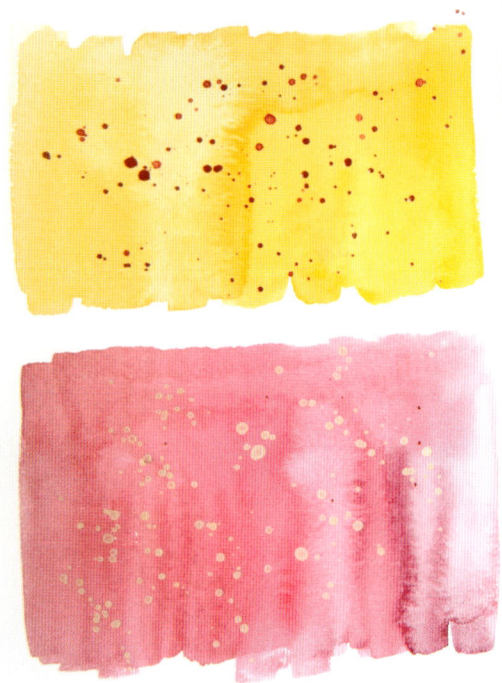

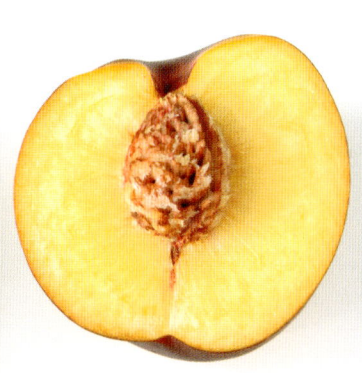

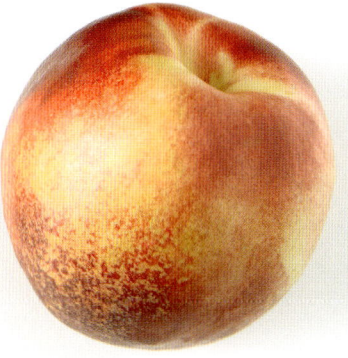

Color Exercise

Paint a light yellow block & a magenta block, then let them dry. Fill your brush with wet paint, then tap the brush to splatter the opposite color over each block. Light colors usually don't show up well over darker ones, but with thick light yellow paint on your brush, it will be visible.

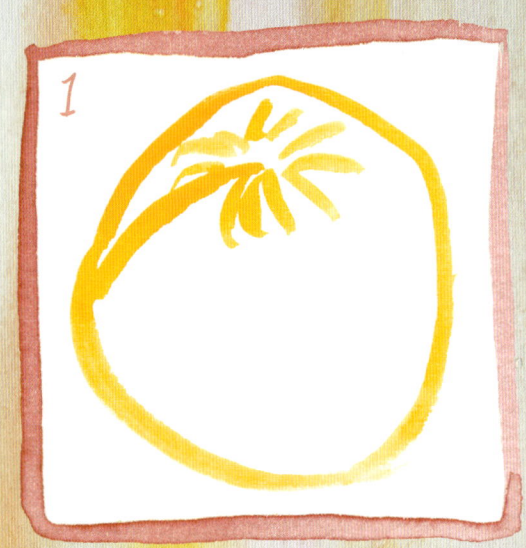

1

Paint a yellow circle. Inside the circle paint a design that resembles a flower with a stem that touches the circle.

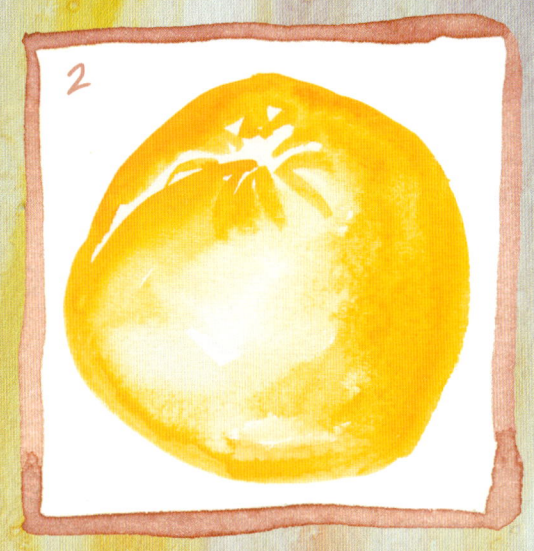

2

Add watery yellow to fill in the outline, making it darker around the edges. Leave some white bits inside the flower design.

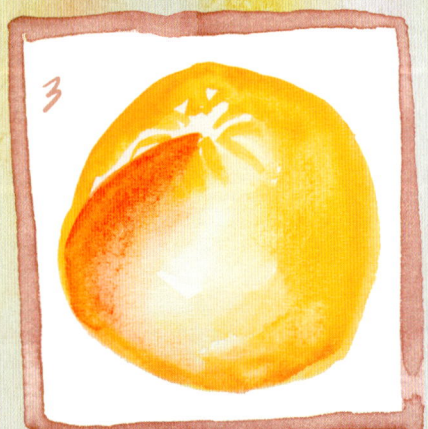

3

Paint over the "stem" part of the design with dark orange.

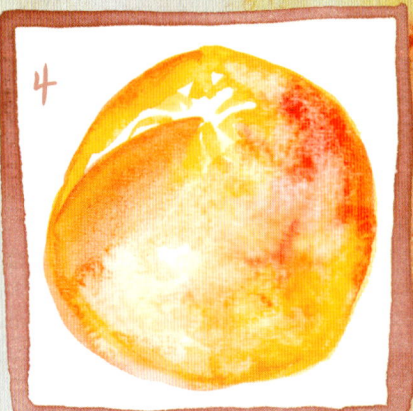

4

While the yellow area is still wet, add some watery drops of red, orange & magenta. Let it bleed.

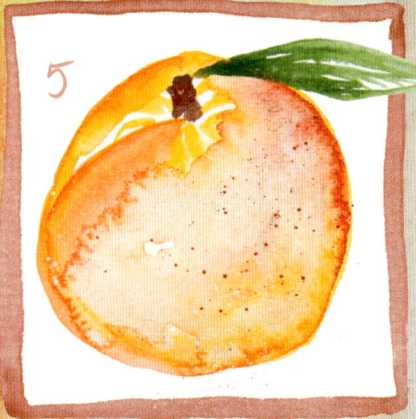

5

Let it dry then add a dark brown stem & a green leaf. Tap a small brush with magenta paint over the paper to splatter speckles.

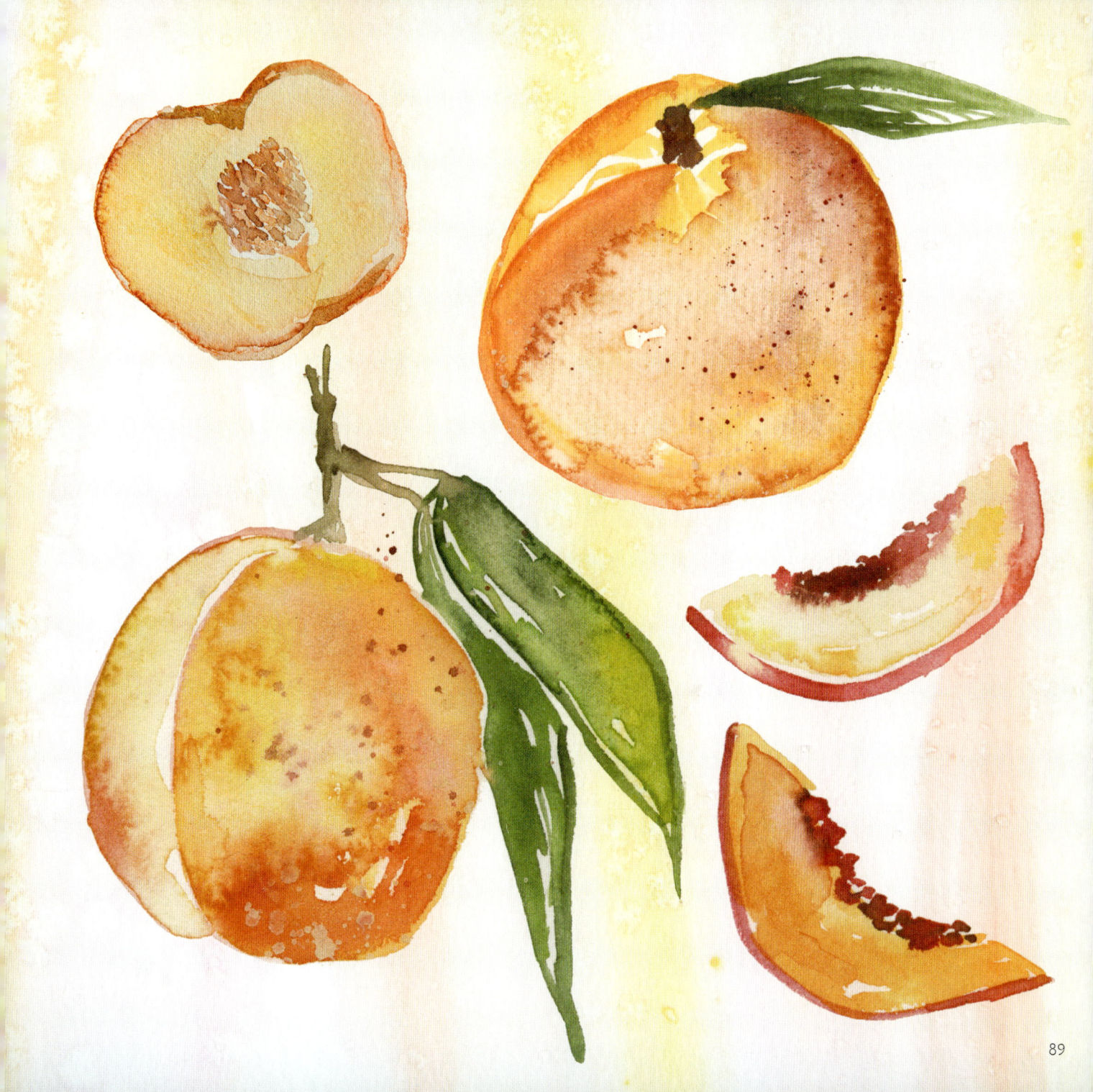

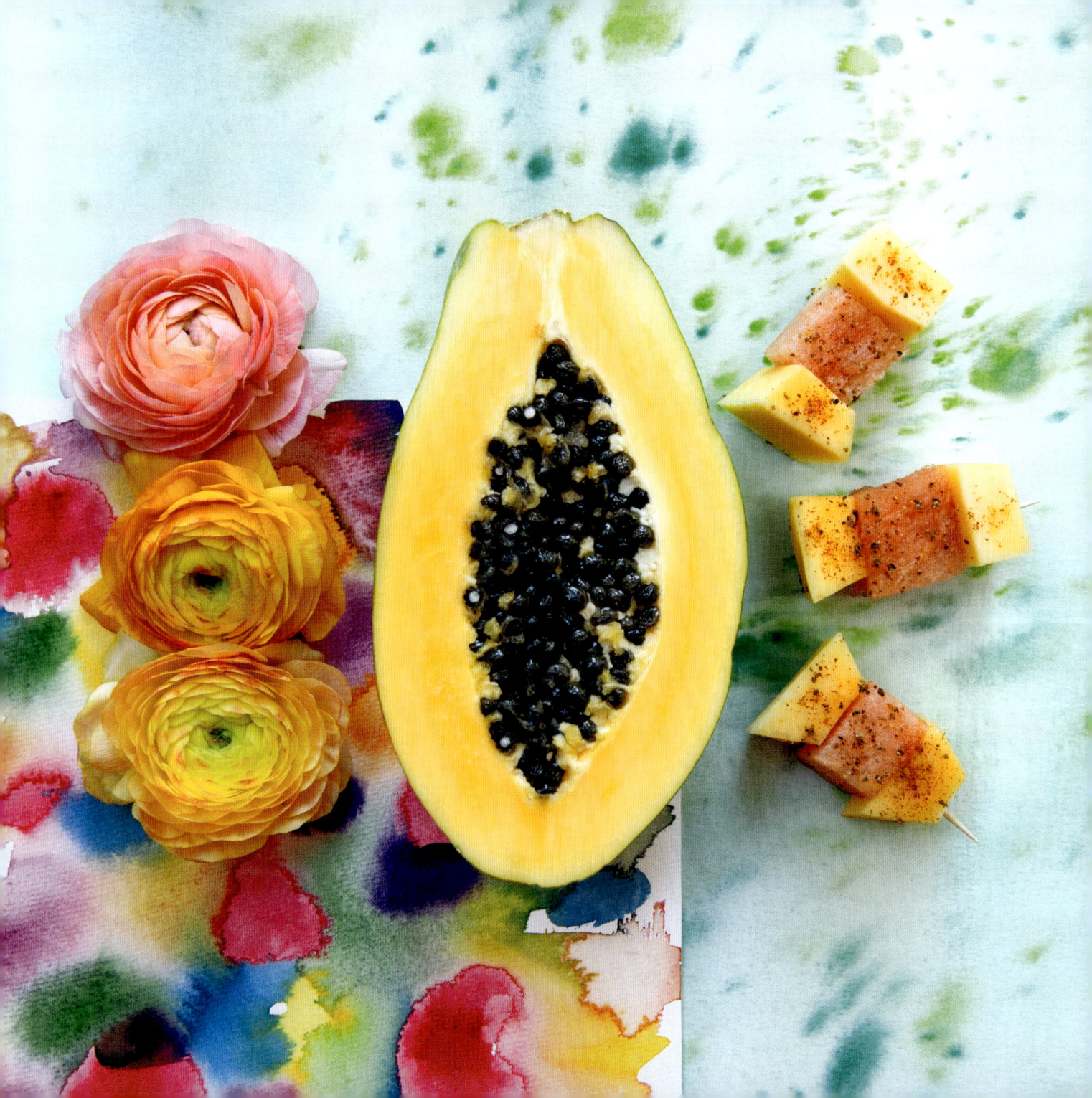

Papaya

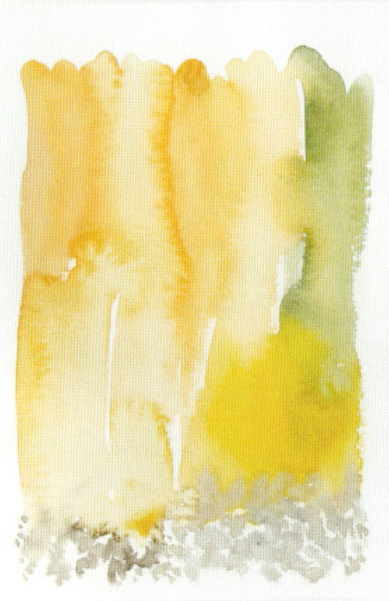

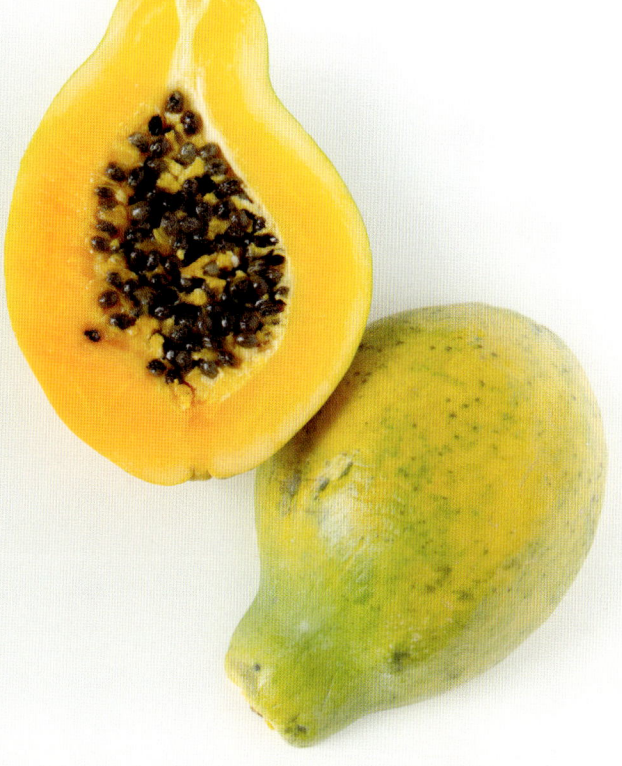

Color Exercise

Mix yellow, orange & a touch of brown to create that beautiful papaya flesh color. Add a strip of green. Using watered-down brown or black, dab your brush to make small markings over the yellow & beside it.

Recipe Idea

Stack cubes of papaya & watermelon onto skewers. Sprinkle with lime juice & Tajín seasoning.

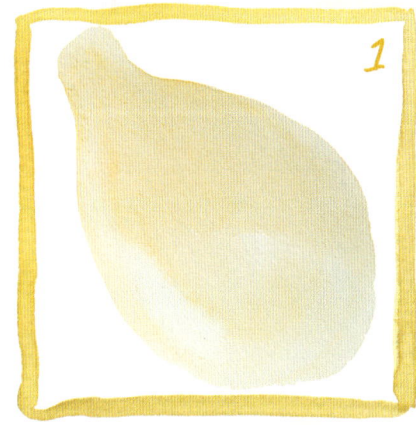

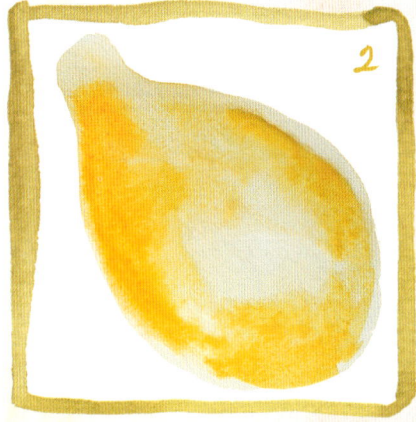

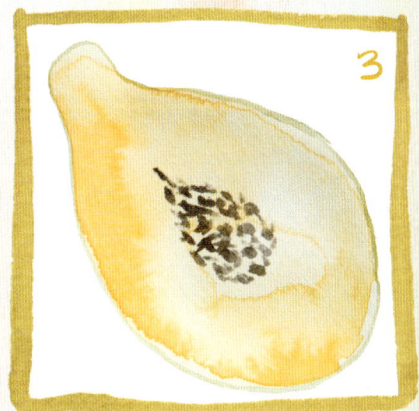

Start by painting a light silhouette of the papaya. If you outline it in pencil, erase the pencil before painting.

While the first layer is still wet, add a deeper hue (yellow + orange + a touch of brown), mostly around the edges.

Let it dry, then dab your brush to make seed-like markings with dark brown.

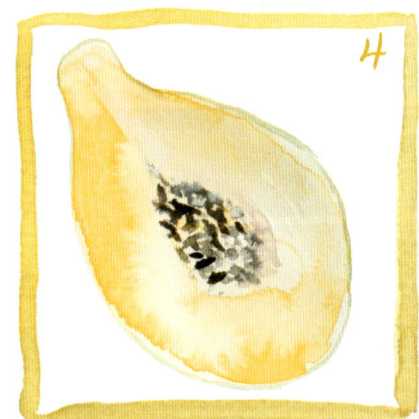

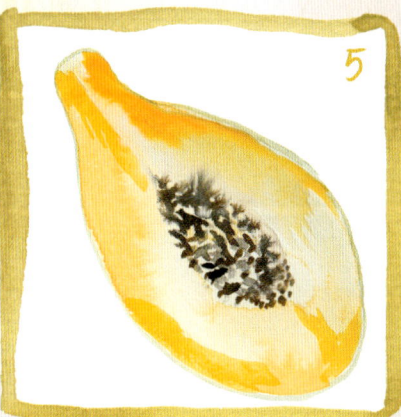

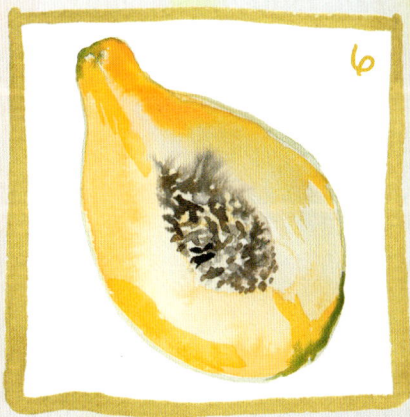

Mine was still damp, so the seeds bled a little, but I don't mind. To remove excess bleeding you can always blot with a cloth, wait for it to dry, then repaint the seeds.

Use a richer color (yellow + more orange) to add some detail to the edges of the papaya flesh.

Add some green to the top & base.

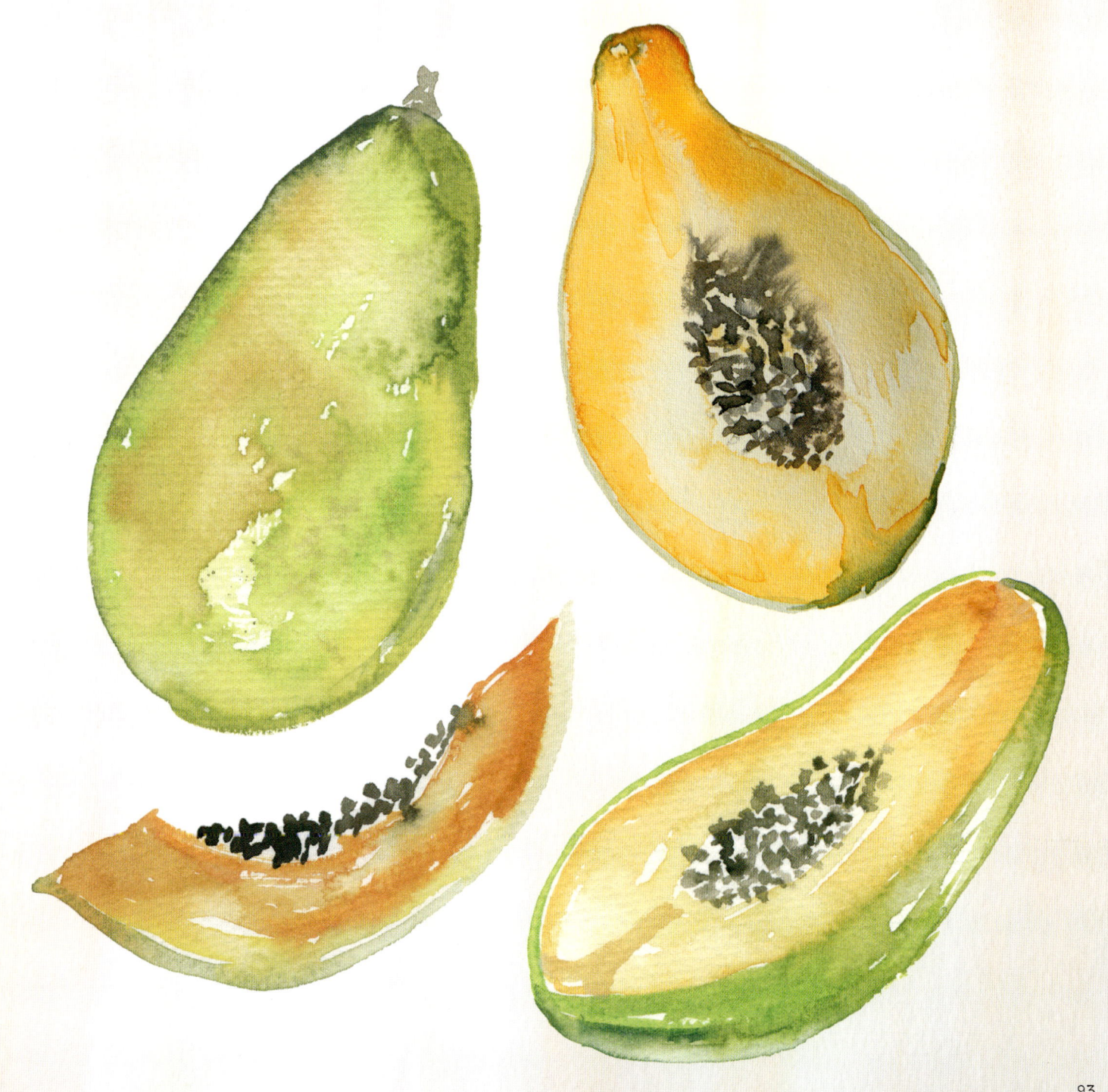

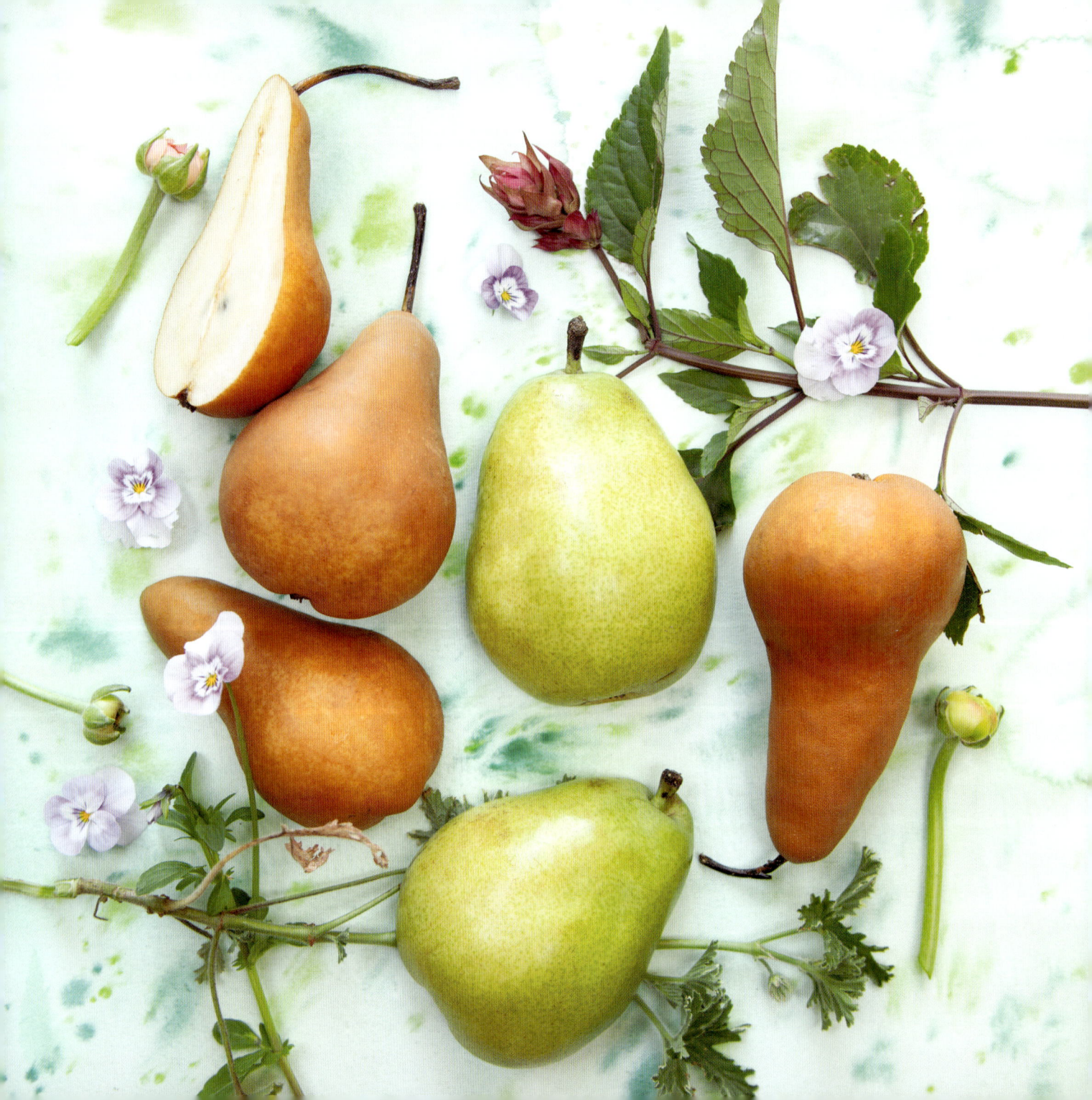

Pear

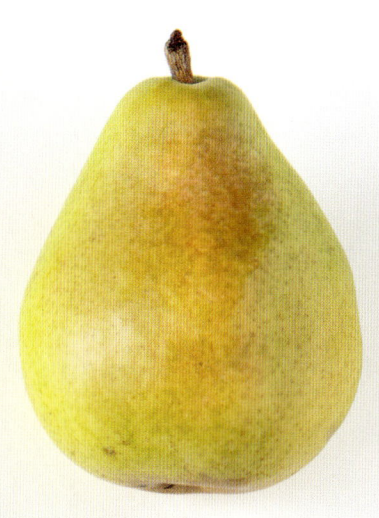

Color Exercise

On your plate, mix some of the colors you see in this pear:

{ green + yellow / green + brown / red + brown }

Paint a watery wash over your paper combining these new colors. Allow it to dry, then load your brush with dark brown paint. Lightly tap the brush over your painting to create speckles.

Recipe Idea

Add diced pear & cinnamon to your oatmeal while it's cooking. Top with honey & chopped walnuts.

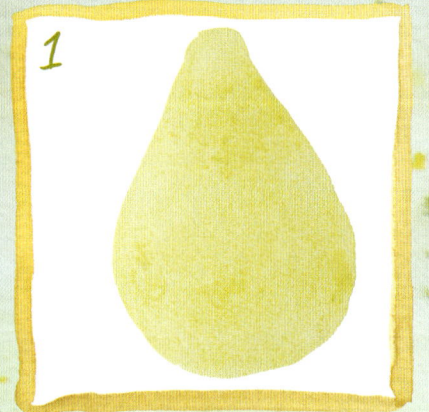

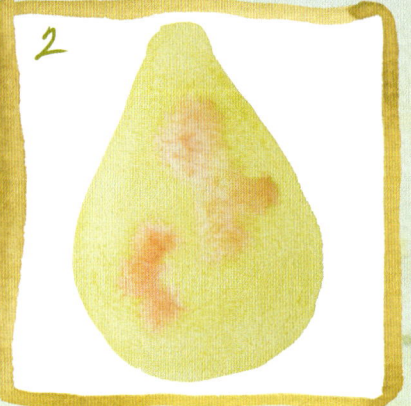

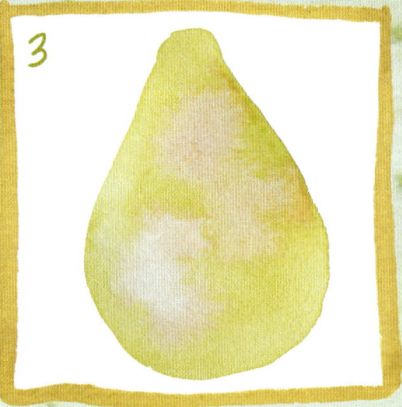

1 Create a greenish-yellow wash in the shape of a pear. If you use a pencil, erase it before you begin painting.

2 While the greenish yellow is damp, add some spots of maroon (red + a little brown).

3 Use a cloth to blot the maroon & lighten it.

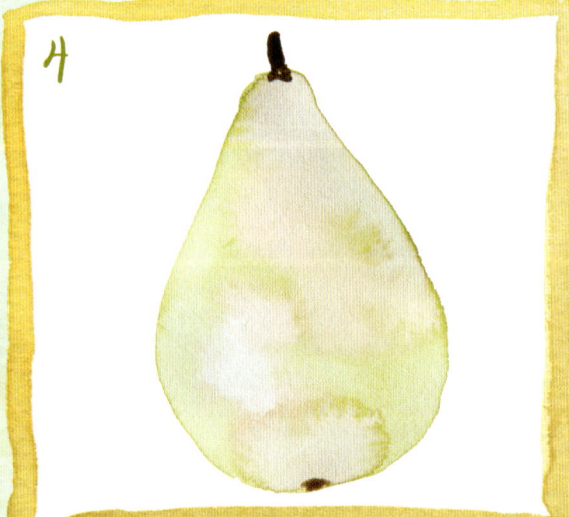

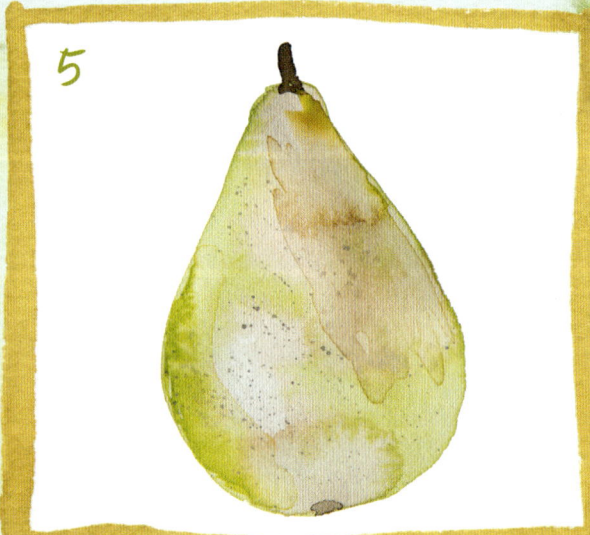

4 Add a dark brown stem & base. If your painting is mostly dry (or you blot it more), the brown won't bleed. Colors may fade as the paint dries.

5 I decided mine needed more color, so I added a bit more green & watered-down maroon at the edges. When it dried, I tapped my brush to add dark brown speckles. Add a leaf if you wish.

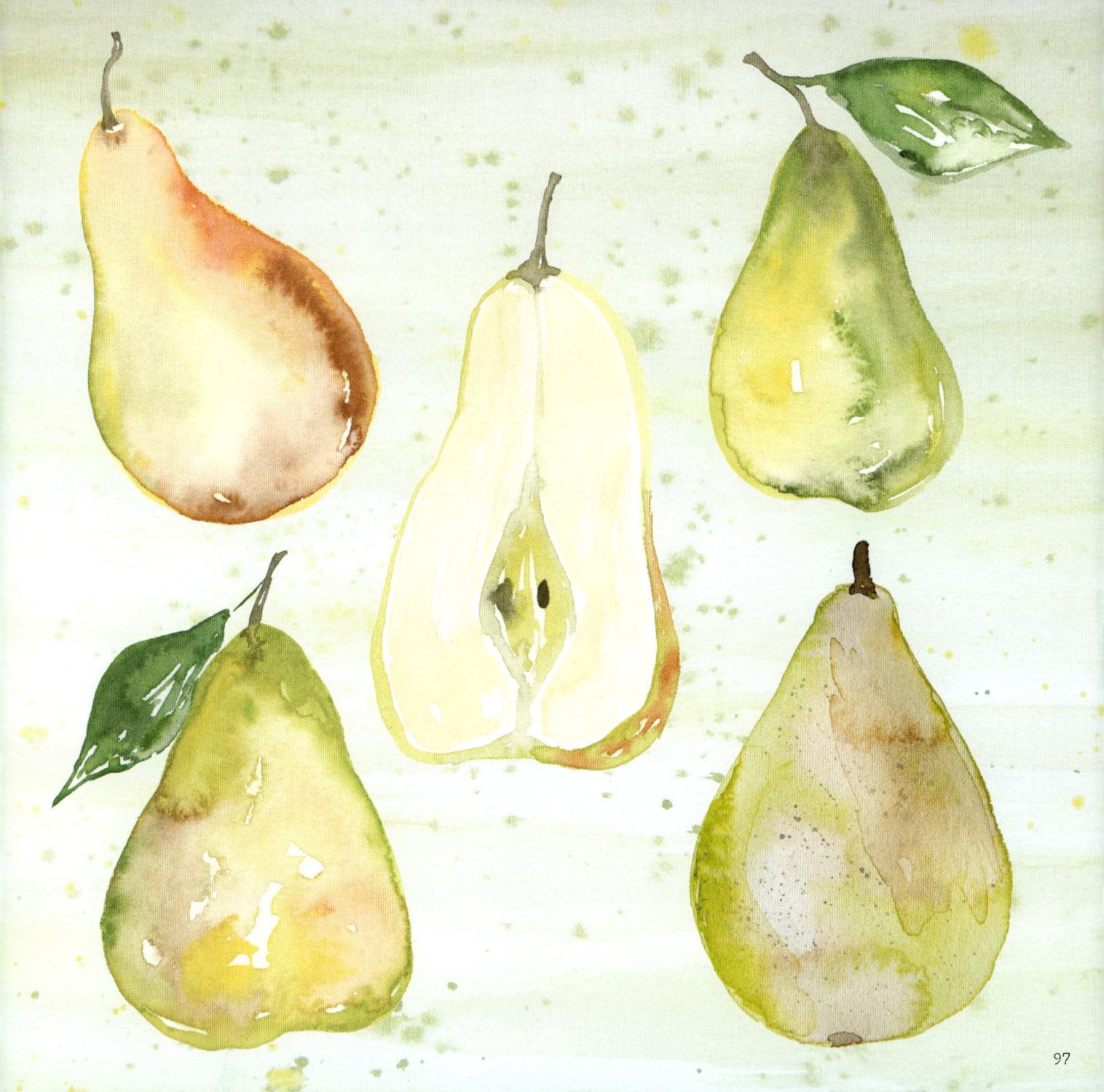

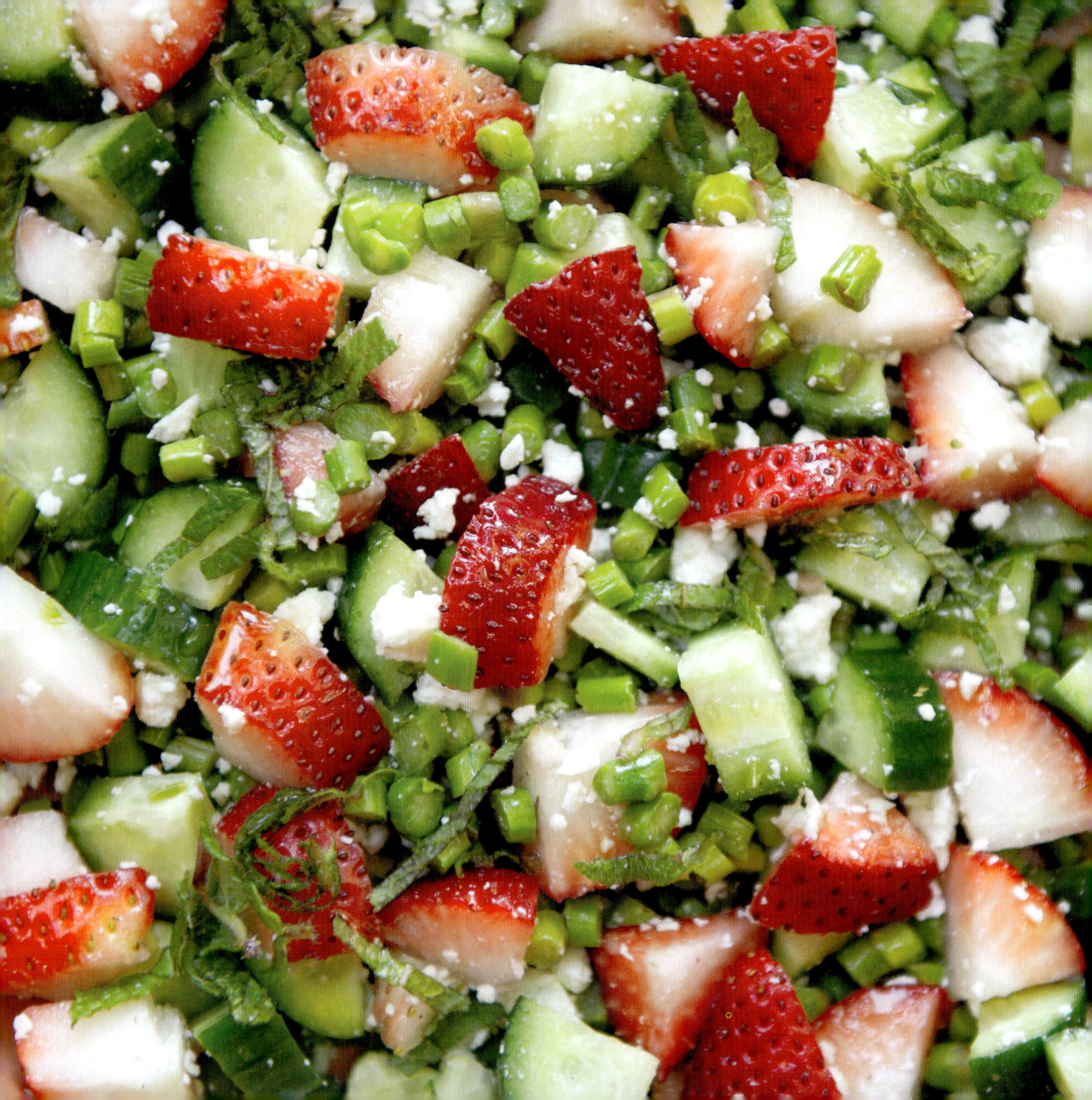

Strawberry

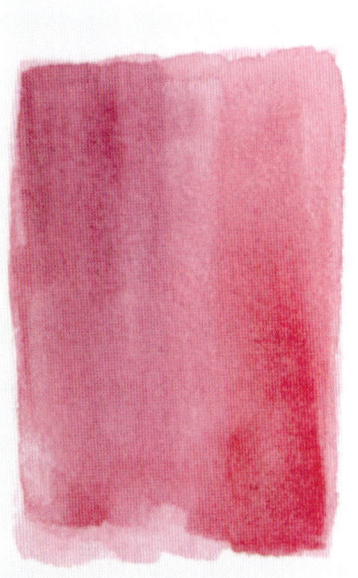

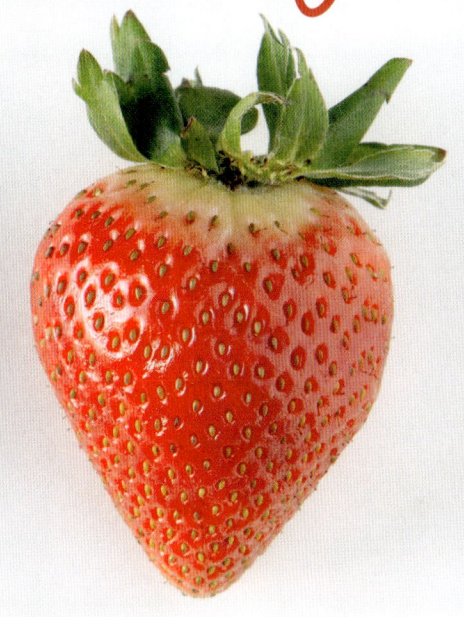

Color Exercise

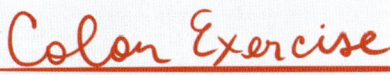

Mix 2 shades of red on your plate.
Mix some purple into one. Combine these
colors in a somewhat even wash over your
paper. Try not to use too much water to
avoid blooming marks when it dries.

Recipe Idea

Make a spring salad
by combining sliced
strawberries, cubed cucumber,
quickly sautéed chopped
asparagus, crumbled feta,
mint & a light vinaigrette.

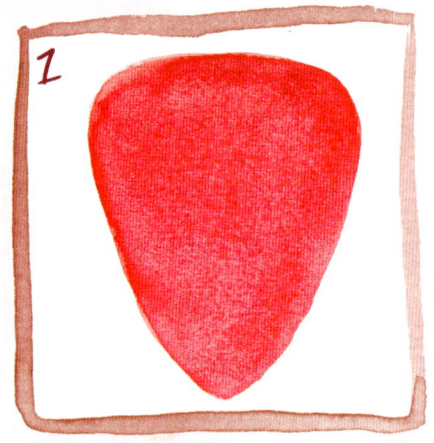

Paint an even silhouette
of the berry using the
red shades you have
mixed. Use minimal water
to avoid rippled blooming
marks when it dries.

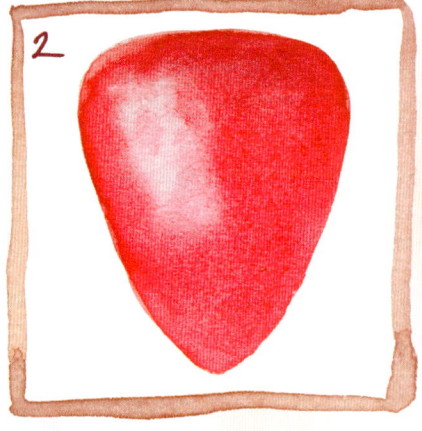

Use a cloth to blot
the upper left to look
like a highlight.

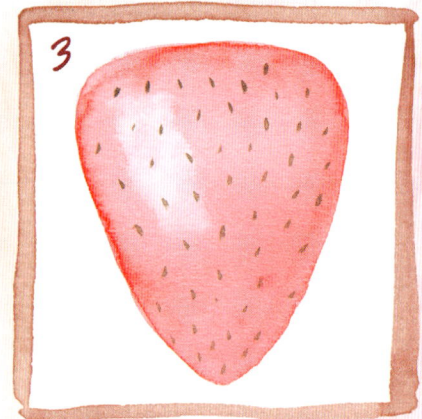

When it dries, add
some dark brown seeds.
Use your smallest brush,
or size 0.

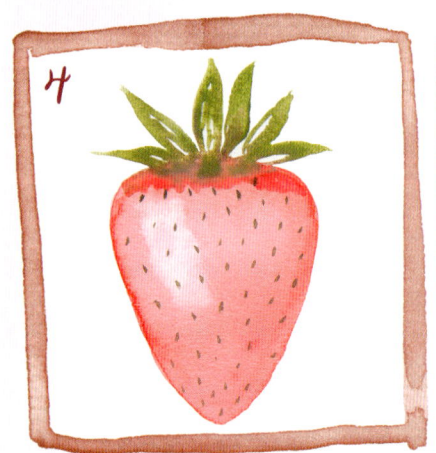

Add some leaves in
a medium green.

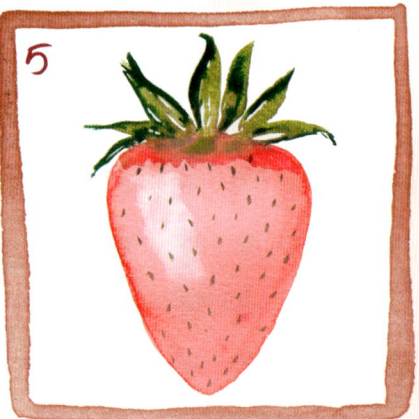

While the medium
green is still wet, add
dark green around the
leaf edges.

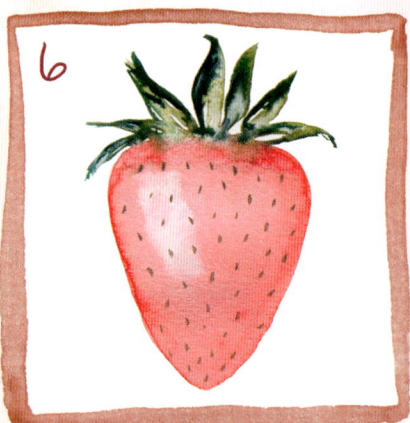

Notice how the colors
lighten when they
dry. Add more seeds
if you'd like.

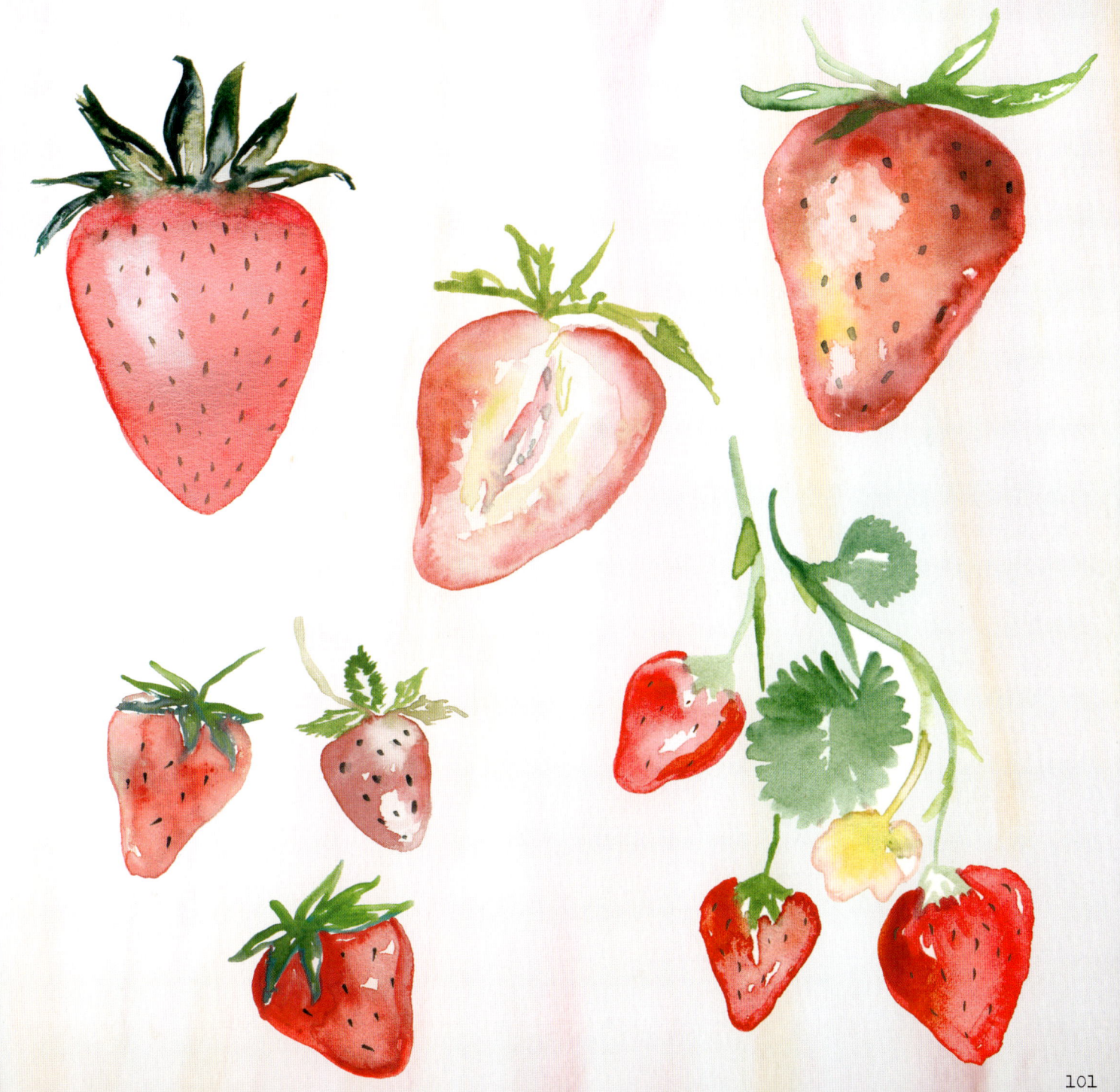

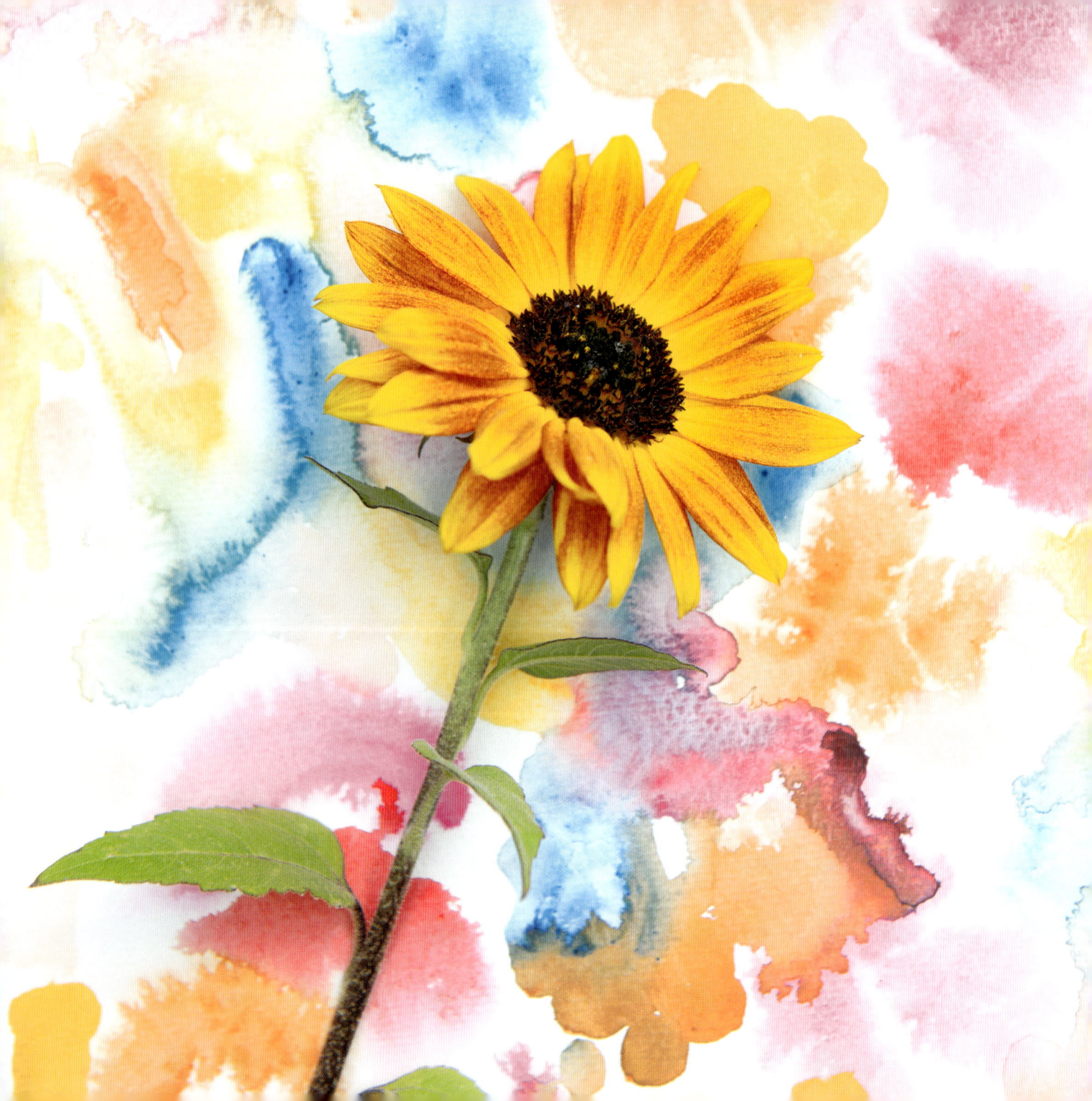

EDIBLE FLOWERS

In this section, follow step-by-step instructions to paint edible flowers. As a reminder, like in the previous chapter, start each tutorial with a size 2 brush. Most of the time I use small brushes (size 0-2) and a larger brush (such as size 6) just to fill in larger areas. See my color mixing tips on page 14. To give your page a background color (like my snapdragons on page 135) paint the entire paper with a light, watered-down color. Let it dry, then paint your item over it.

While these flowers are technically edible, in some cases I just use them as decoration. I grow many of these flowers myself, since they're easy to cultivate in pots (and flowers from a florist may be grown with pesticides). I also buy edible flowers online or in the herb section at Whole Foods. I offer recipe suggestions alongside each painting tutorial so that you can use the flowers after you paint them. These paintings generally take about 15 minutes, but sometimes a little more if you need to let a layer dry between steps. I like to paint on postcard-size watercolor paper so it feels fun and easy, and so I can mail my art to someone afterward.

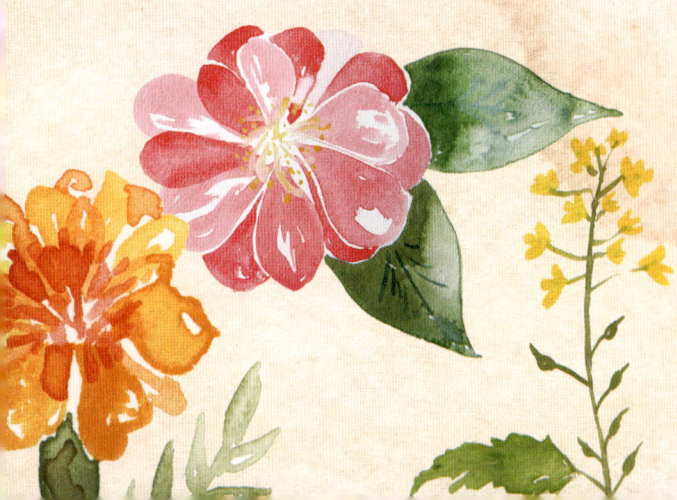

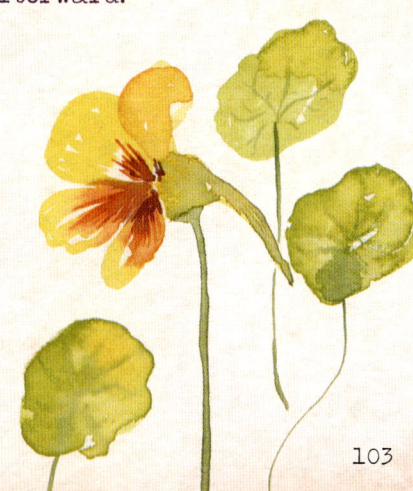

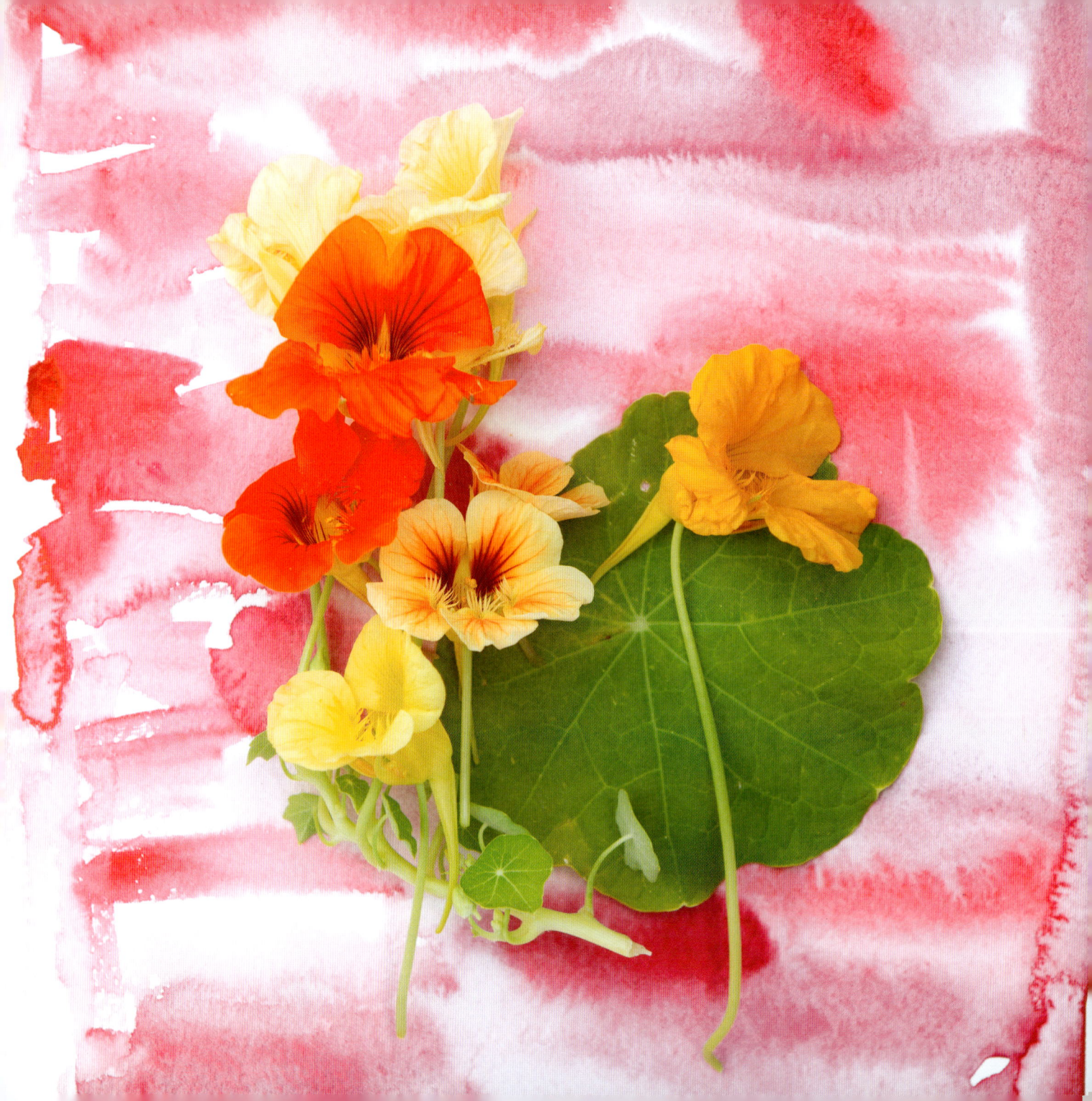

Nasturtium

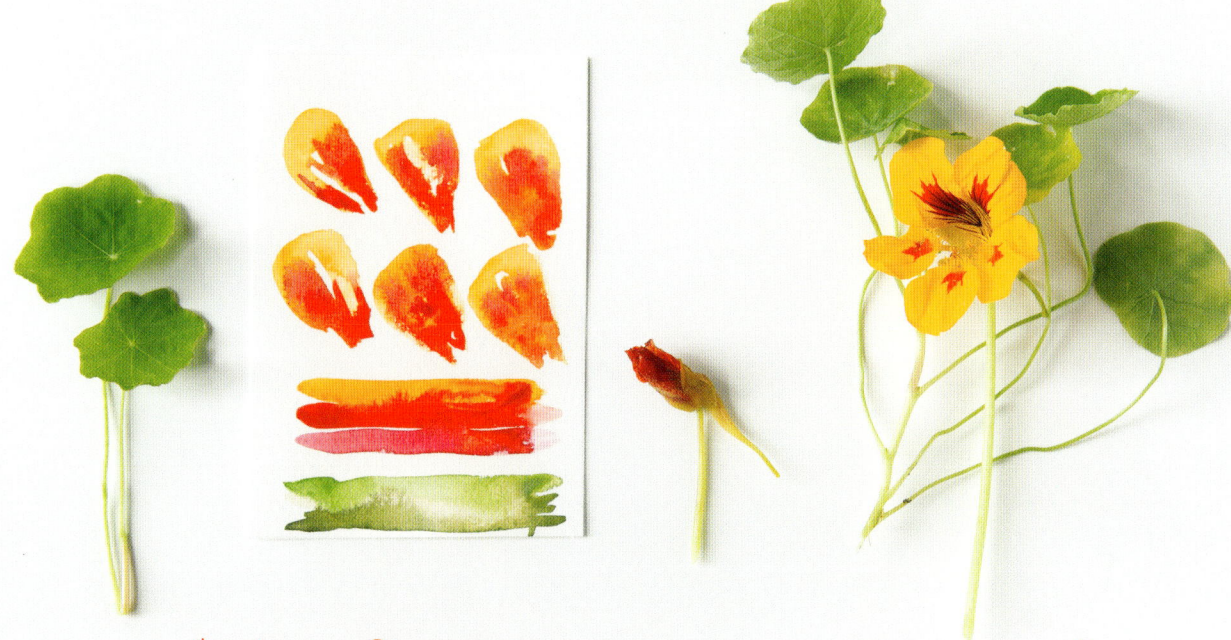

Color Exercise

Let's explore adding a dark color over a light color without the light color being overtaken. Paint yellow petal shapes, then dab a bit of orange on one end. Let it bleed, but if it's very wet or you add too much orange, it could cover up the yellow entirely, which we'd like to avoid.

Recipe Idea

Make a green herb salad by tossing torn butter lettuce, mint, dill & cilantro with your favorite vinaigrette. Add a pop of flavor and color by placing nasturtium flowers on top.

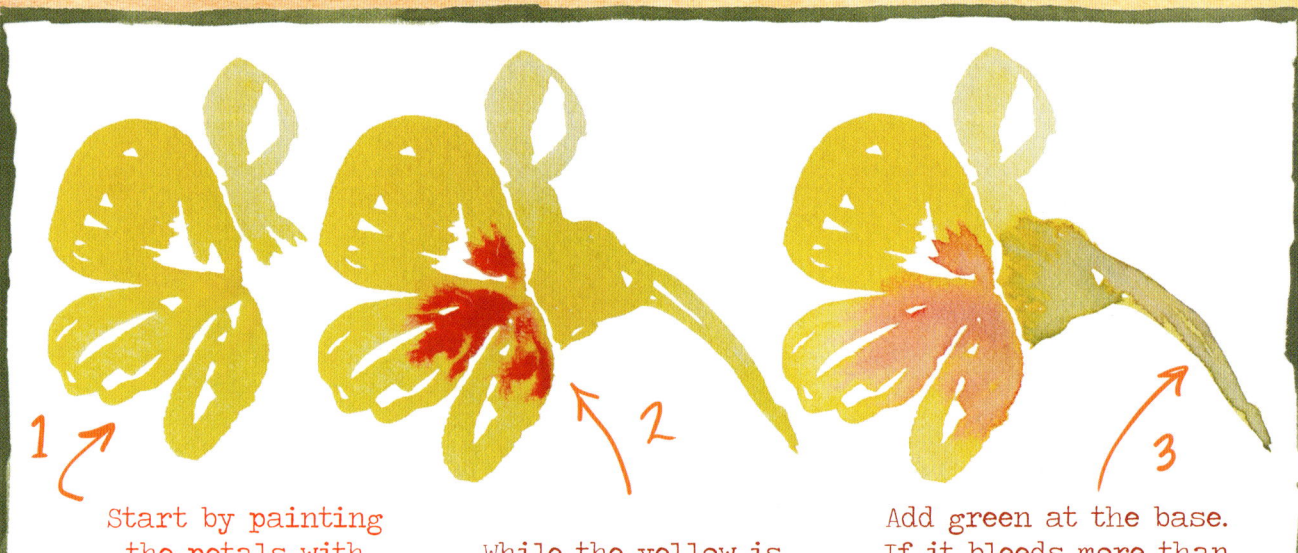

1 Start by painting the petals with a watery light yellow. Leave some white bits.

2 While the yellow is wet, dab dark orange paint in the center.

3 Add green at the base. If it bleeds more than you anticipated, blot with a cloth & repaint with yellow, then green.

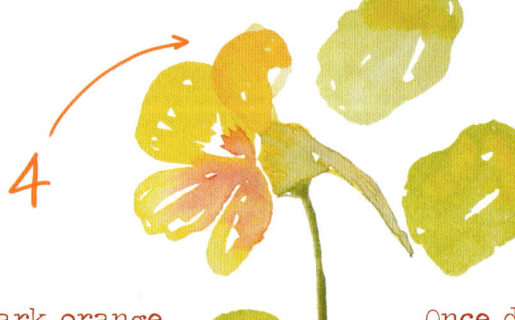

4 Add dark orange to the upper petal to bring it to the foreground. Add a thin green stem & paint round green leaves with a touch of yellow.

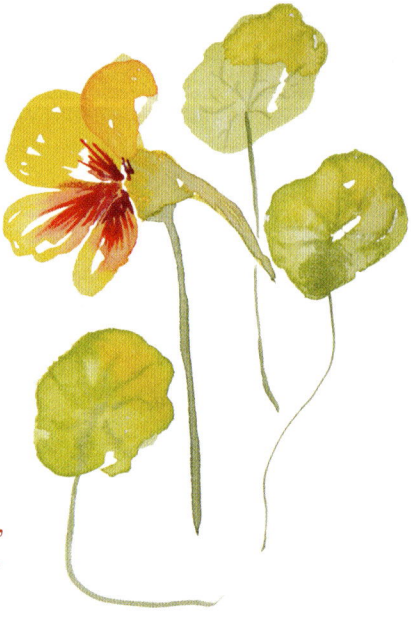

5 Once dry, add red lines at the base of the petals, plus green veins & stems on the leaves. Notice how my lower leaves weren't quite dry yet, but I don't mind that the veins bled a bit.

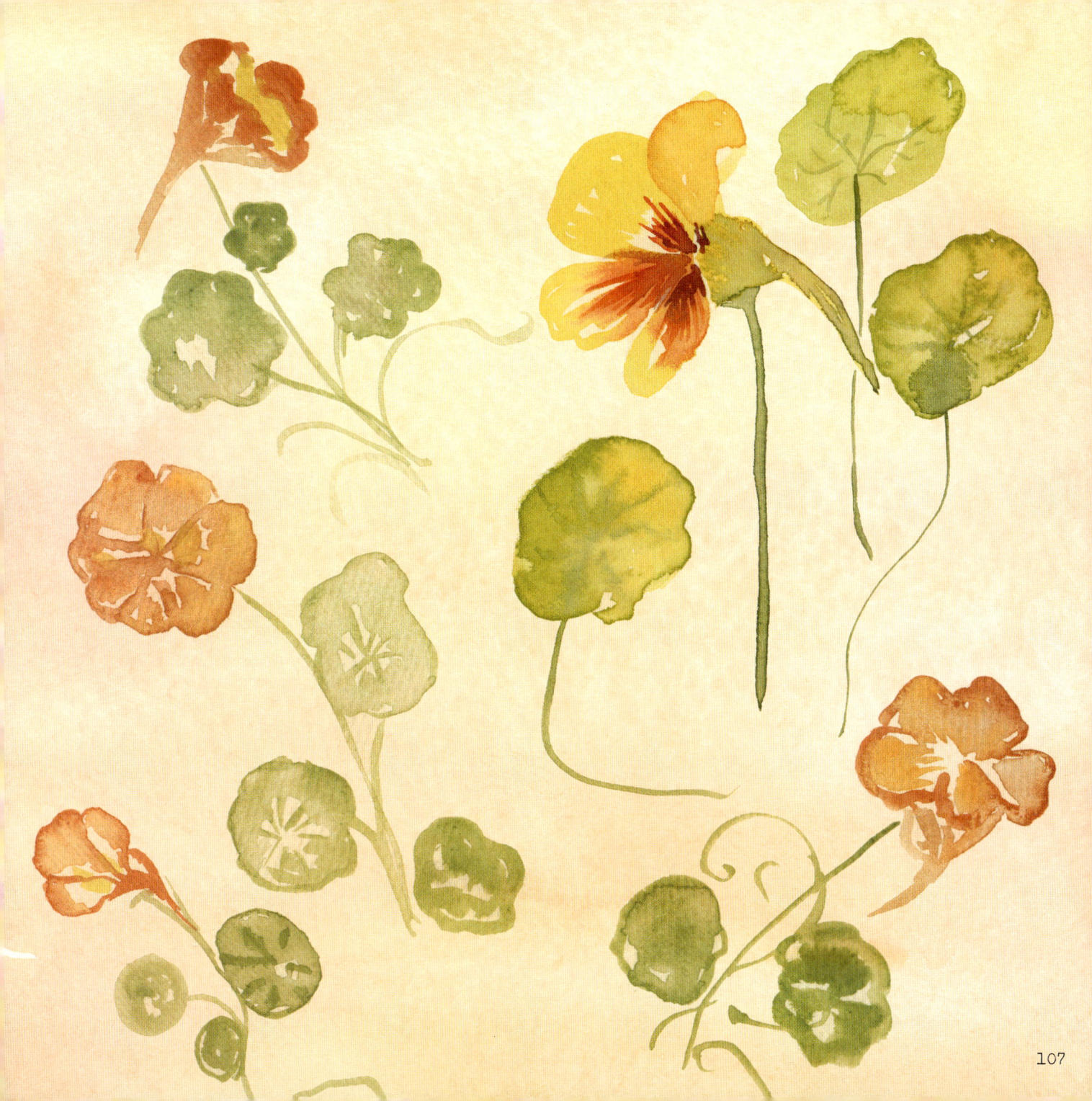

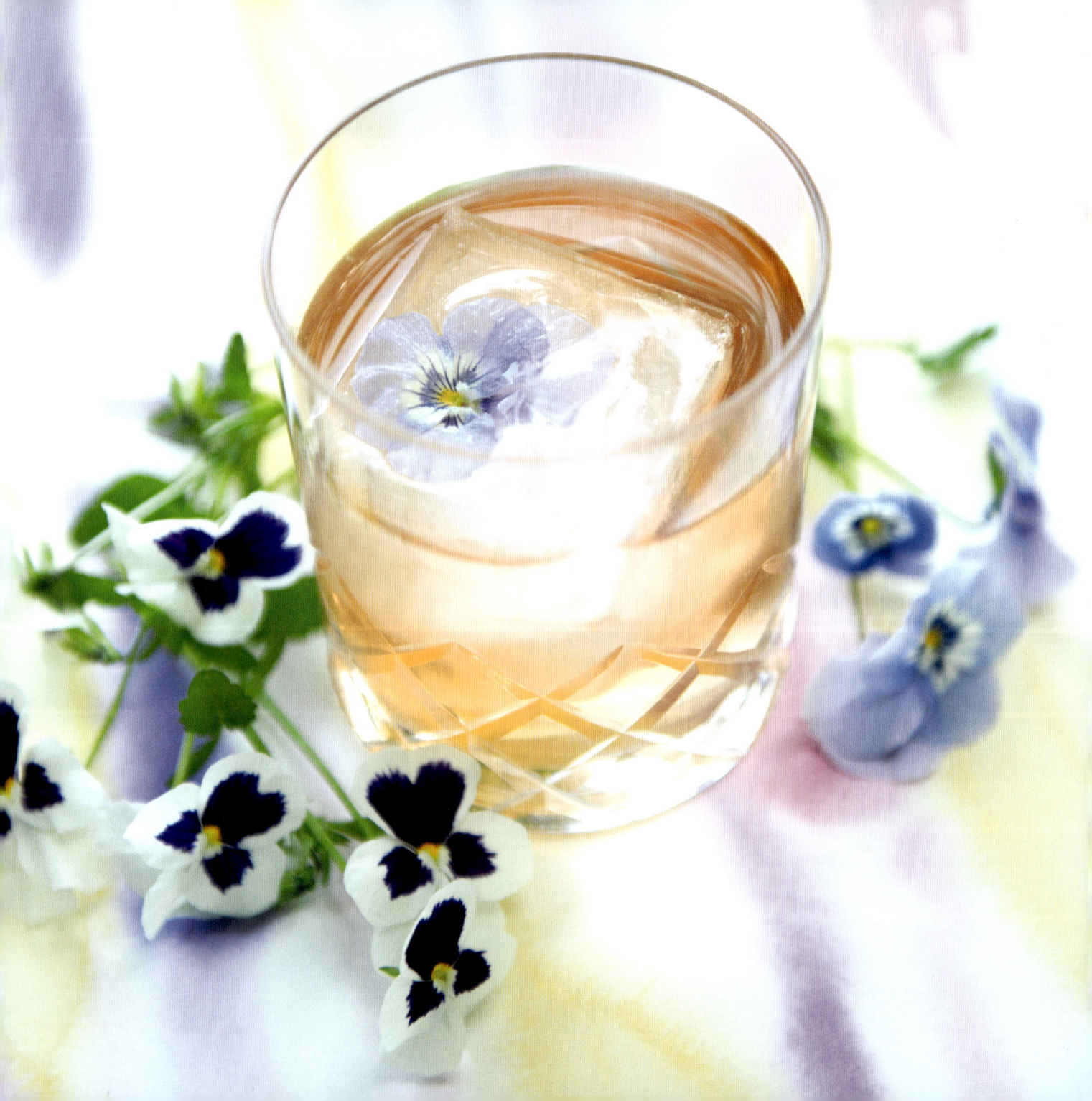

Viola

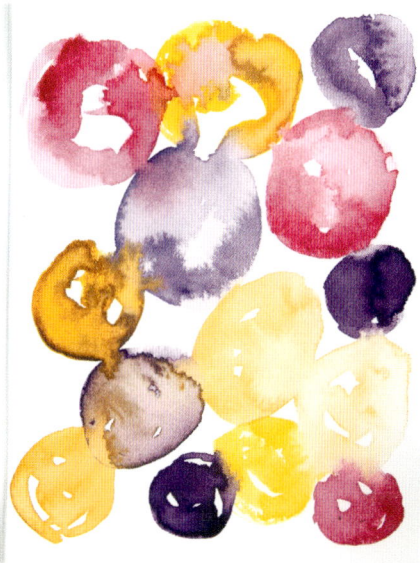

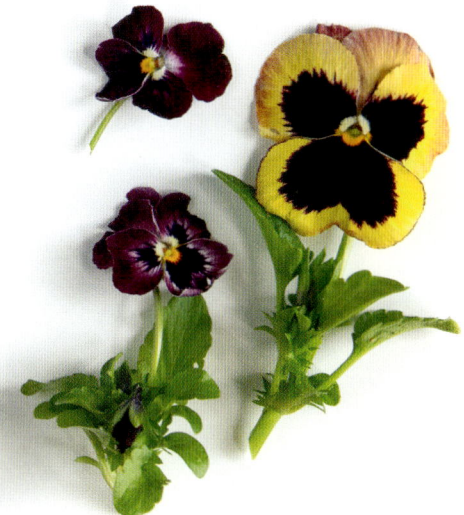

Color Exercise

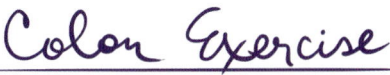

On your plate, try mixing shades of yellow, green & purple that you see in these violas. Create a series of intersecting circles & notice how the colors change when the wet paint touches.

"Recipe" Idea

Floral ice cubes! Fill an ice cube tray (I use a silicon one that makes large cubes) with water, then float a viola on each section. Freeze & enjoy in your favorite drink.

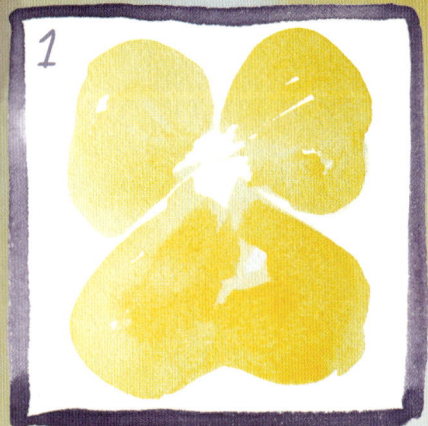

1

Using watered-down
yellow, paint 3 petals
with an unpainted white
spot in the middle.

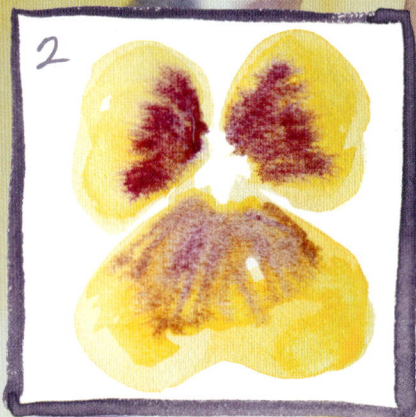

2

While the yellow is
wet, paint tiny lines
outward from the center
with a small amount of
reddish purple.

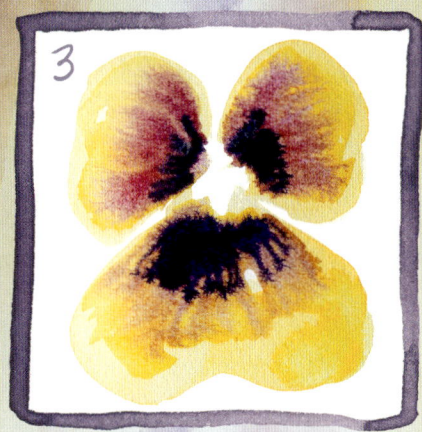

3

Let the purple bleed
outward. Add a very
small amount of dark
purple. (Careful: if it's
too wet, the purple could
take over the yellow.)

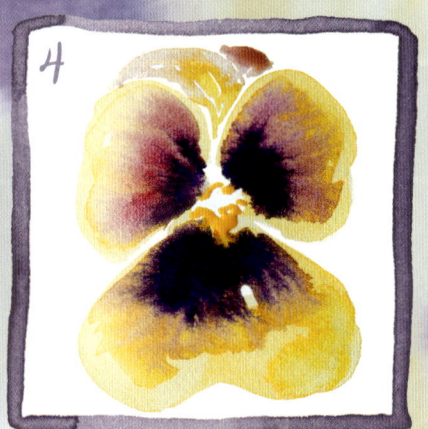

4

Add some yellow dots
to the center. Leaving
a thin white gap, add a
petal or 2 at the top.

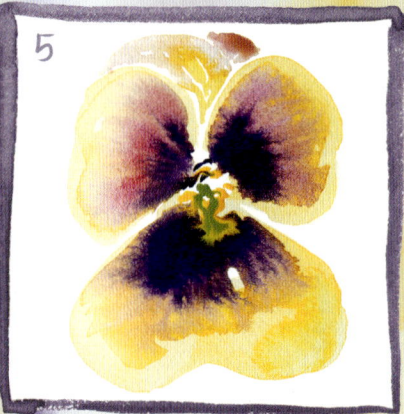

5

Add a bit of green
to the center. Oops!
Mine bled too much.

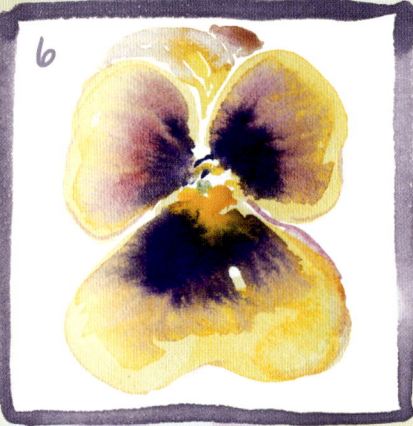

6

I blotted the green with
a cloth & added a bit
more yellow instead.

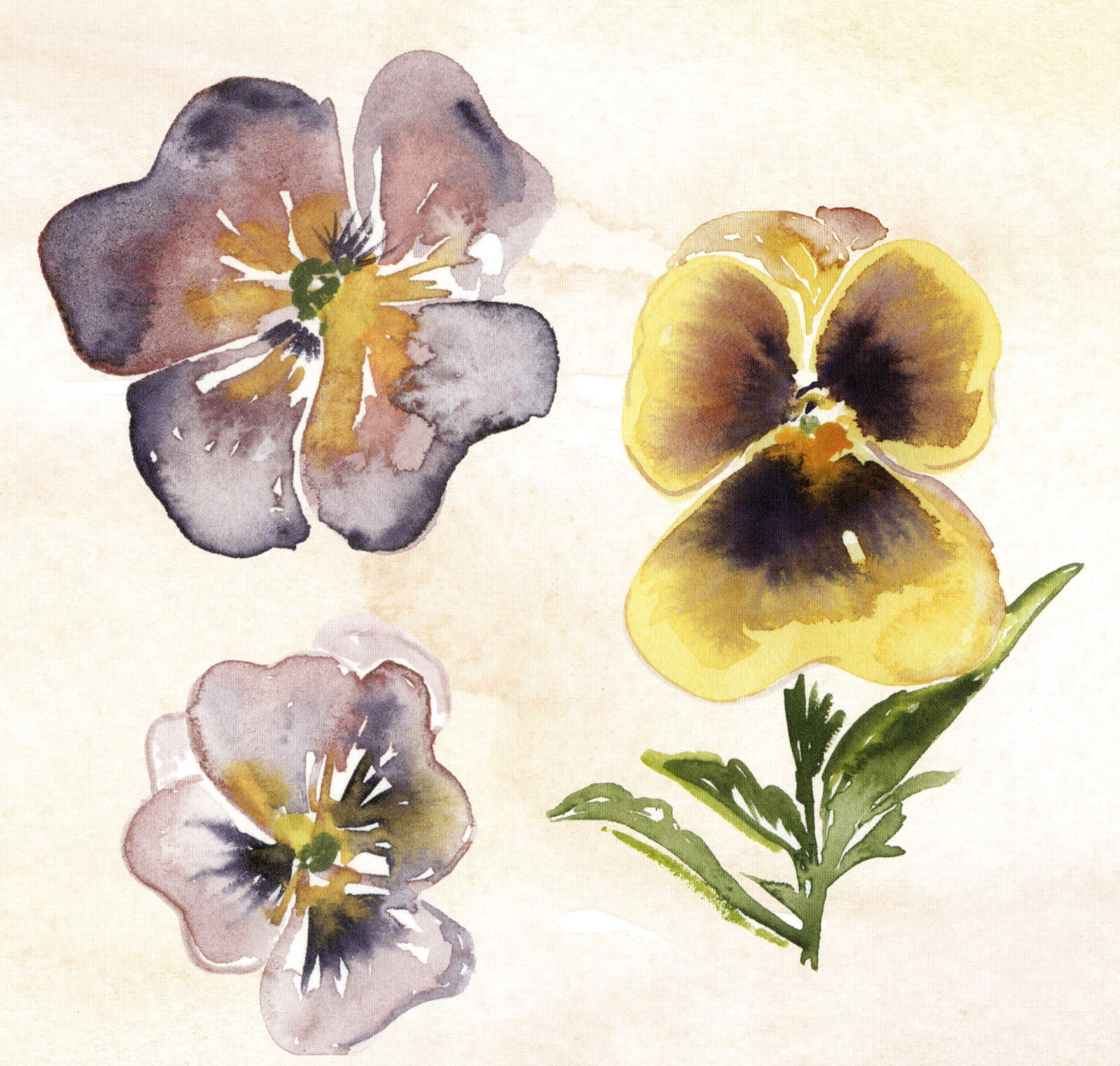

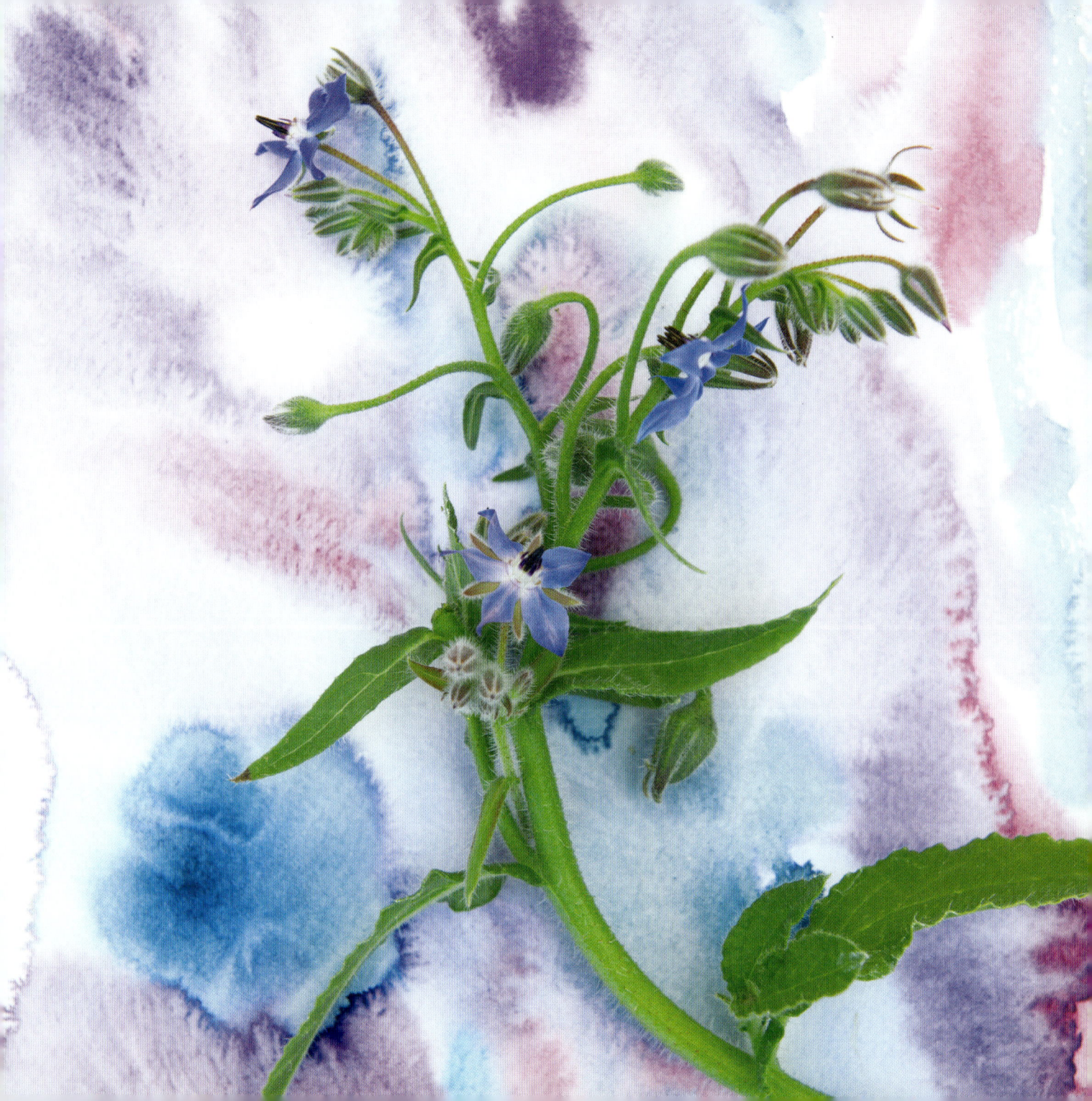

Borage

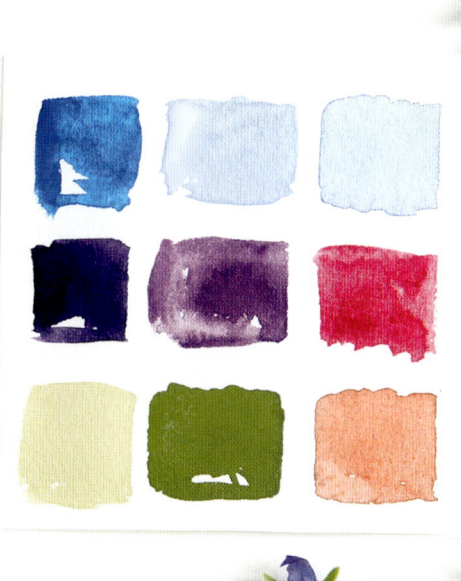

Color Exercise

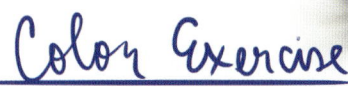

How many shades of blue &
green do you see? Do you
also see a bit of purple, red,
brown, or pink? Paint a grid
of small squares. Notice how
more water on your brush
makes any color lighter.

Recipe Idea

Borage is easy to grow! Put these
pretty blue flowers on your salad or
use them as a topping for ice cream.

113

1 2 3

Paint the outline of the flower, then fill it in using small strokes toward the center, leaving some white in the middle. Then dab the points of the flower with a darker shade of blue & let it bleed inward.

4

Add another blossom (side angle), then add a stem using a mix of brown & green.

5 Allow the blue areas to dry, then...

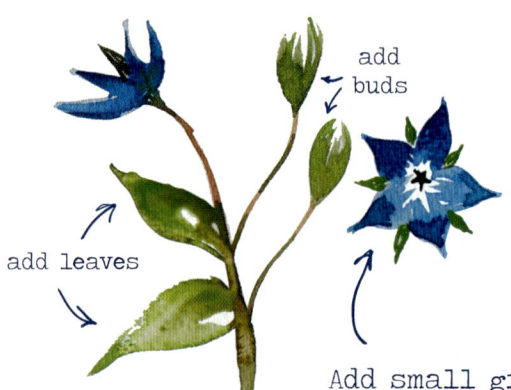

add buds

add leaves

Add small green leaves between the blue petals & a small black star-shaped stigma in the center.

6

Once it dries, you can add dark blue detail around the edges of the flowers if you think it's needed. Notice how different the leaves look once they're dry!

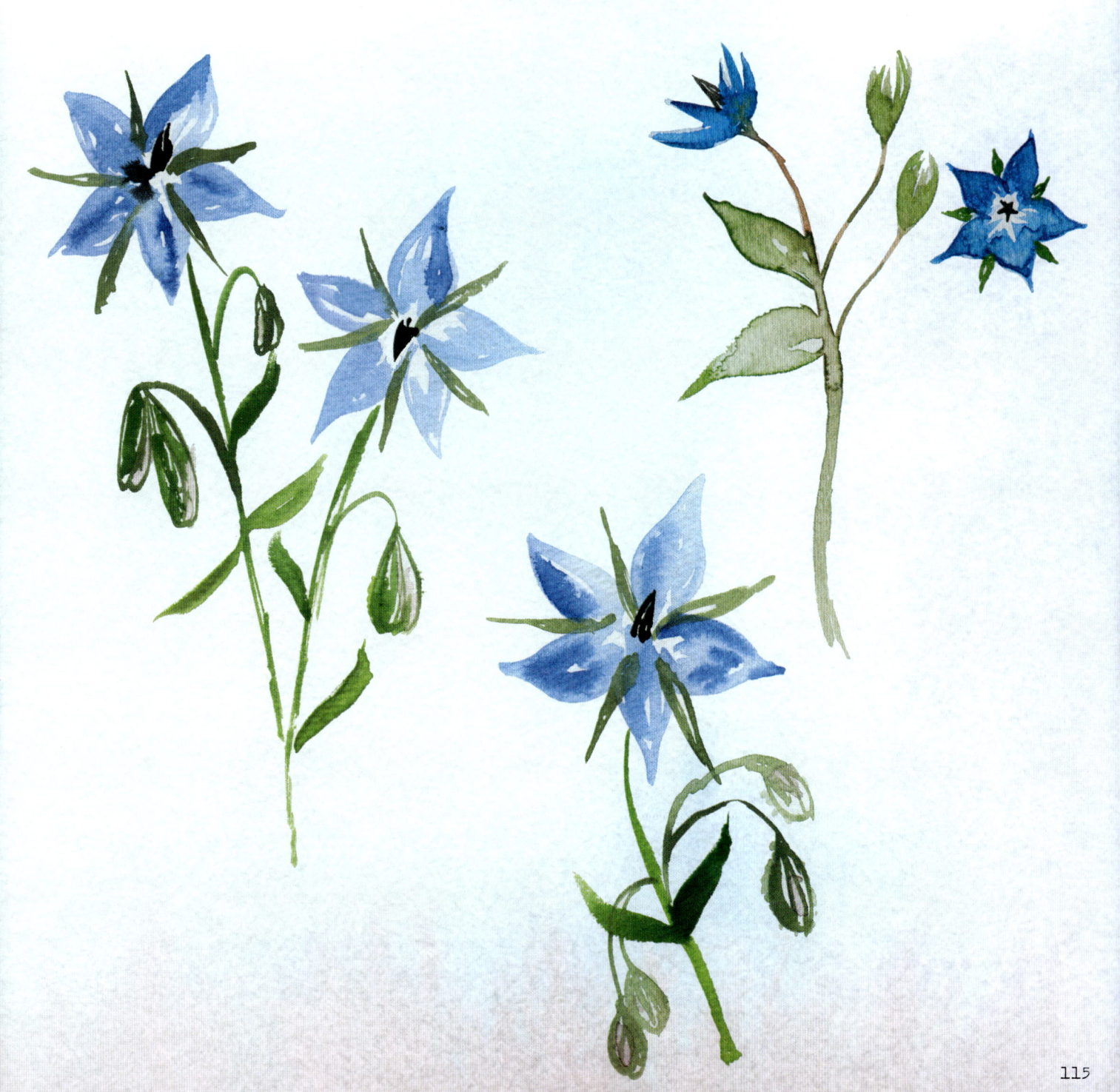

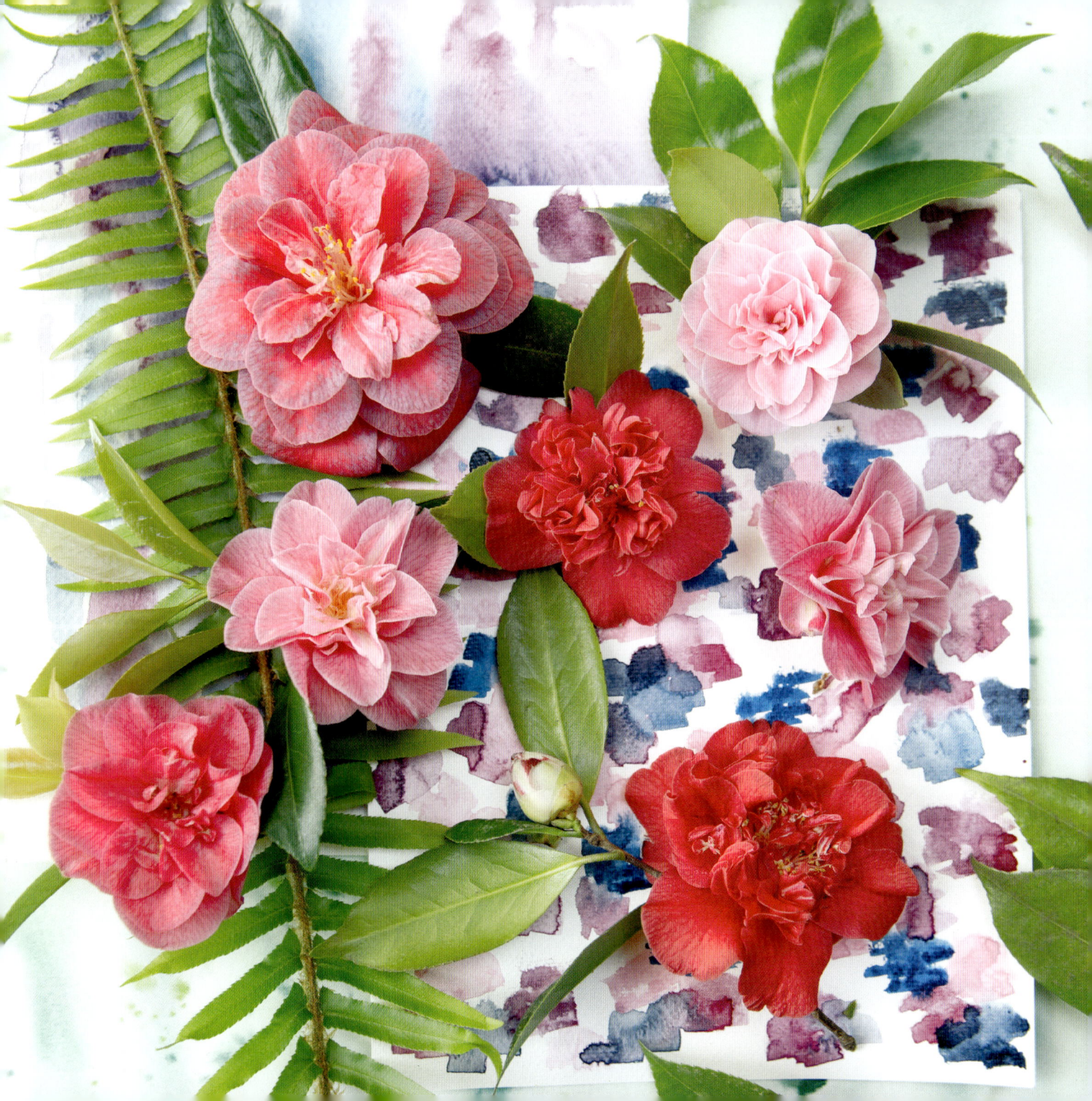

Camellia

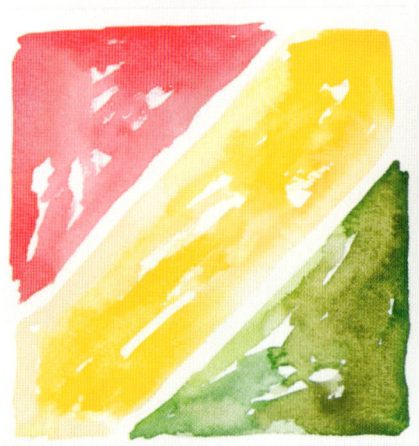

Color Exercise

Explore the separate shades in this flower by painting stripes of pink, yellow & green. On a plate, mix a custom shade of each.

{ pink + red
yellow + white
green + brown }

Intentionally leave some unpainted white bits.

Recipe Idea

I am lucky to have a camellia tree at home in California that blooms from January to June! I often lay branches down in the center of a dinner table or use the blooms on a cheese board as decoration.

1

Start by painting a light pink base of petals. Leave some unpainted white bits. Allow to dry.

2

Add red to your pink to create a darker shade of pink. Paint darker petals "behind" the lighter ones & also a couple that overlap the light petals. Try to leave a thin unpainted white line between each petal. Using 2 shades of green, add leaves that don't quite touch the pink petals. Allow to dry.

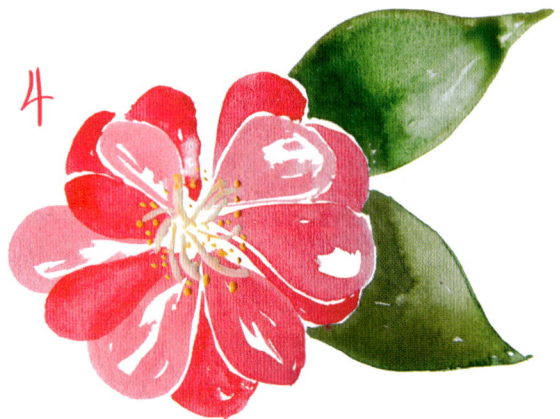

4

Generally, light colors don't show up well over darker paint, but try putting a thick amount of light pink on your brush (not too watery) & paint small lines for the stamen. Then add yellow dots.

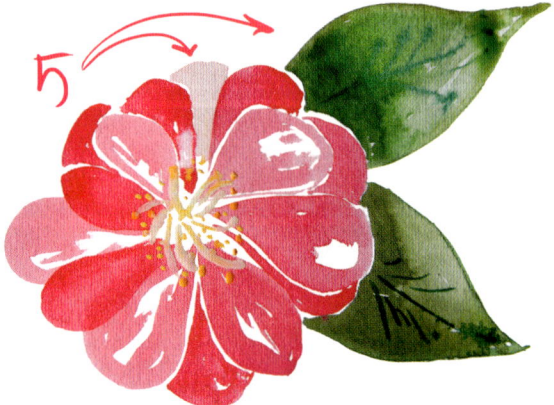

5

Use dark green to make veins on the leaves. Notice my upper leaf was not quite dry, so the paint bled (I like it!). Add more light pink petals if it feels right.

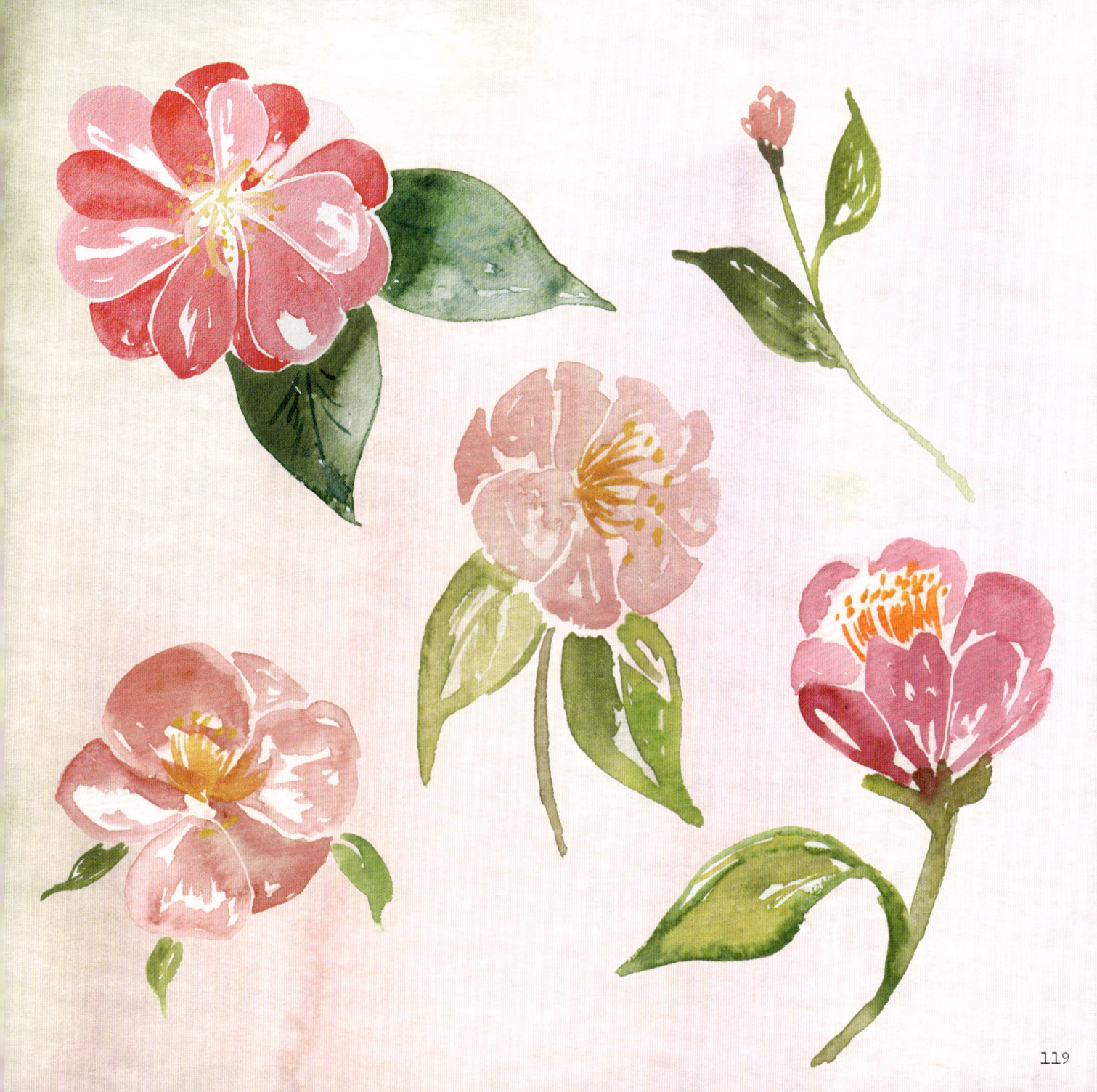

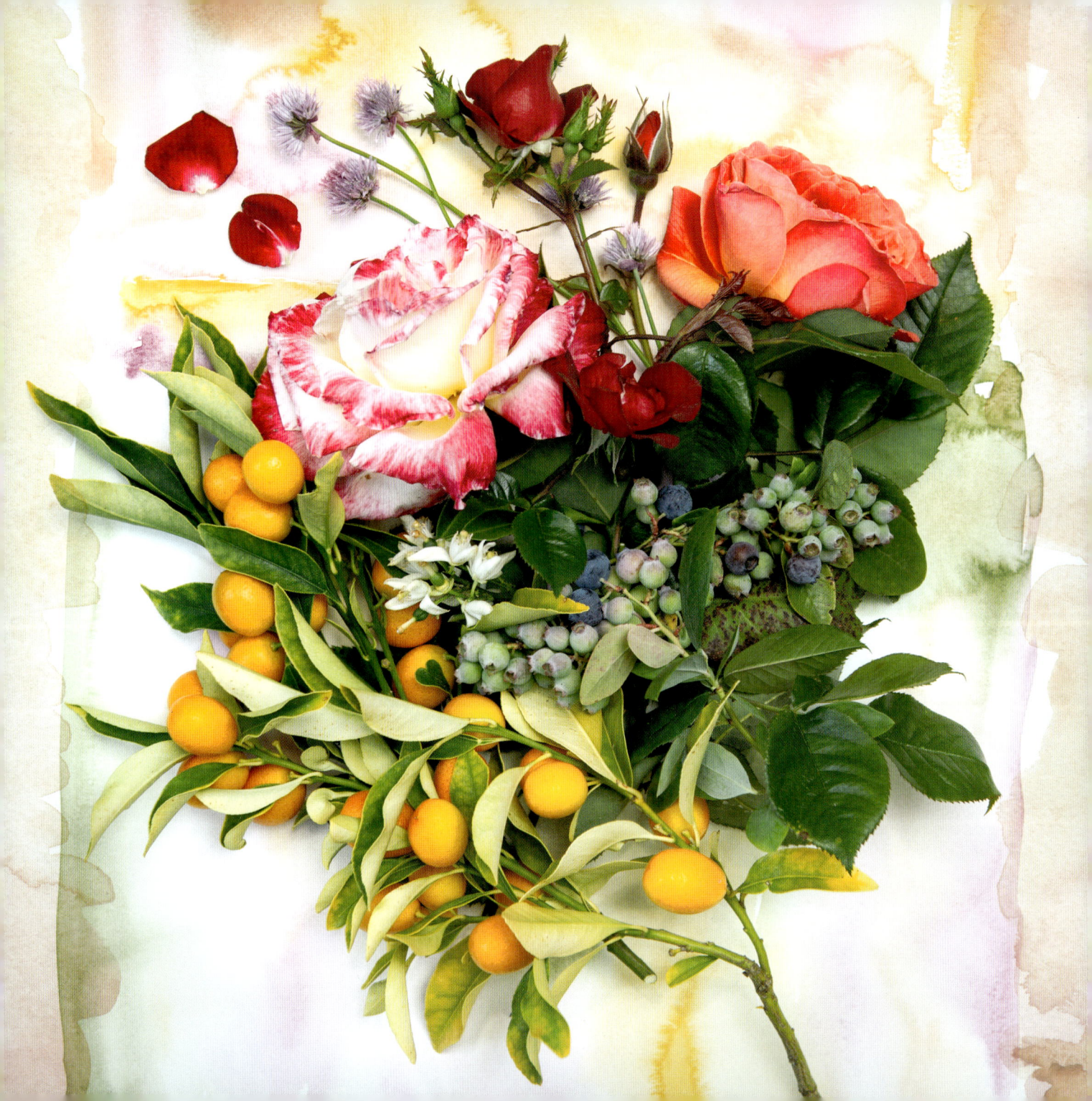

Rose

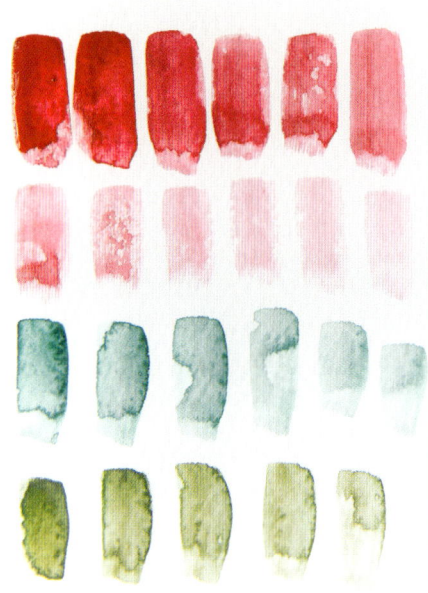

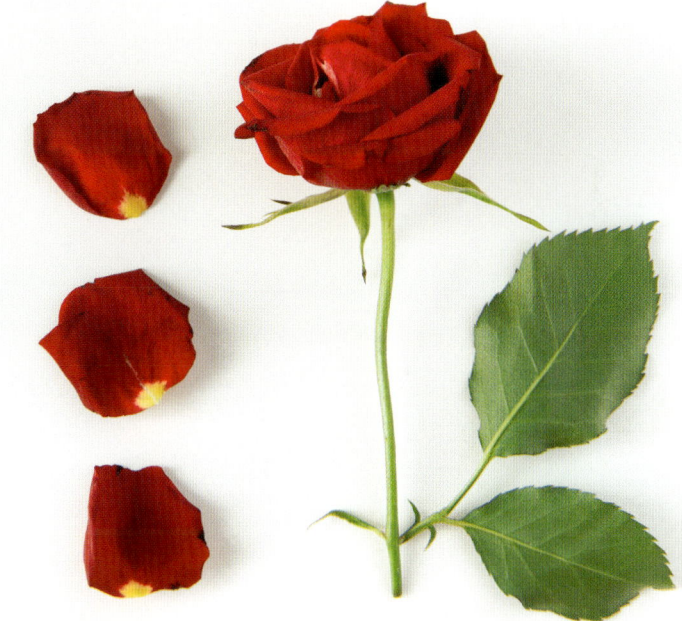

Color Exercise

Use a larger brush (approx. size 6) to paint a grid of strokes with shades you see in this rose. Notice how if you have more water on your brush, the color is lighter.

Recipe Idea

Sprinkle rose petals over a fruit platter for a colorful decoration.

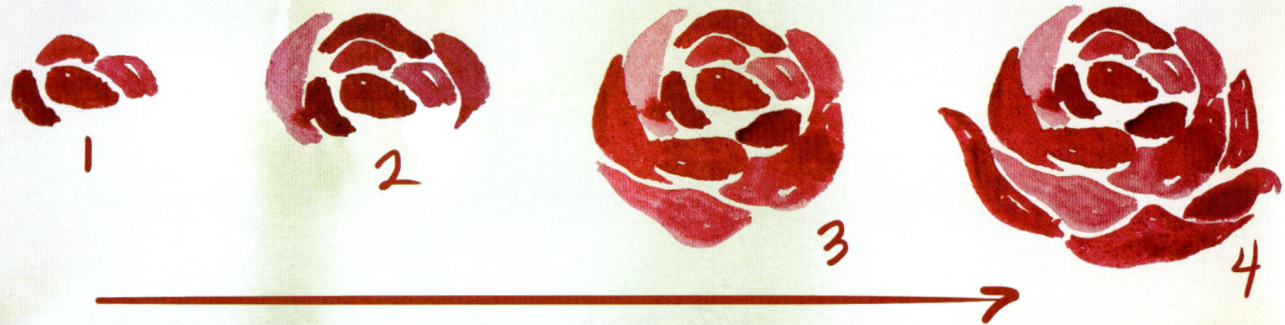

Working out from the center of the rose, paint small petals with a single shade of red. If you add water to the red paint, it becomes lighter. Use more pigment (& less water) on your brush & it'll be a deeper red. Leave white space between the petals, but don't worry if some bleed together.

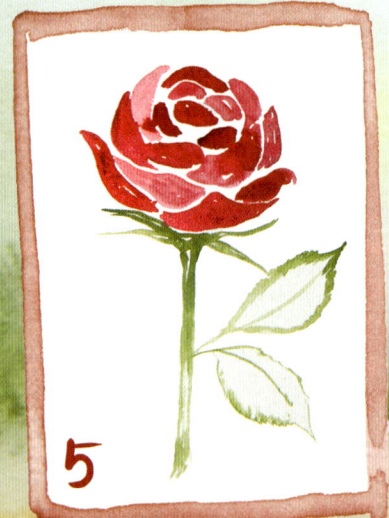

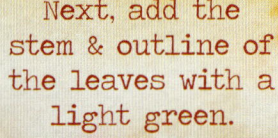

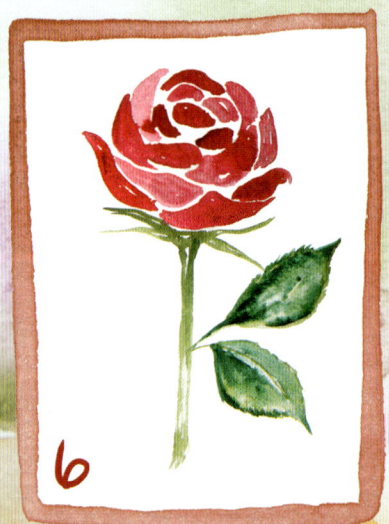

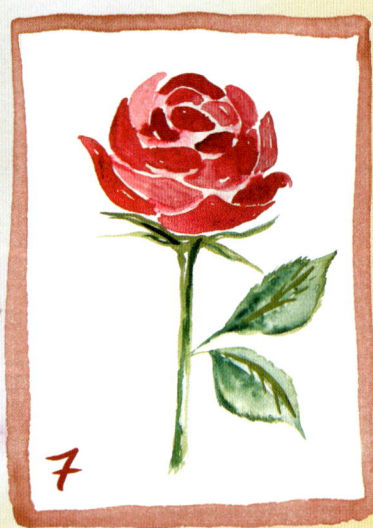

Next, add the stem & outline of the leaves with a light green.

Fill in the leaves with just water on your brush, then add some strokes with darker green paint.

When dry, add dark green line details to the stem and leaves. Then, using just water, brush lightly over some of the white spaces between the petals to soften the gaps.

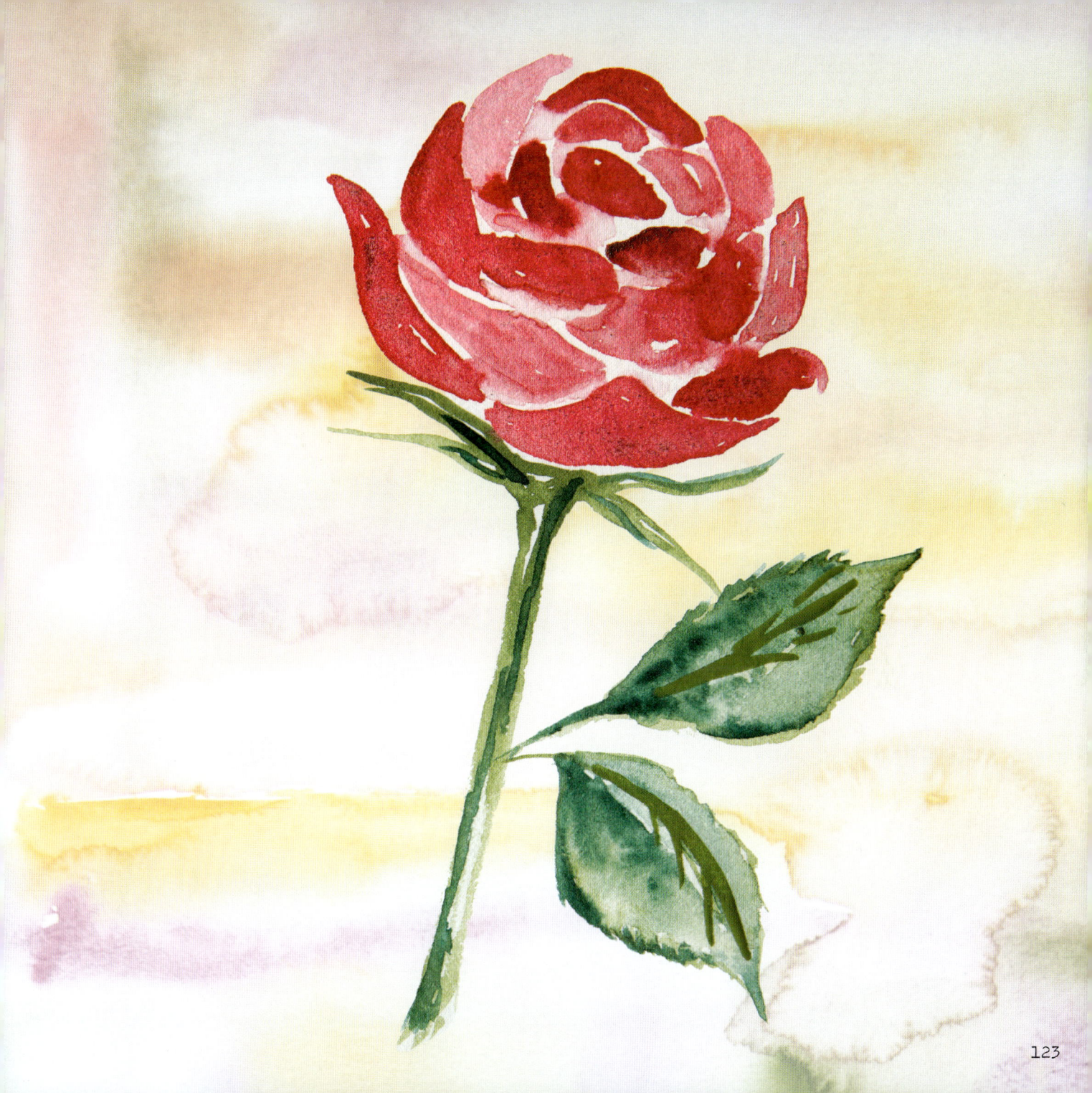

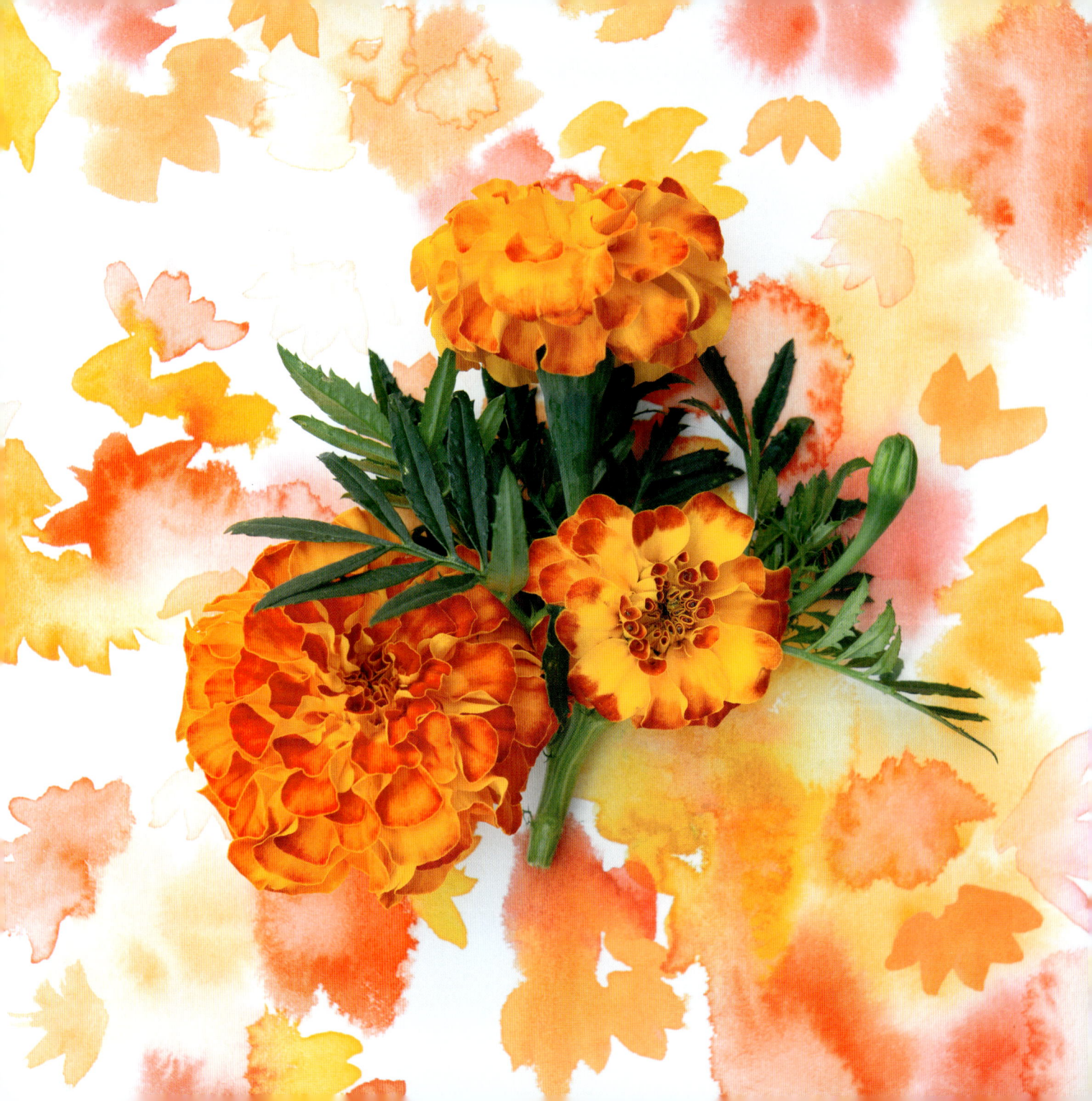

Marigold

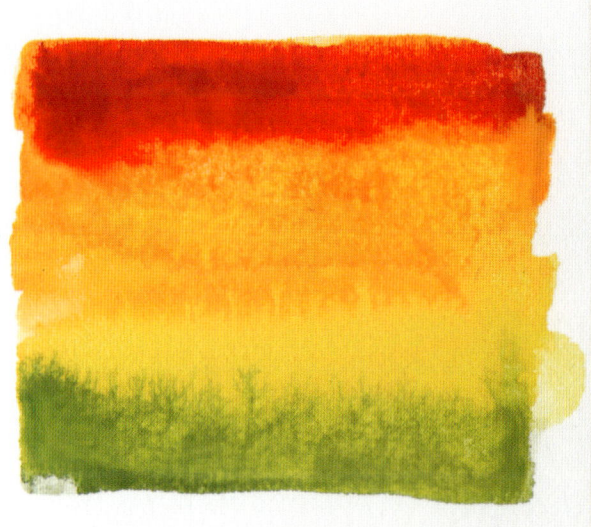

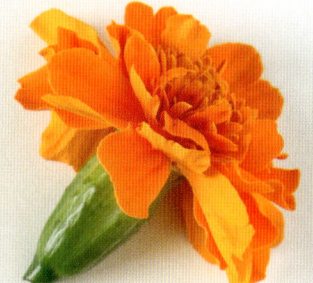

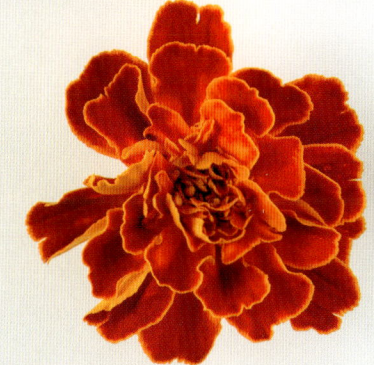

Color Exercise

Mix a few colors on your plate that you see in these marigolds. Create a gradient of color from red to orange to yellow to green, letting the colors bleed into each other.

Recipe Idea

Sprinkle marigold petals & everything bagel seasoning over avocado toast.

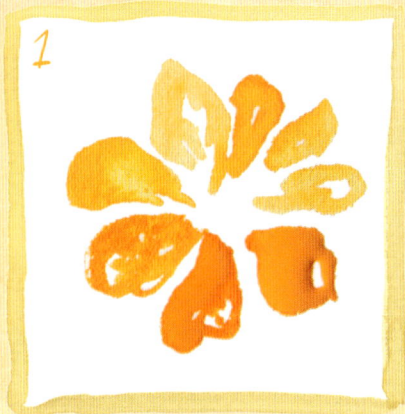

1

Using 1 shade of orange & varying amounts of water, paint several petals.

2

Trying not to touch the orange, add the green stem base.

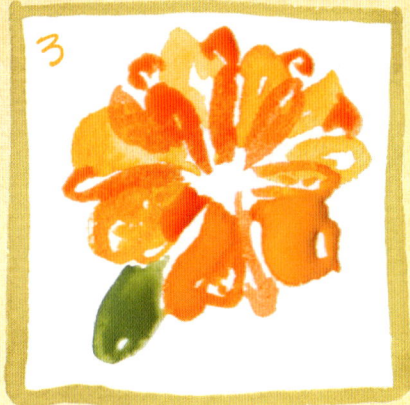

3

When some petals have dried, add more petals in a darker orange shade on top.

4

Allow it to dry, then add some red markings in the middle.

5

Add some greenish brown to the stem base.

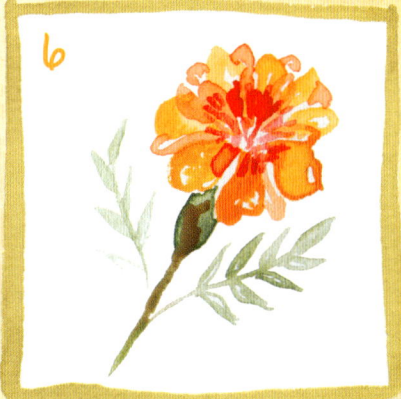

6

Extend the stem & add green leaves.

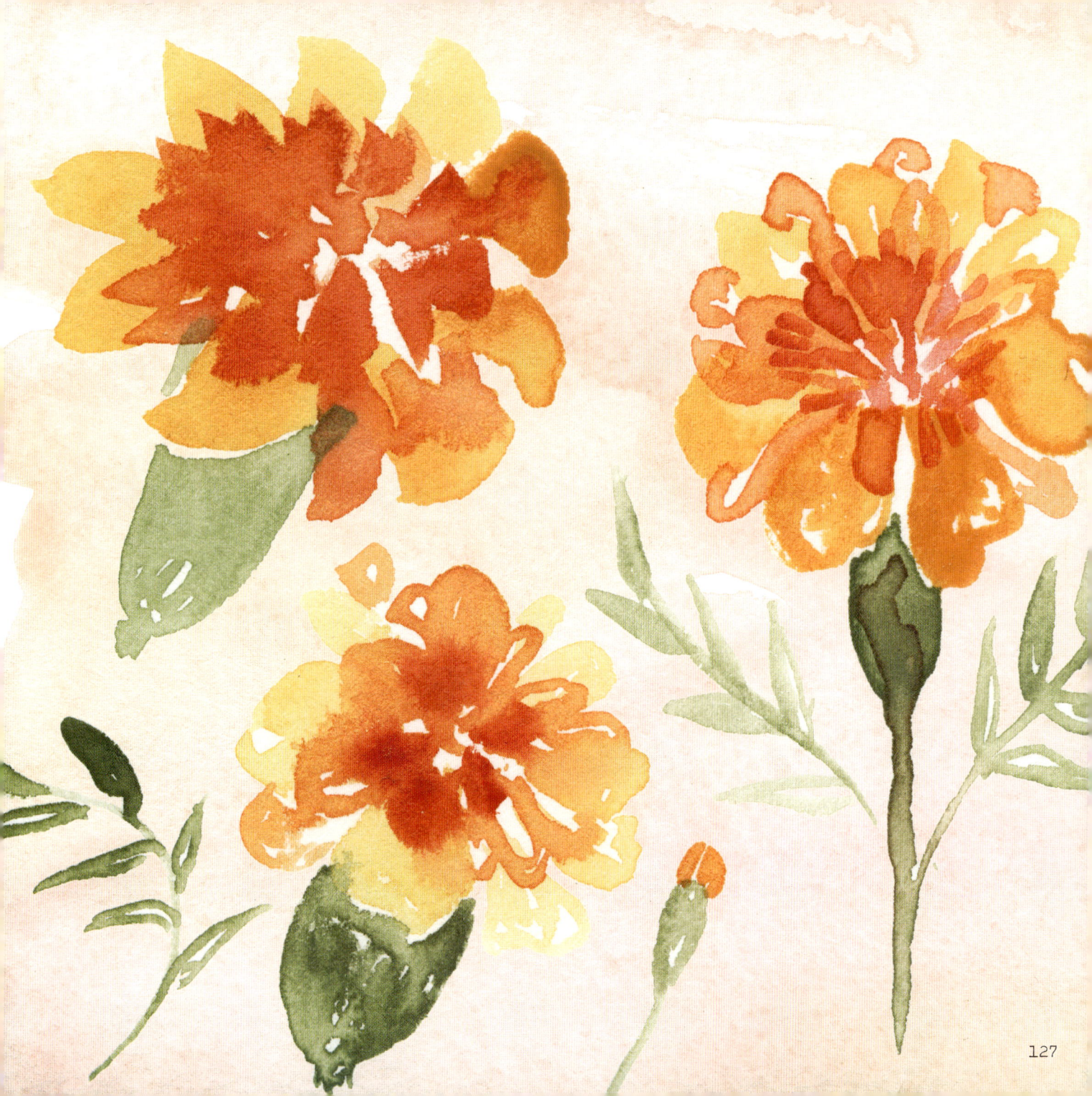

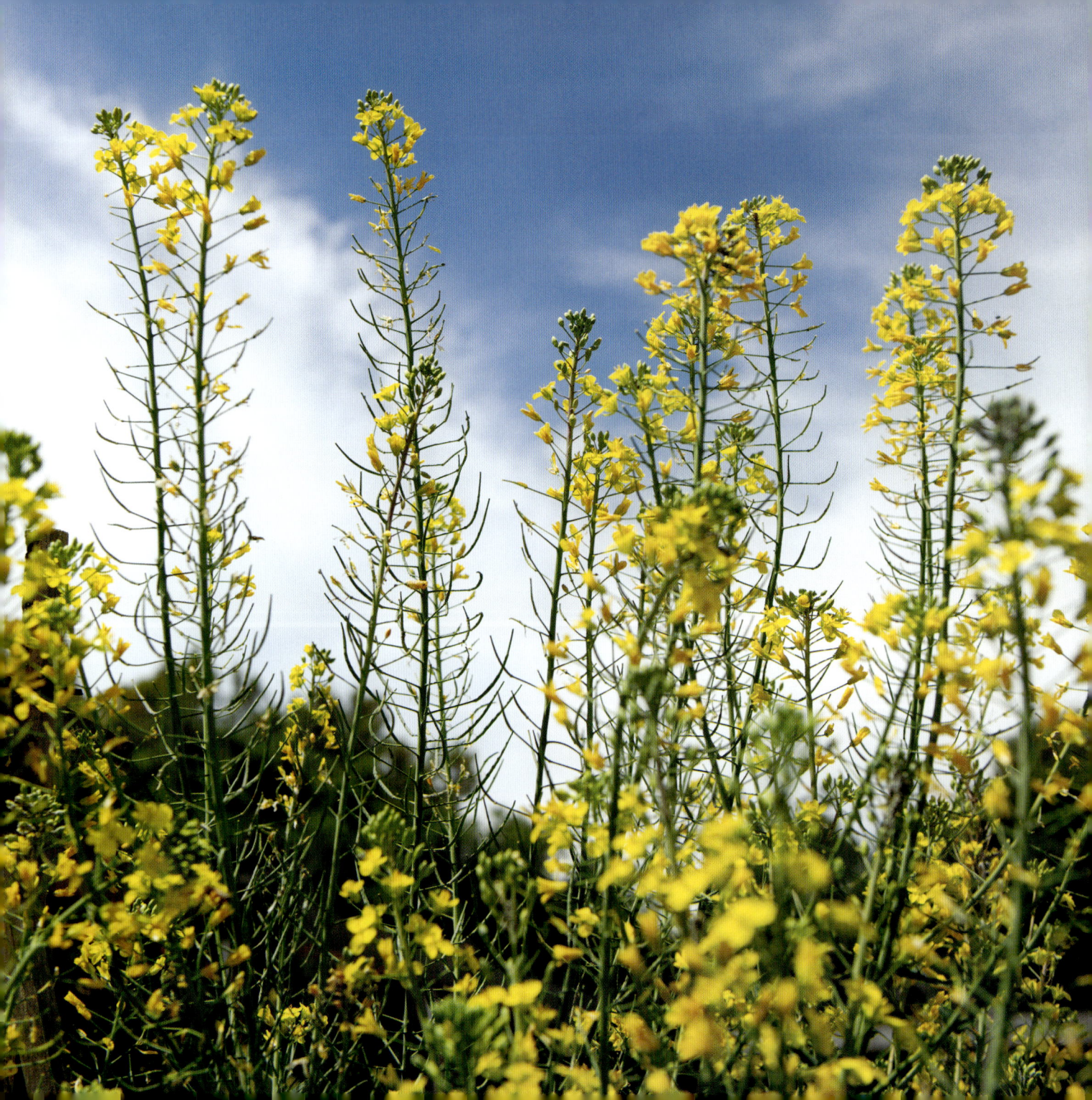

Mustard

Wild mustard grows everywhere in early spring in California where I live. If you grow broccoli in your garden and it goes to flower, the edible blooms look similar to mustard. (Please always consult a professional before eating foraged items.)

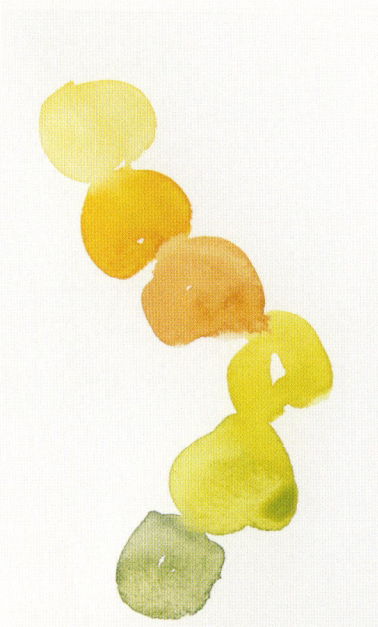

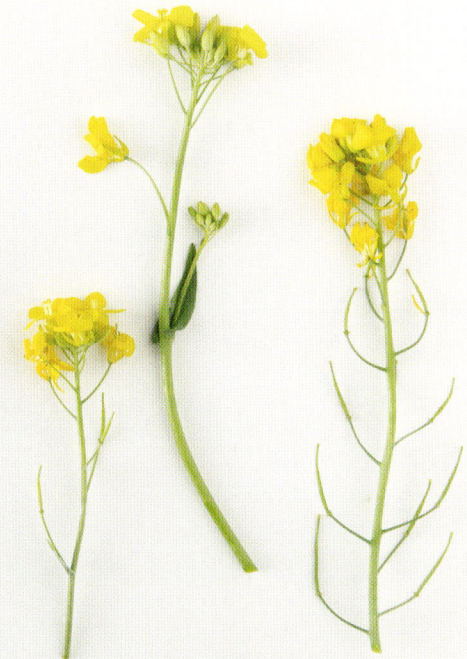

Color Exercise

Mix custom shades of yellow & green:

{ yellow + white + orange
yellow + green }

Paint a series of "bubbles" that connect slightly.

Recipe Idea

For a spring dish, sauté asparagus with butter & garlic. Lay it out on a platter & top with crumbled feta & chili crisp. Sprinkle with yellow mustard flowers.

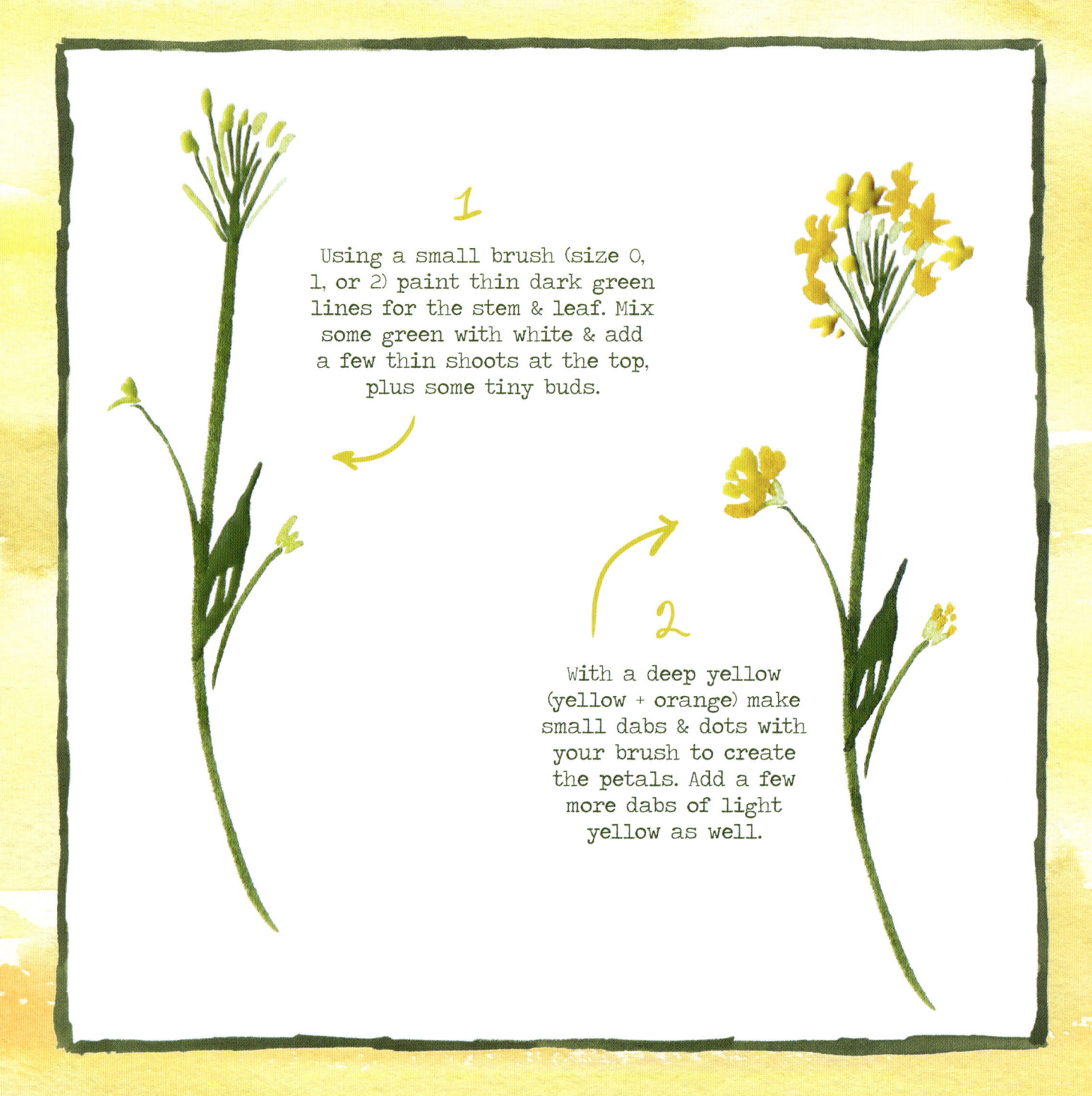

1

Using a small brush (size 0, 1, or 2) paint thin dark green lines for the stem & leaf. Mix some green with white & add a few thin shoots at the top, plus some tiny buds.

2

With a deep yellow (yellow + orange) make small dabs & dots with your brush to create the petals. Add a few more dabs of light yellow as well.

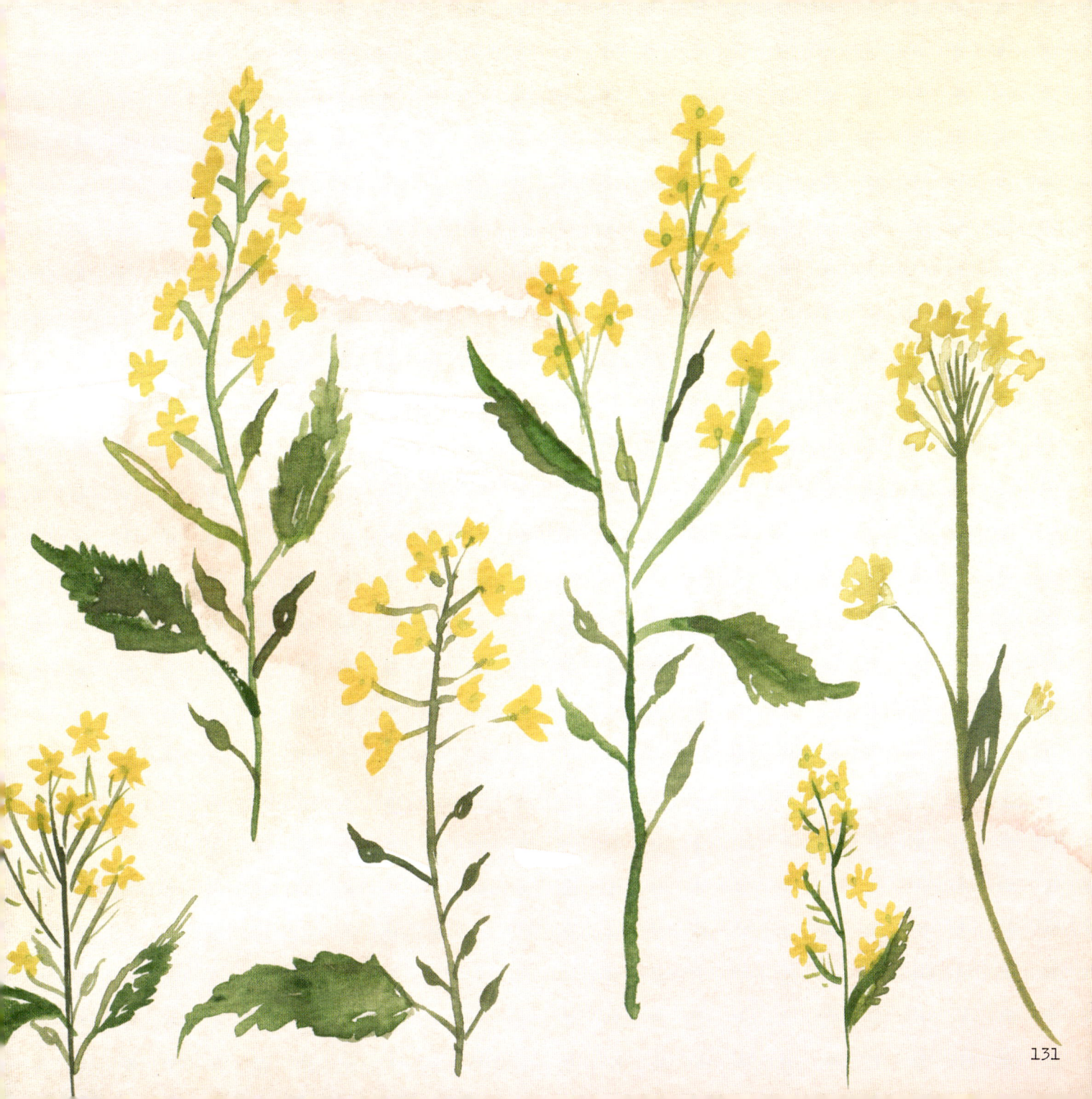

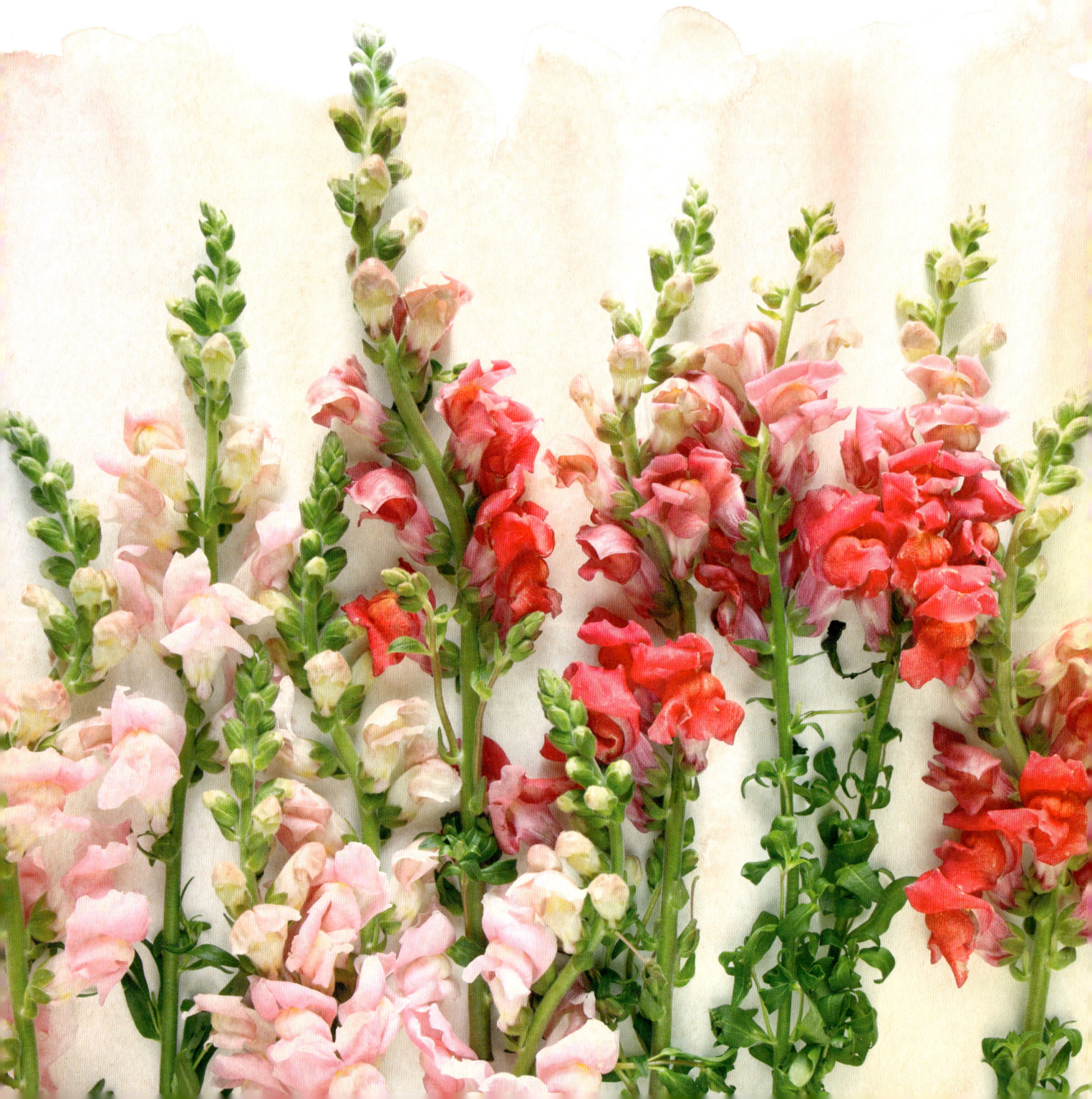

Snapdragon

Try pressing your brush down on the paper & twisting as you pull up to achieve irregular petal-like shapes.

I dipped my brush in 2 different colors for these.

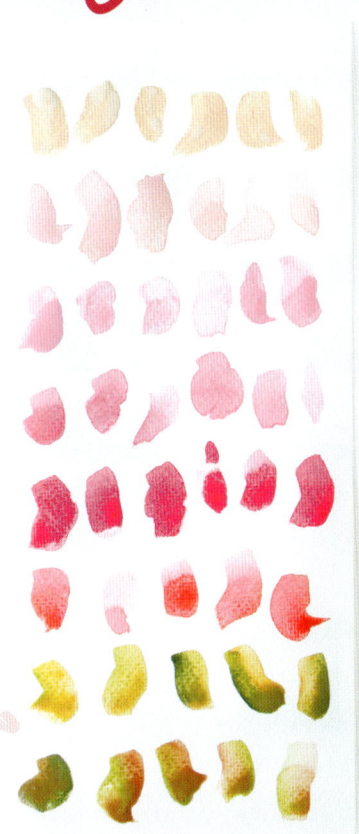

Color Exercise

Instead of "painting" petals, try "dabbing" or pressing down & pulling up with your brush to create petal shapes. Try a couple different brushes & various shades of pink. I used a size 6 brush with a rounded tip.

Recipe Idea

Use snapdragon blooms to decorate a cake or tart.

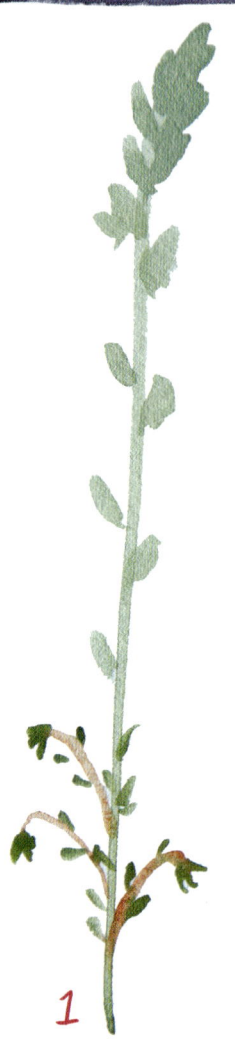

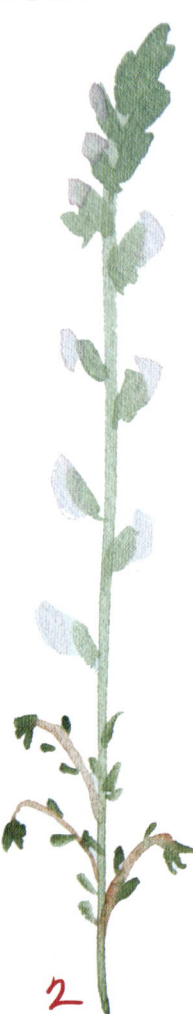

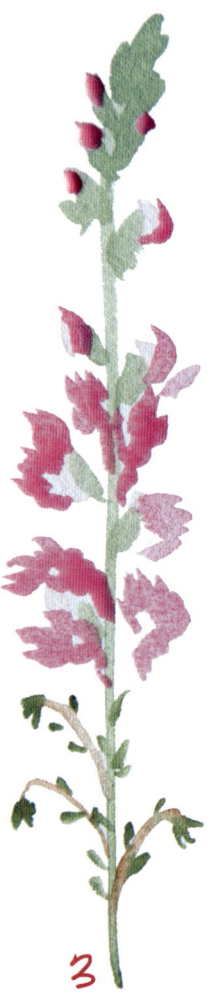

1

Using light green
(green + white) paint a
long stem with buds on
either side. Add some brown
shoots at the bottom with
small green leaves.

2

Add a small dab of light
purple to the buds by
briefly pressing your
brush on the paper.
Allow the painting to
partially dry.

3

Mix a darker pink
(pink + red) &
continue dabbing
your brush to
create additional
flower petals.

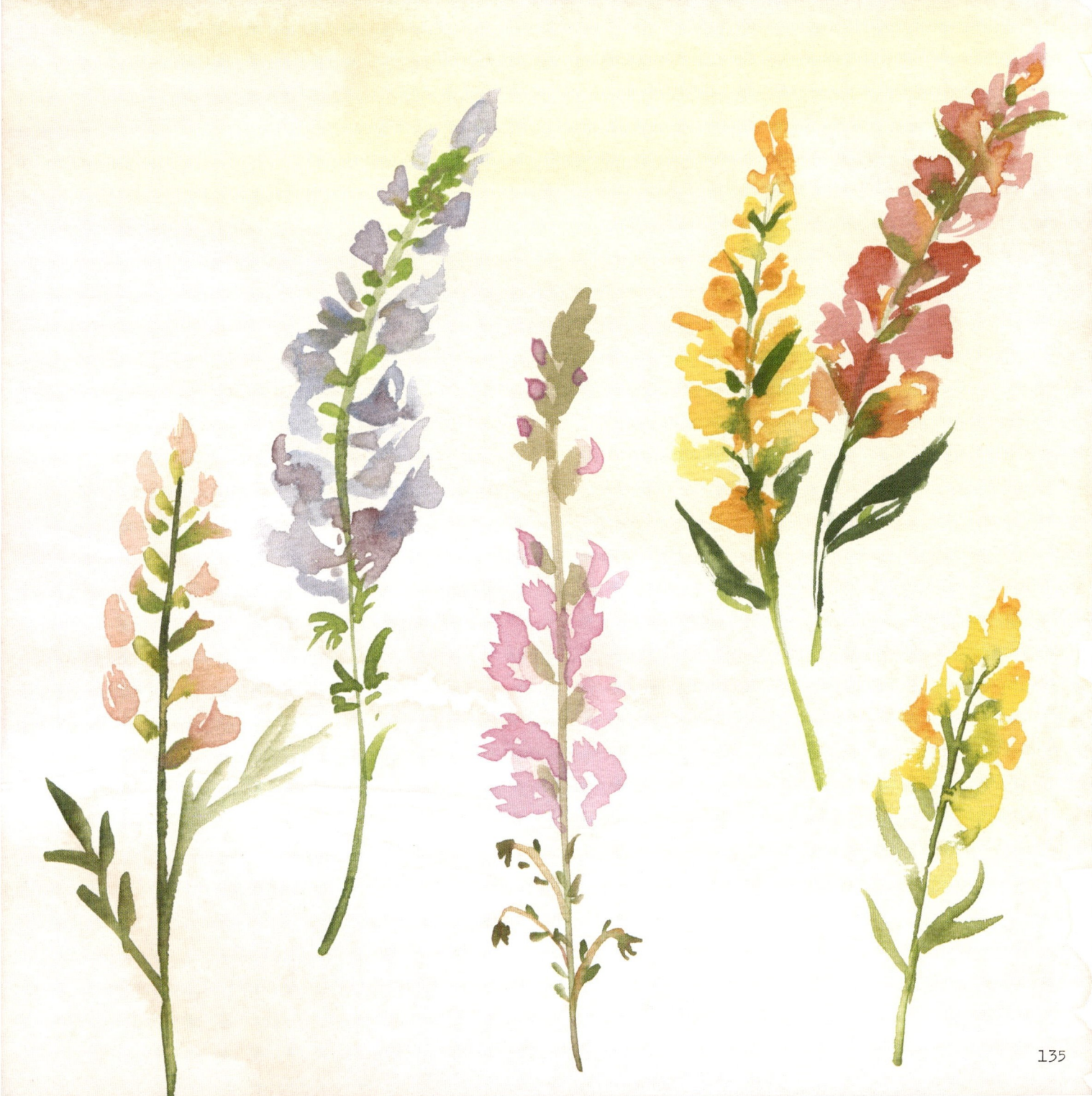

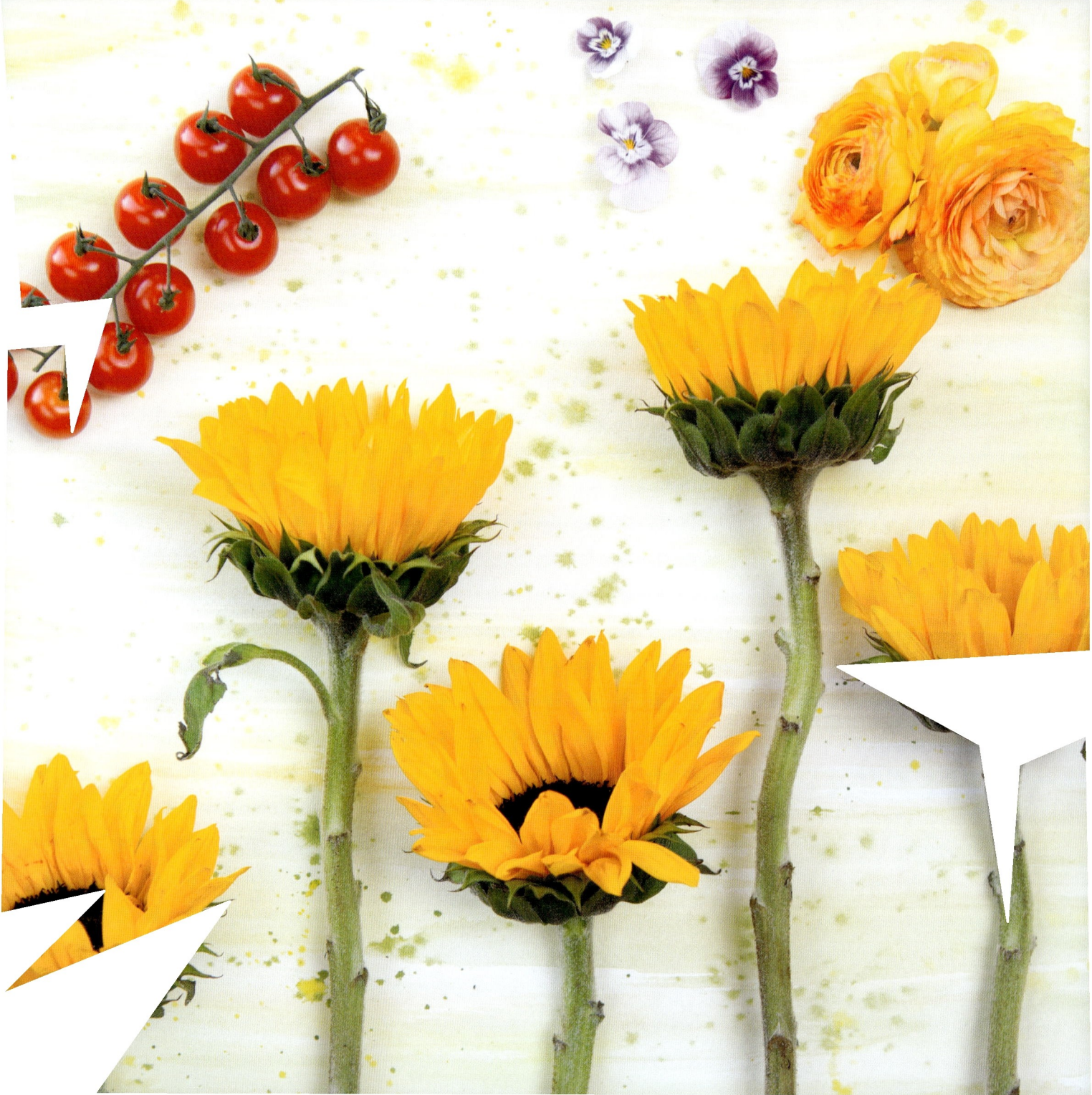

Sunflower

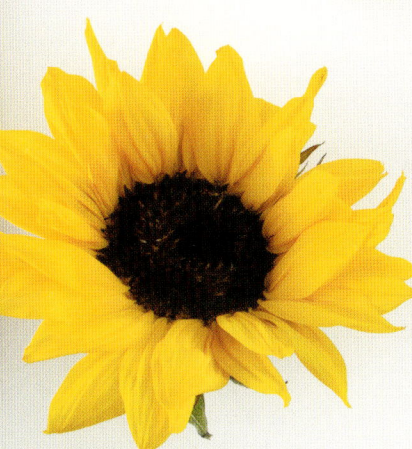

Recipe Idea

Sprinkle yellow
sunflower petals
over a platter of
sliced red watermelon
as a garnish.

Color Exercise

Instead of painting the outlines of petals & leaves, try this:
using a larger brush with a pointed tip (approx. size 6) hold
your brush at a 30° angle relative to the paper. Press, then drag
just a little, pulling up at the end to create the point. Practice
making a series of these markings using yellow & green.

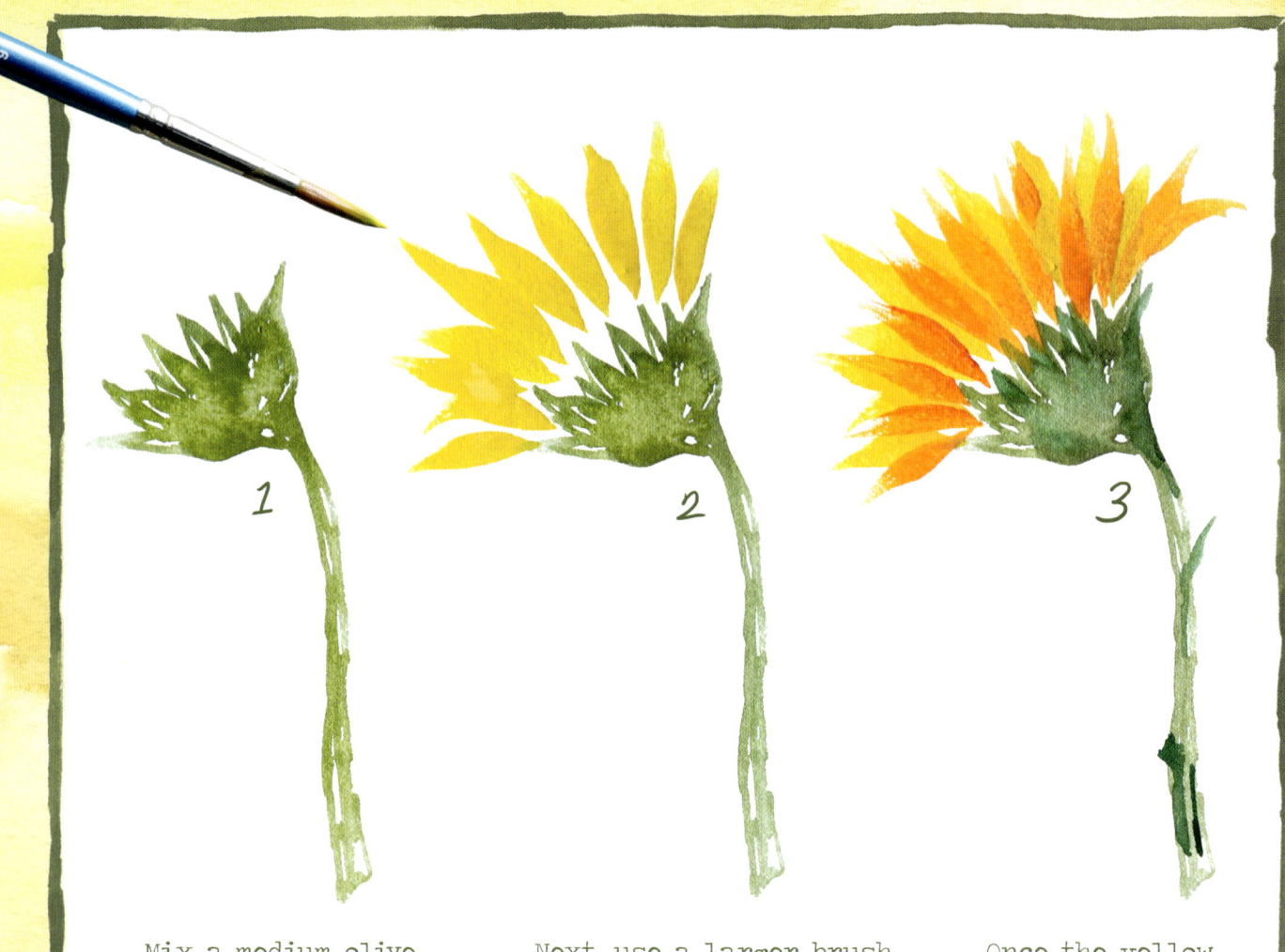

1

Mix a medium olive
green (green + brown)
& paint the stem.
Leave a few unpainted
white bits. If you use
a pencil, erase the
outline before you
start painting.

2

Next, use a larger brush
with a pointed tip (I used
size 6) to make yellow petals.
Holding the brush at a 30°
angle, lightly press the whole
side of the brush. Drag &
pull up at the end to create
pointy petal-shaped markings.

3

Once the yellow
petals dry,
add a layer of
light orange
petals over
them. Add dark
green details
to the stem, too.

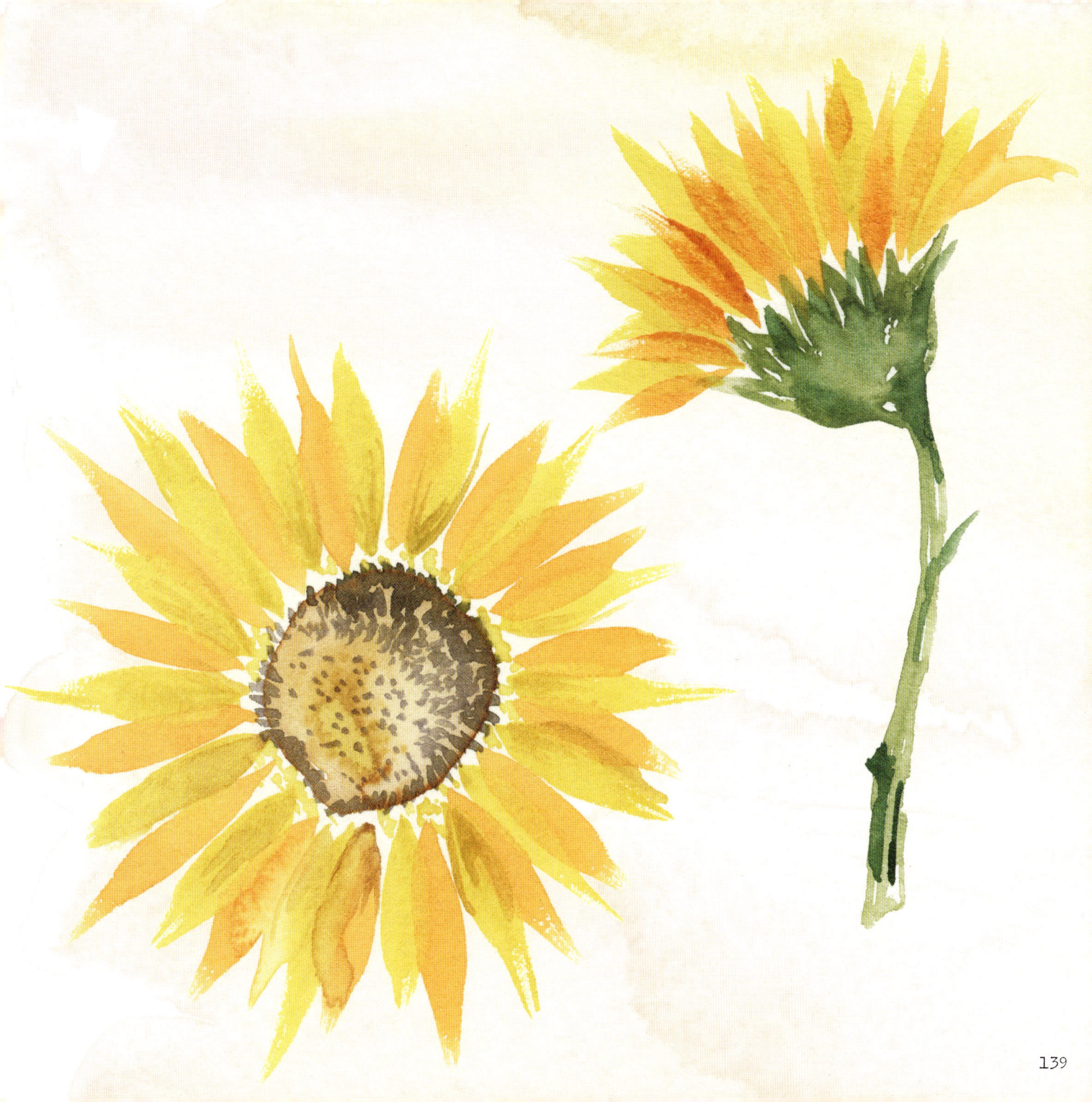

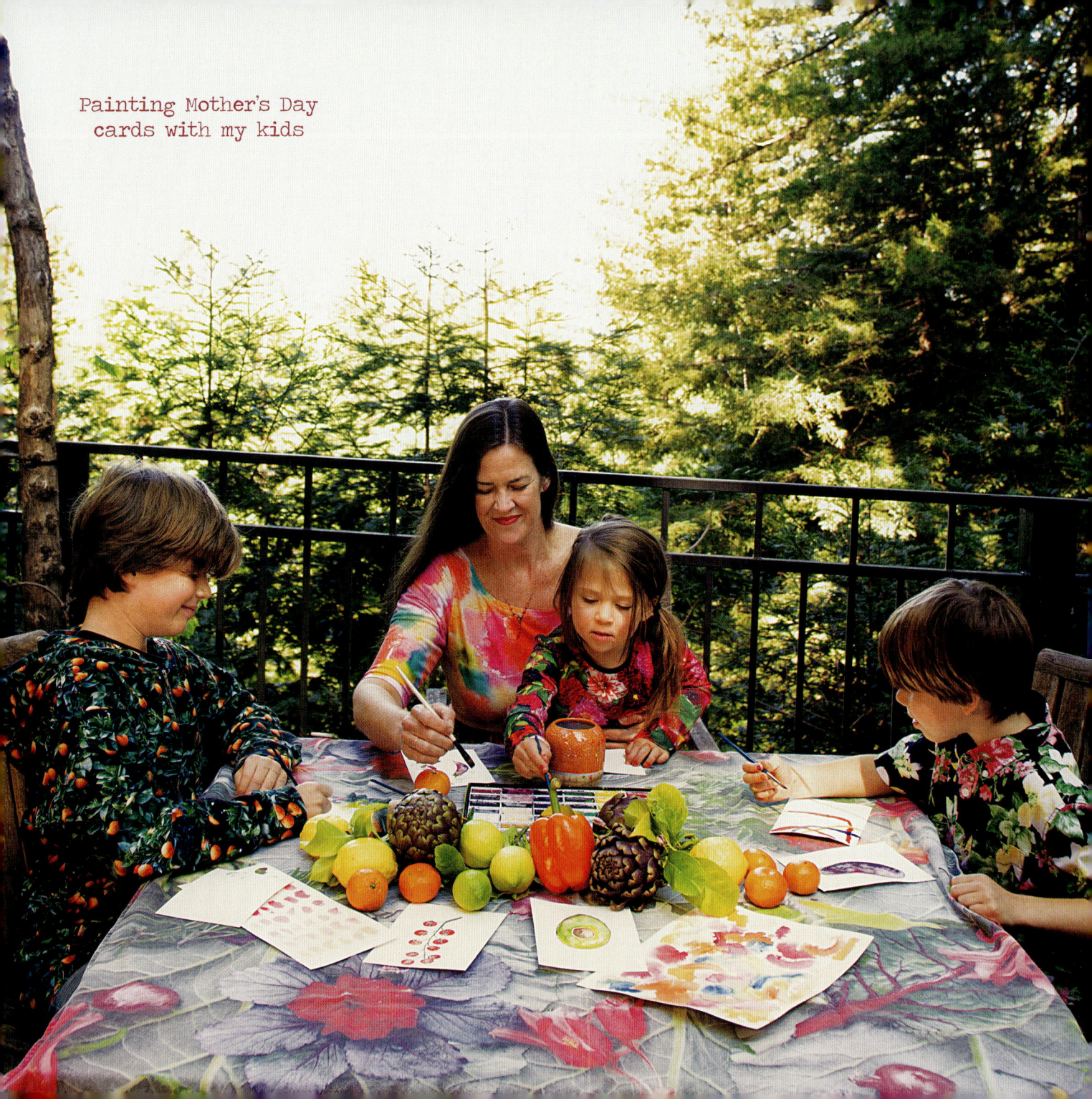

Painting Mother's Day
cards with my kids

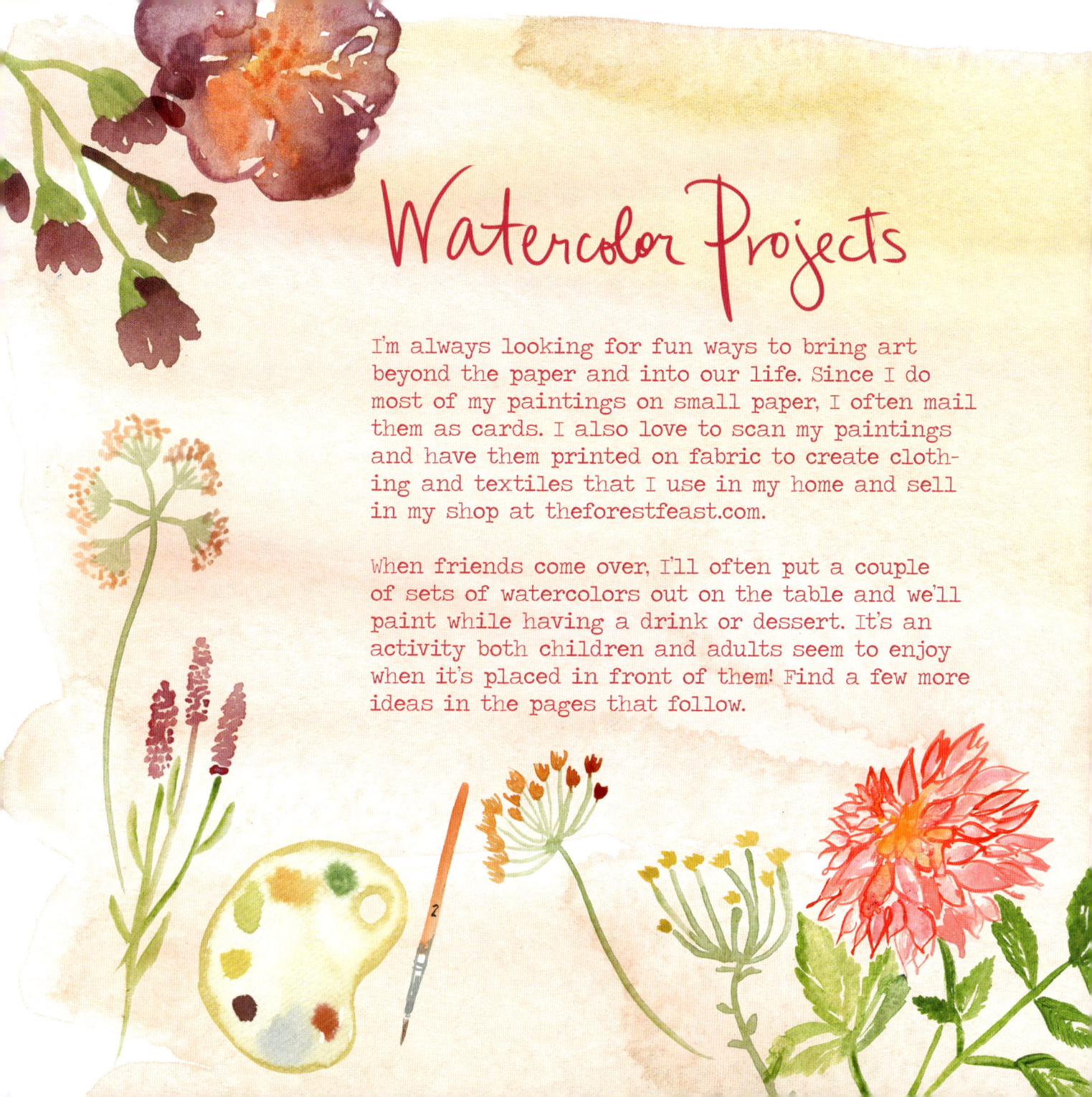

Watercolor Projects

I'm always looking for fun ways to bring art beyond the paper and into our life. Since I do most of my paintings on small paper, I often mail them as cards. I also love to scan my paintings and have them printed on fabric to create clothing and textiles that I use in my home and sell in my shop at theforestfeast.com.

When friends come over, I'll often put a couple of sets of watercolors out on the table and we'll paint while having a drink or dessert. It's an activity both children and adults seem to enjoy when it's placed in front of them! Find a few more ideas in the pages that follow.

I love taking my travel paint set and postcard-size paper on day trips and vacations. Painting can be a welcome break in the middle of a long hike, or a fun activity with kids. I pack a cup for water or use the lid of a water bottle. Mail your postcard to a relative or tuck it into a photo album as a sweet souvenir.

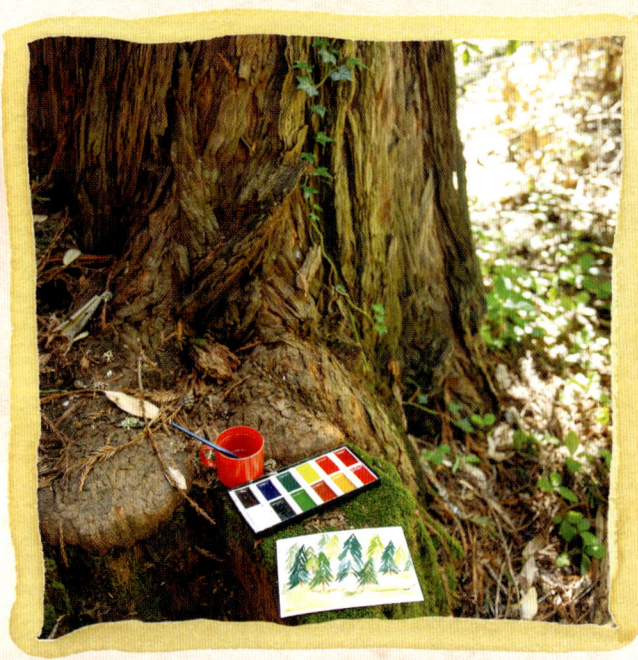

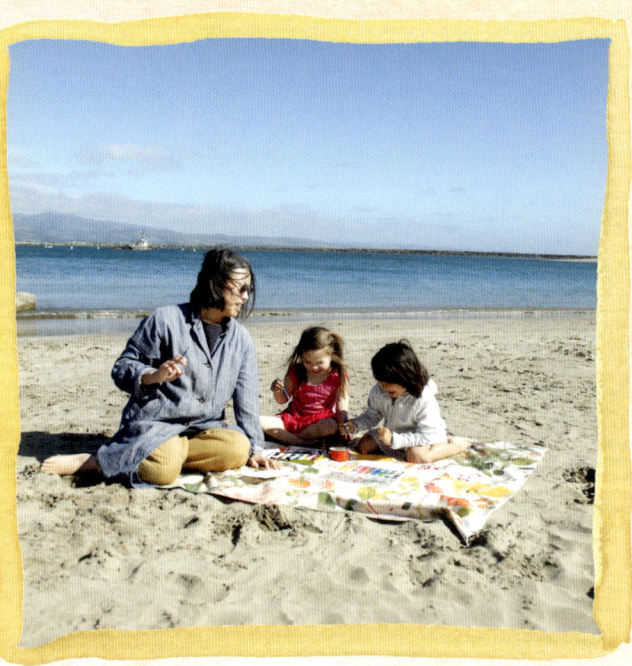

We did some seaside painting on a day trip to Half Moon Bay, California, with my friend Kayoko.

On a hike through the redwoods near our home in the Santa Cruz Mountains, I took a break and painted the trees.

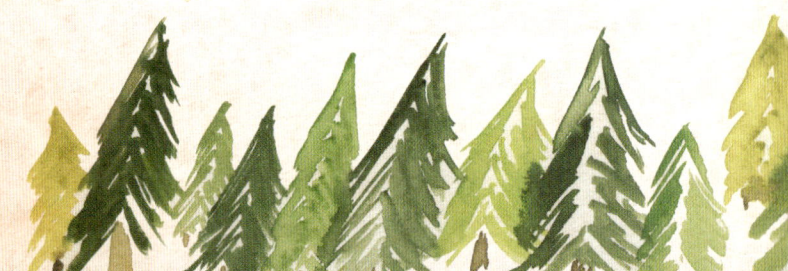

Hand-Painted Cards

It's been years since I've bought a greeting card! Sometimes I use my own handwriting, but it's also fun to trace a font for a more polished and consistent look. I find a font I like, print out my text, then use a light table (see below; these are easy to find online) to trace the letters with a small paintbrush.

THANK YOU

Try dipping your brush in a few different colors as you go & leave some unpainted white bits.

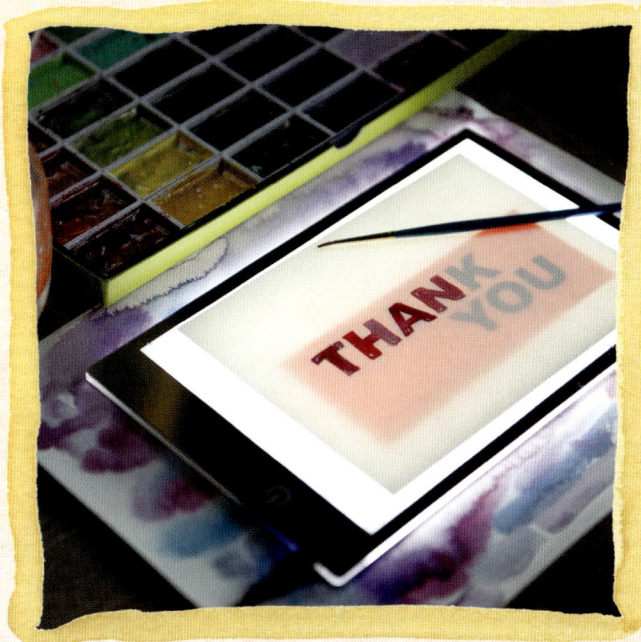

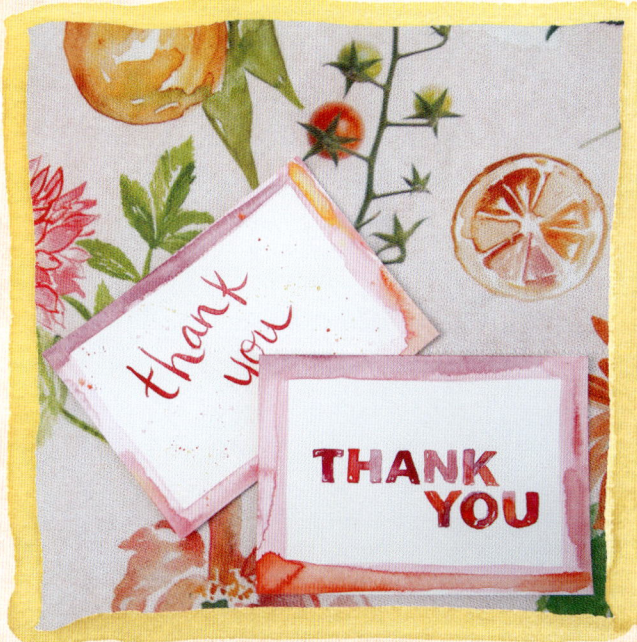

Watercolor Table Settings

I love to host, and I'm always looking for ways to infuse art into our gatherings. I recently painted some lemons, inspired by a vintage lemon napkin that belonged to my grandmother. I then scanned the painting and had it printed on fabric and sewn into napkins using spoonflower.com. I've turned other artwork into various linens and home goods to sell in my shop at theforestfeast.com. Find links to printing and textile-making resources on my website as well. Designing your own textiles is easy; everyone should try it!

For holiday meals, I love making watercolor place cards and buffet cards. Start by folding watercolor paper into a tent, then flattening it so you can see the fold mark. Paint a light base color on the lower portion, let it dry, then add your painted handwriting on top. Use your smallest brush for the lettering (I used size 0).

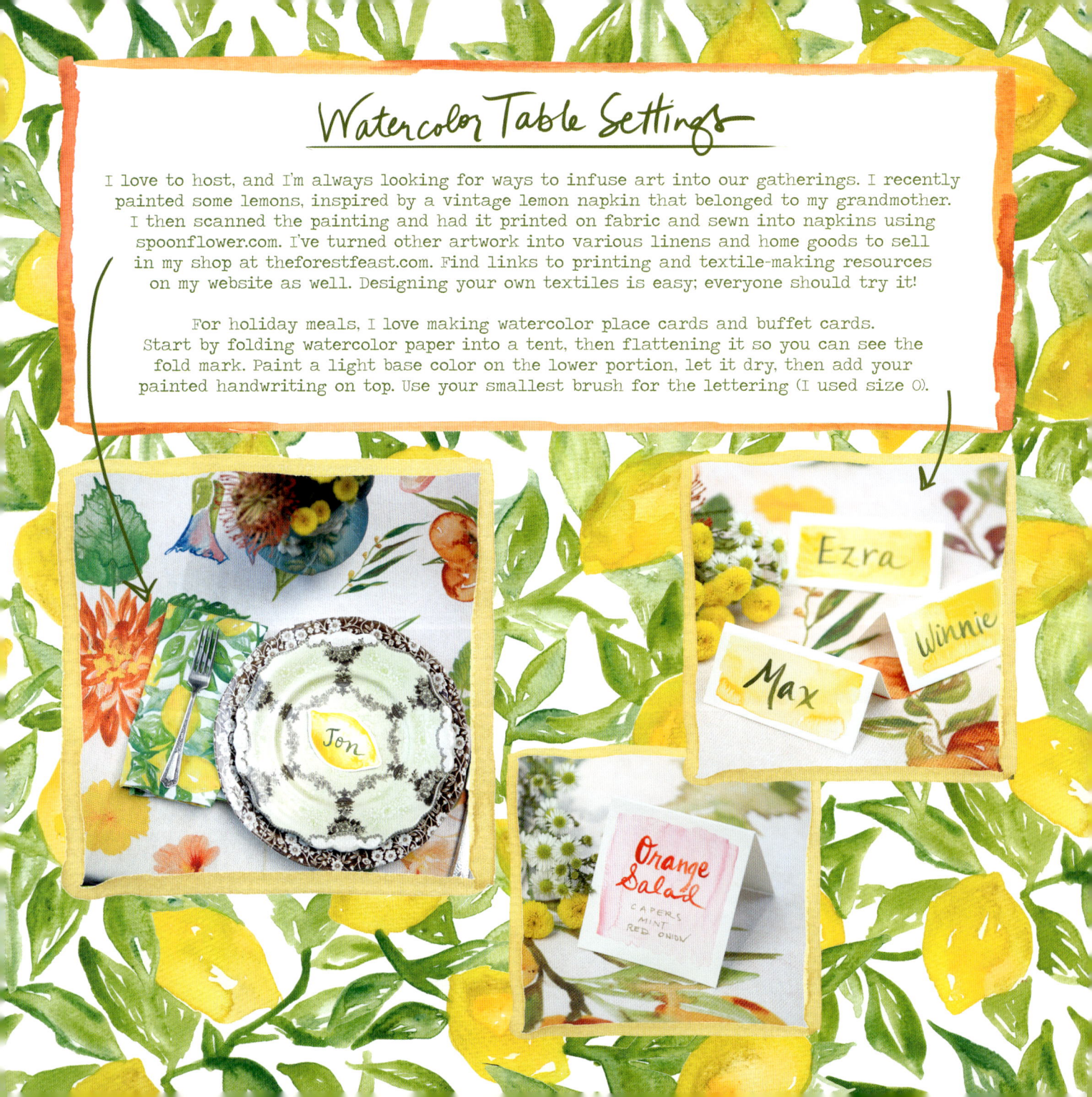

Watercolor Home Furnishings

I scanned the abstract color exercises below and had them printed on fabric at gooten.com to create these throw pillows for my living room.

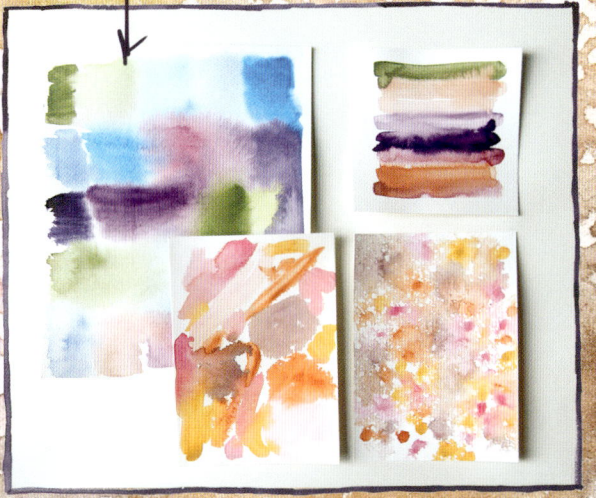

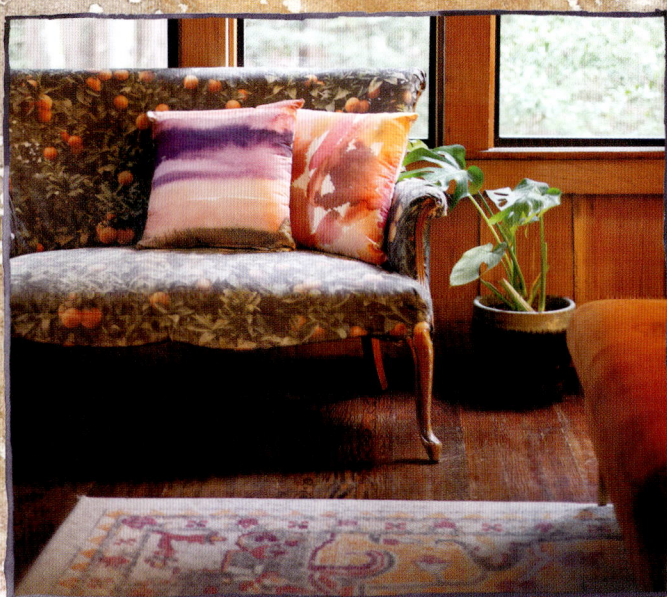

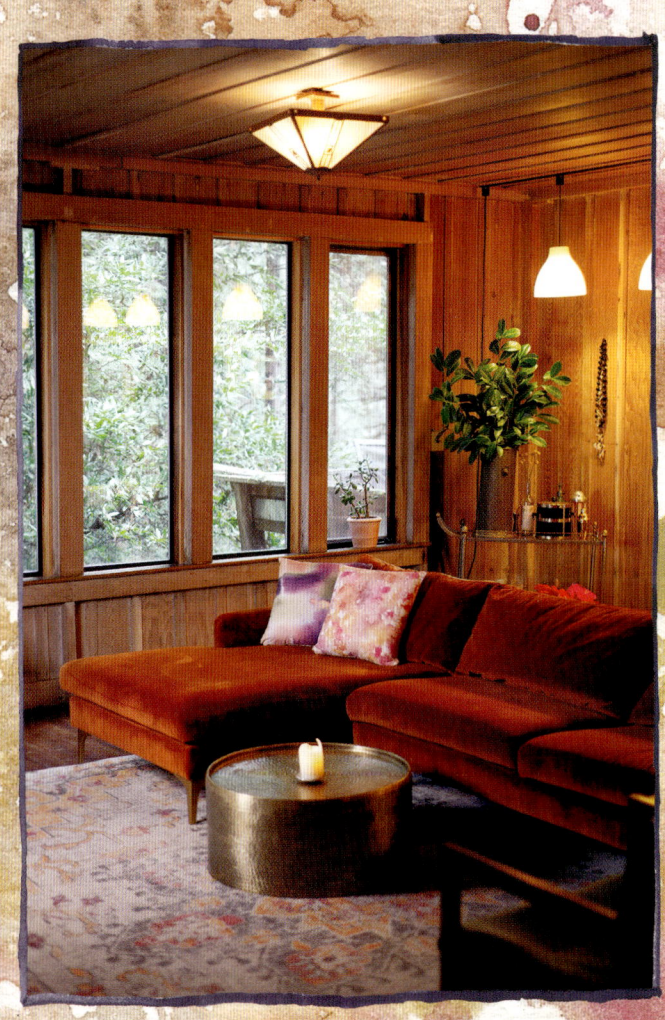

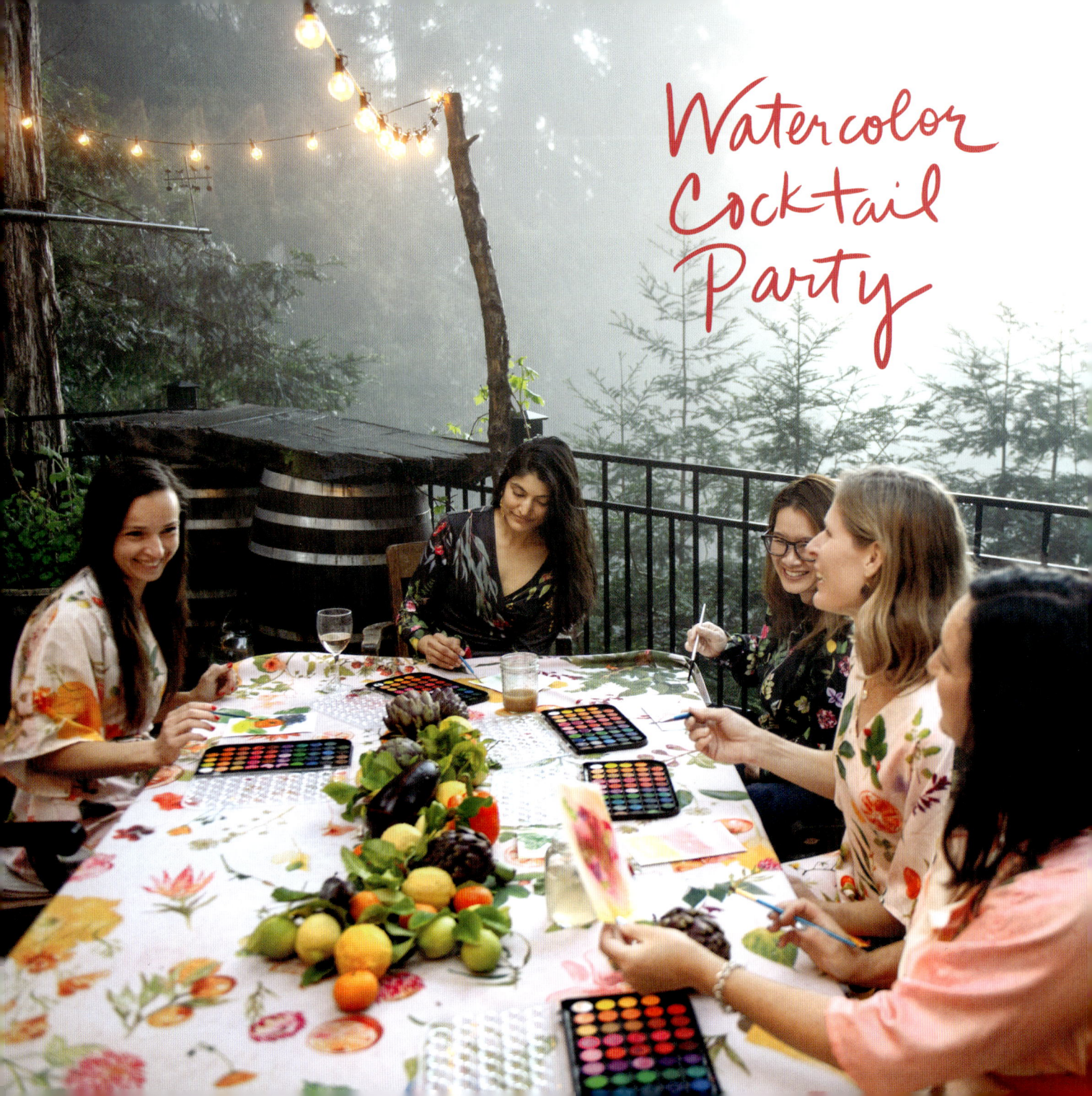

Watercolor
Cocktail
Party

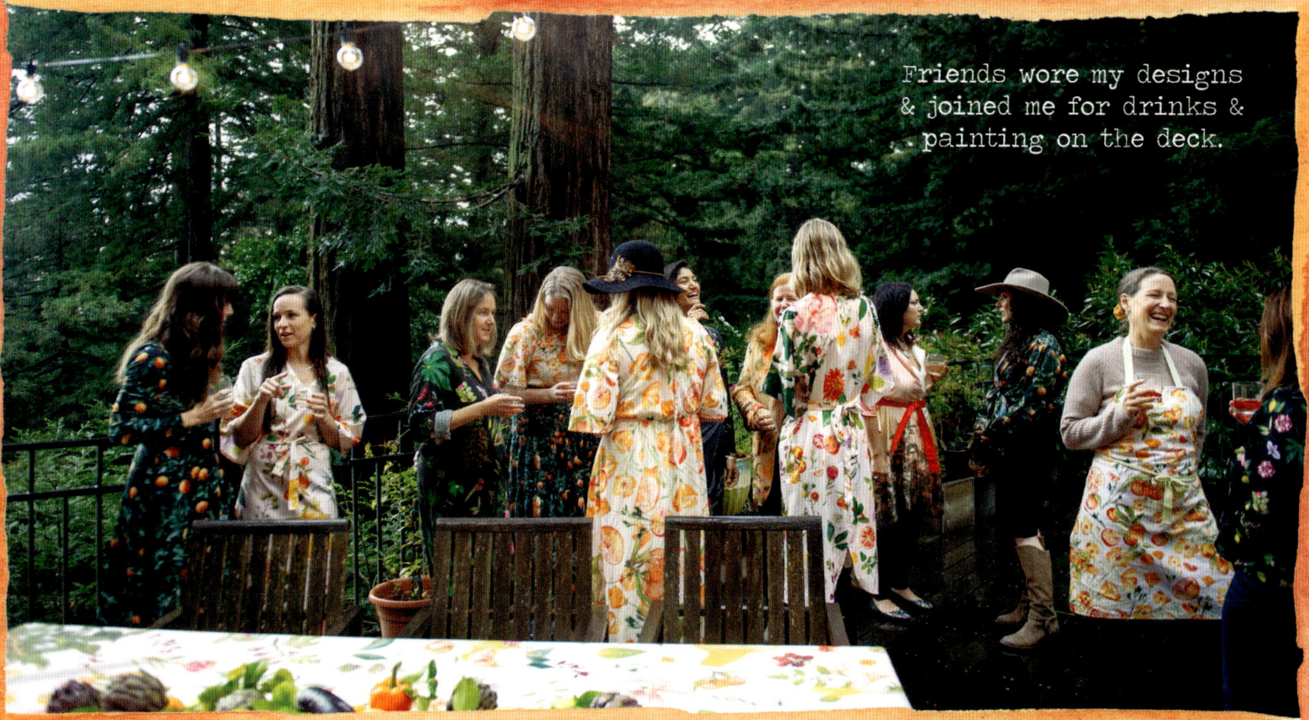

Friends wore my designs
& joined me for drinks &
painting on the deck.

We love to host late afternoon cocktail parties on our deck in the redwoods with fun drinks and small bites from the Forest Feast cookbooks. Making watercolor a central activity to the gathering can act as an icebreaker and calming exercise over conversation with friends. We rarely get a chance to sit down and be creative in our busy lives, and this is a fun way to do it socially. I scatter fruits, vegetables, and flowers down the center of the table and let guests paint freely on postcard-size paper to take home. Make the gathering a potluck and it becomes a Watercolor Dinner Party!

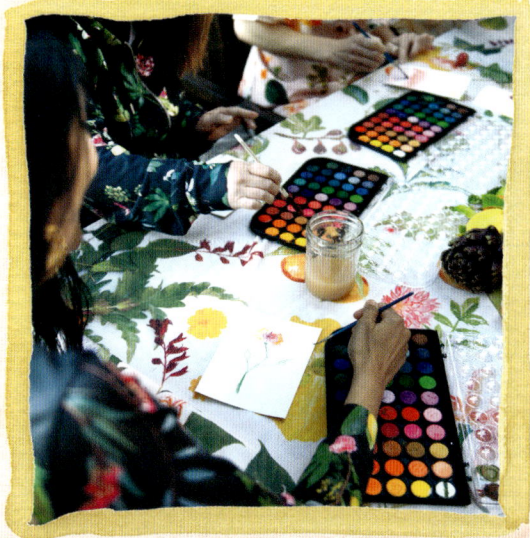

WATERCOLOR COCKTAIL PARTY

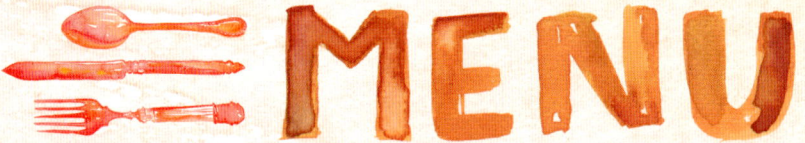

MENU

1
Negroni Sbagliato

Mix equal parts Campari, sweet vermouth & prosecco over ice. Garnish with an edible flower.

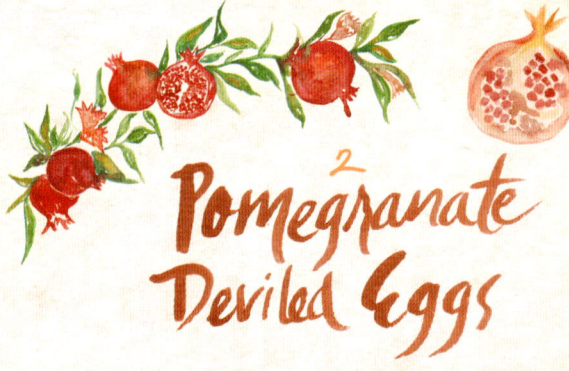

2
Pomegranate Deviled Eggs

Top deviled eggs with smoky paprika & fresh pomegranate seeds.

3
Chili-Peach Crostini

Top slices of toasted baguette with Brie, a slice of peach & chili crunch.

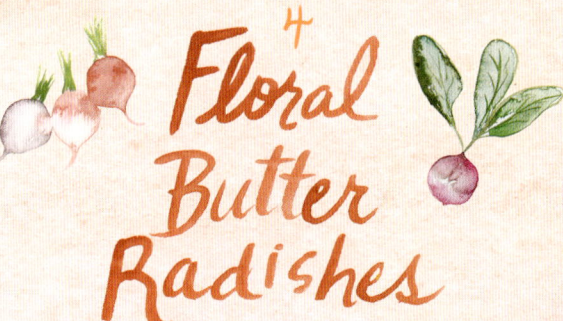

4
Floral Butter Radishes

Top halved radishes with butter, coarse salt & small edible flower petals.

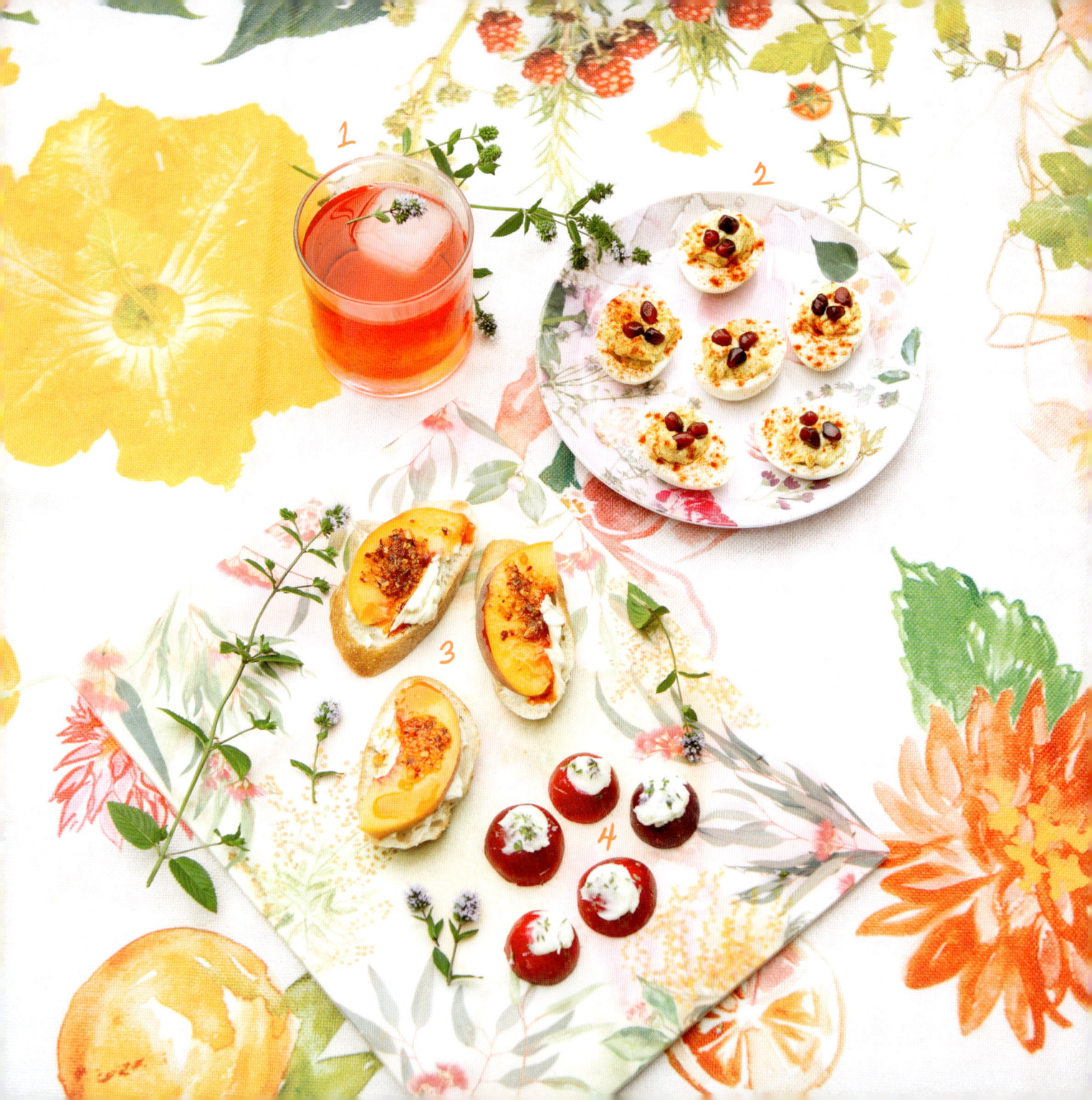

Artist Inspiration

There are many artists I love to follow for inspiration. There is so much you can do with watercolor, and styles vary a lot! Here are a few artists and illustrators who work in watercolor and other mediums.

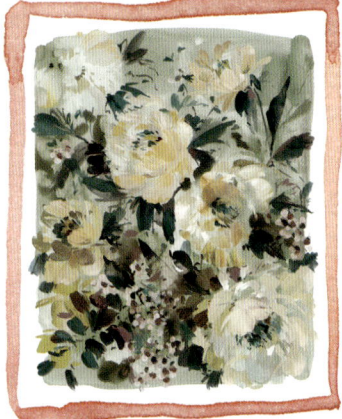

Kelly Ventura
@KellyvVenturaDesign

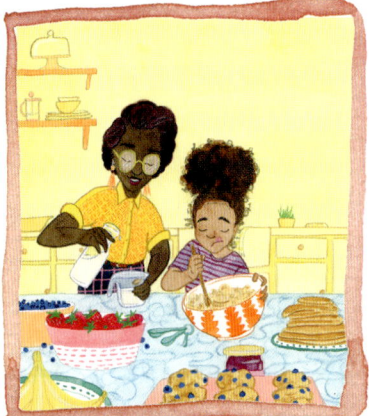

Charnelle Barlow
@callmechartreuse

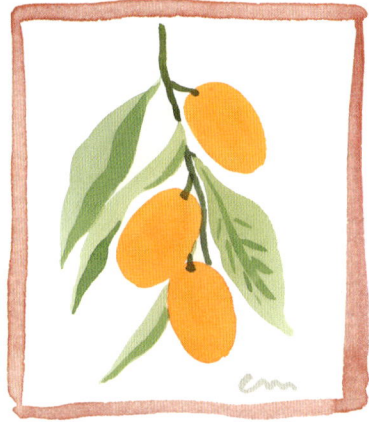

Caitlin McGauley
@caitlinmcgauley

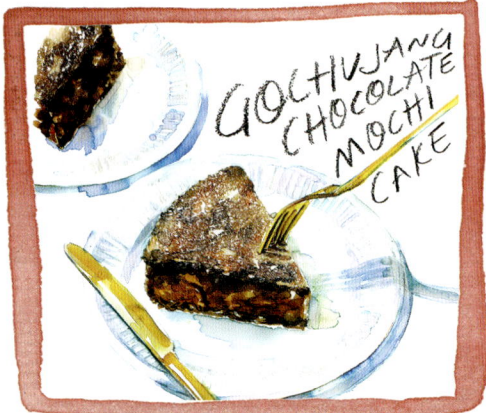

Samantha Hahn
@SamanthajHahn

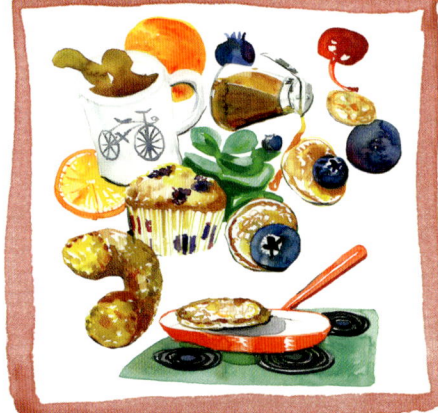

Jessie Kanelos Weiner
@JessieKanelosWeiner

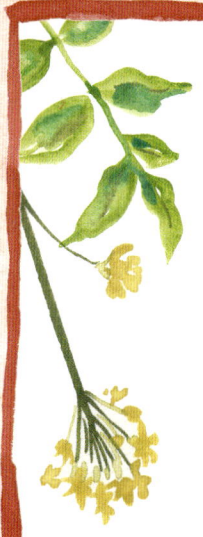

Resources & Videos

Find links to my painting videos, favorite supplies & textile printing resources: theforestfeast.com/watercolor

Paint & cook with me!

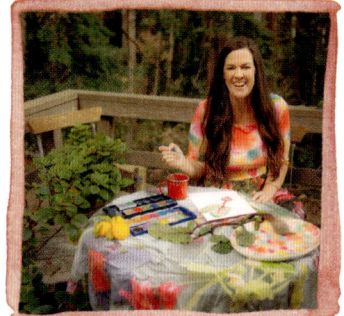

YouTube: youtube.com/theforestfeastcooks
Cookbooks, Shop & Recipes: theforestfeast.com
Instagram & Facebook: @theforestfeast
#thewatercolorfeast

→ tag me!

Thank You

I'm so grateful to all the friends, family, colleagues, collaborators, and readers who have supported me in creating this book. Thank you most of all to my husband, Jonathan—you are the best. Thank you, Ezra, Max, Winnie, Mom, Dad, Ry, and Shan. Thank you to my agent, Alison, my editor, Laura, and the entire team at Abrams, especially Liam, Lisa, and Diane. Thank you, Kim, Daphne, Christine, Aurelie, Margaret, Laura, Mara, Neera, Devon, Kayoko, and everyone who sipped, tested, and painted with me along the way. Thank you, Debbie and Brook, for growing much of the beautiful produce in this book and for allowing me to pick so freely in your gardens! And a big thank-you goes out to my readers! Thank you to everyone who has bought, gifted, and cooked from my cookbooks over the years. It's because of your unwavering positive support and enthusiasm that I am able to keep sharing my work. Thank you!

Editor: Laura Dozier
Managing Editor: Lisa Silverman
Designer: Erin Gleeson with Liam Flanagan
Production Manager: Kathleen Gaffney

Library of Congress Control Number: 2024942513
ISBN: 978-1-4197-7679-3
eISBN: 979-8-88707-398-9

Abrams books are available at special discounts when
purchased in quantity for premiums and promotions as
well as fundraising or educational use. Special editions
can also be created to specification. For details, contact
specialsales@abramsbooks.com or the address below.

Abrams® is a registered trademark of Harry N. Abrams, Inc.

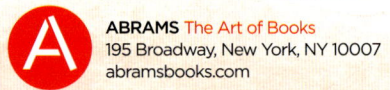

ABRAMS The Art of Books
195 Broadway, New York, NY 10007
abramsbooks.com

Use the following rip-
out watercolor pages to
practice the exercises and
tutorials in this book
or to create your own
unique artwork. Remember,
it doesn't need to be a
masterpiece—just play
around, let it flow, and
have fun with color!

When creating
recipes and eating
edible flowers,
it is essential
that readers use
extreme caution
and consult
physicians or
other medical
professionals as
needed. The Author
and Publisher
disclaim any and
all liability in
connection with
information in
this book about
the foraging and
use of wild plants.

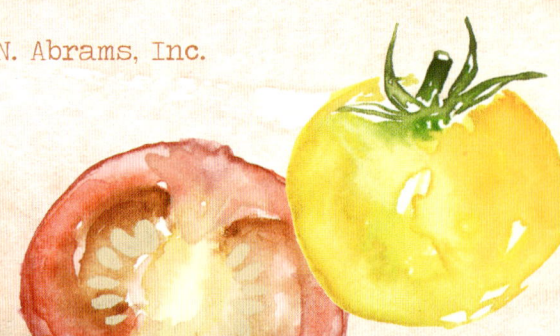

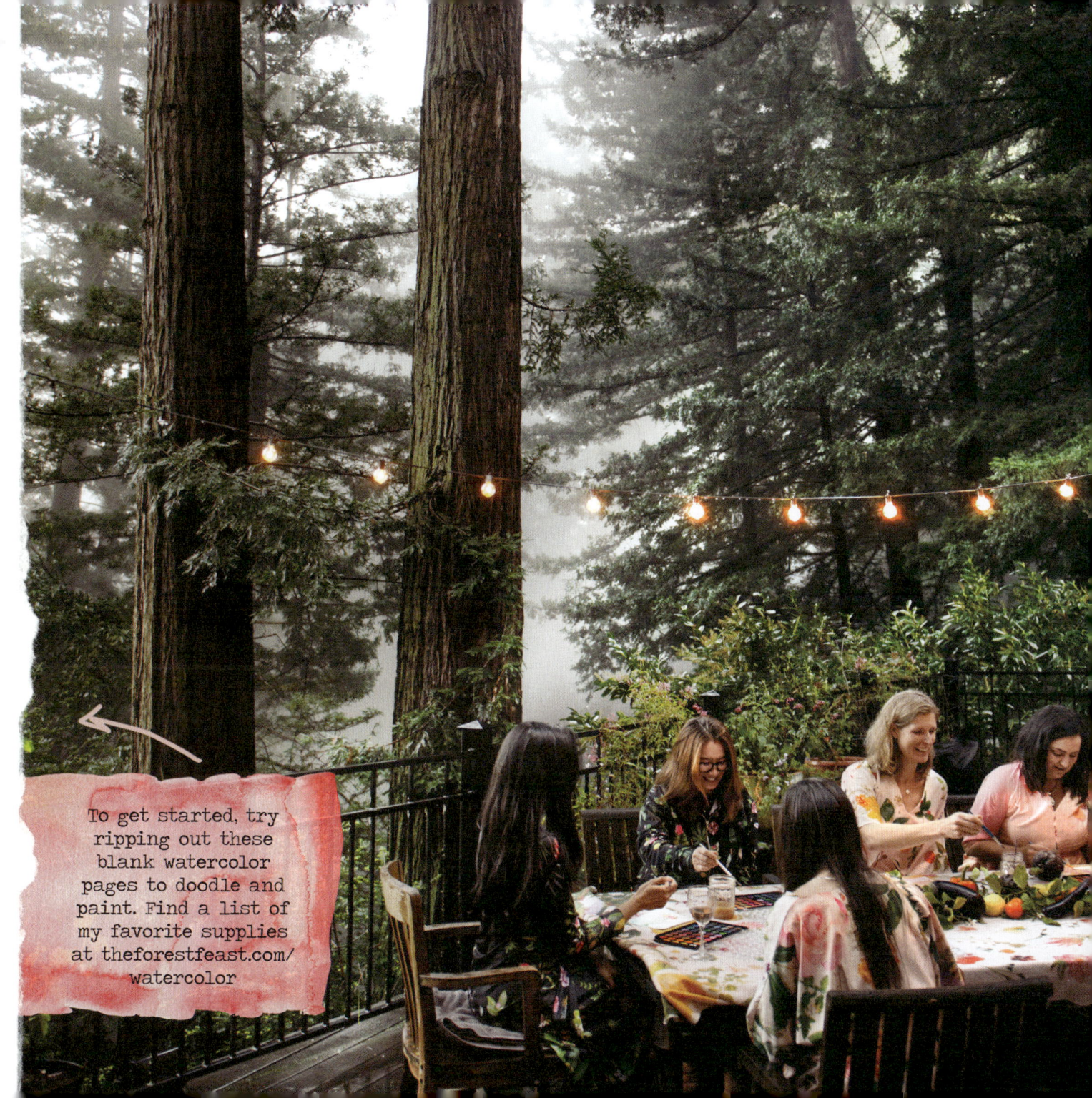

To get started, try ripping out these blank watercolor pages to doodle and paint. Find a list of my favorite supplies at theforestfeast.com/watercolor

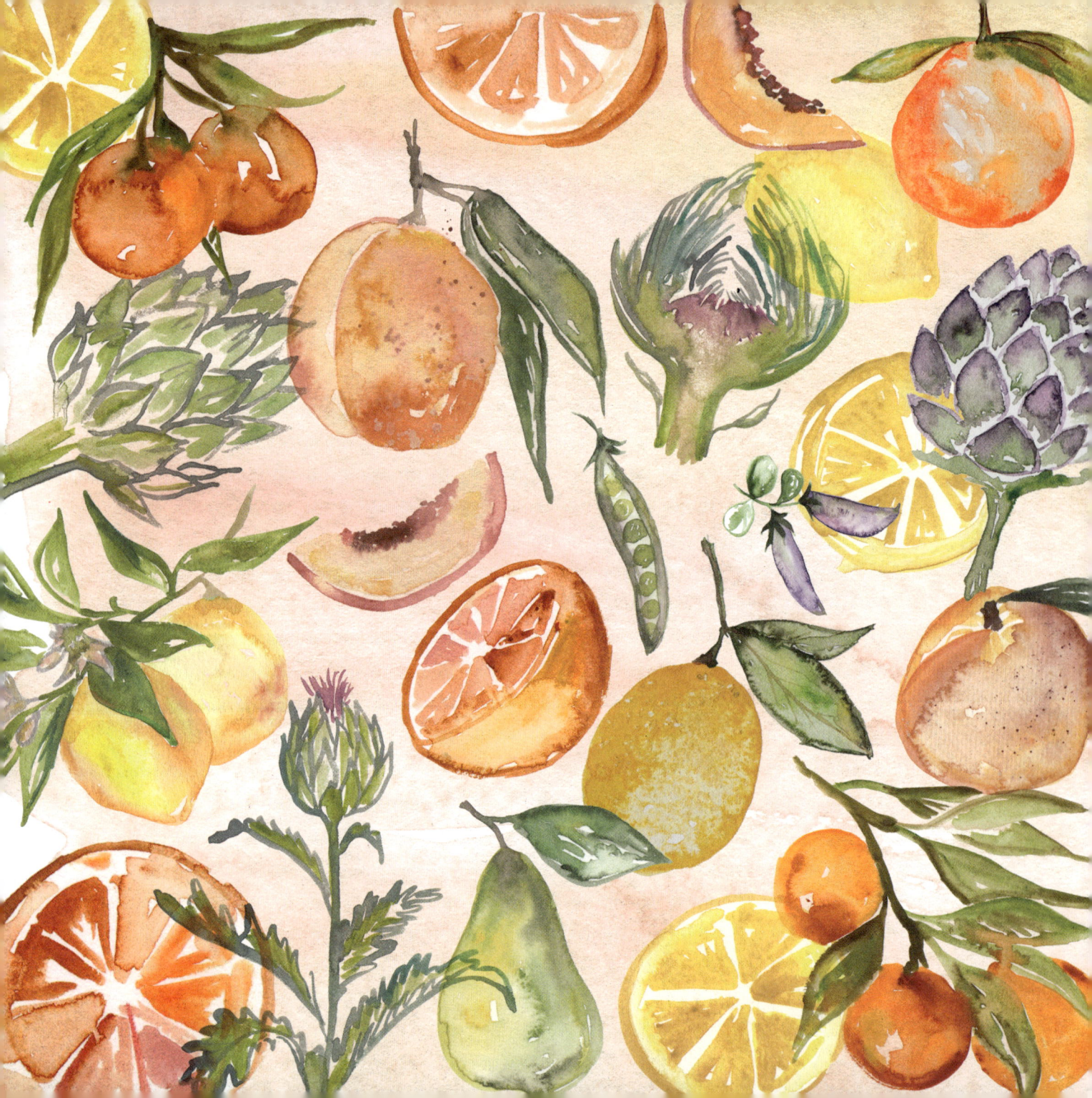